SO-EIC-860

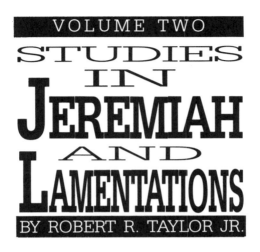

VOLUME TWO

STUDIES IN JEREMIAH AND LAMENTATIONS

BY ROBERT R. TAYLOR JR.

GRACE BAPTIST CHURCH LIBRARY

© Copyright 1992 by Robert R. Taylor, Jr.

All rights reserved. No part of this publication may be reproduced, stored in a retrieval system, or transmitted in any form by any means—electronic, mechanical, photocopy, recording, or otherwise—without prior permission of the copyright owner and Quality Publications.

IBSN: 0-89137-140-0

DEDICATION

In loving tribute this volume is dedicated to Sherra Williams Taylor who became my esteemed daughter-in-law on May 30, 1987. She is lovely of person, radiant of disposition, talented of mind and body, possessive of a winning smile, devoted to the Lord and His church and is an excellent companion and worthy wife to my son, Tim. To know her is to love, admire and respect her. She has added a delightful dimension to our family. Holy Writ inquires, "Who can find a virtuous (worthy) woman?" Jon Gary and Betty Williams reared her to be such and Tim found her to be such. She graces womanhood with a beauty rarely found in our day. I am delighted to dedicate this book to our own sweet Sherra.

FOREWORD

The books of Jeremiah and Lamentations properly belong to the prophetic section of Old Testament Scripture. Bible students frequently place both of these prophetic productions in the specific category of books belonging to the major prophets—Isaiah, Ezekiel and Daniel being the other three.

Appreciation, deep and wide, is expressed to Bennie Whitehead and Quality Publications for the unsolicited invitation to research and then pen this volume. Two other of my books—**Christ In The Home** and **Studies In Psalms**—bear the Quality label. Quality Publications has invited me to do a fourth work for them—**Studies in Romans.** This is my next planned volume and work has already begun on it. It will be my 1990-1991 literary challenge.

Studies In Jeremiah And Lamentations is the longest book I have written and this one numbers my nineteenth published volume over the last twenty years. It is also the most difficult and time-consuming book I have written even surpassing the Version Volume in these departments. I began work on it during late 1986 and am putting the finishing touches to it in late 1989. It had to be sandwiched in with much other writing, my local work and a heavy schedule of gospel meetings and lectureships each year. Yet hundreds and hundreds of hours have gone into the background research, writing it out first in longhand and then typing it with my own hands. Many of these hours were early in the morning before most people arise. Upon completion of these aspects of book composition, there are many tedious hours of careful proofing again and again to catch as many errors as possible and still some slip through.

I have read widely from both ancient and modern students on Jeremiah and Lamentations. Most of these have been conservative. Some have been modernistic for I wanted to examine their hostile criticisms against

Jeremiah and his two books. I am therefore a literary benefactor from so many who have written previously on these two Old Testament books.

I owe gratitude not only to the foregoing but to many others as well. My wife, Irene, continues to be my main human inspiration in my writing, preaching, teaching and lecturing. She has done much writing herself and knows how exacting and time-consuming it is. I continue to stand in constant debt to a great eldership—brethren Fred Faulk and Everett Presson—who generously allow me time for a writing ministry. In sixteen years of laboring under their shepherding care, at NO time have they requested me to reduce the time I spend in writing. Writing on Biblical matters is studiously exacting of a man and they realize that such gives me a better and broader knowledge of the Book. They know it is a complement to my preaching, teaching and the writing I do for our weekly church bulletin. I owe much also to the Ripley congregation which does not saddle me with a mass of ministerial incidentals but allows me to do the real work of an evangelist as per II Timothy 4:5. I owe much to a number of my regular readers who have inquired frequently as to how the work on Jeremiah and Lamentations was progressing. I owe much to Bennie Whitehead and Quality who have given me no deadline to meet on this literary production, but have patiently waited for it for three years now. I sincerely appreciate such literary patience from a publisher. Much of what I write for Bible School Literature and for lectureship volumes each year, by their very nature, have to meet pressing, publishing deadlines. I owe my ALL to the Gracious Godhead, whose servant I am, for strength of mind and body to begin, prosecute and finish a lengthy, literary endeavor like this one.

This book is sent forth with the breathed prayer that it will help every reader to understand a little better Jeremiah the man, the worthy, wonderful and wise books he penned some twenty-six centuries ago and come to a deeper faith and richer love in and for the same Gracious God that Jeremiah served so well and for so long.

Robert R. Taylor, Jr.

TABLE OF CONTENTS

CHAPTER SIXTEEN

JEWISH DISOBEDIENCE VERSUS RECHABITE FIDELITY
Jeremiah 34, 35

This lesson will again zero in on Jerusalem's destruction and the captivity that is certain to come. Obstinate Jews have paved the sure way of its coming by their atrocious and adamant wickedness. Yet sharply contrasted with their flagrant disobedience is the admirable case of the obedient Rechabites. Rechabite obedience is praised while Jewish disobedience is soundly condemned.

JEHOVAH'S MESSAGE TO ZEDEKIAH

Paragraph 1 of Jeremiah 34 reads,

> **The word which came unto Jeremiah from the Lord, when Nebuchadnezzar king of Babylon, and all his army, and all the kingdoms of the earth of his dominion, and all the people, fought against Jerusalem, and against all the cities thereof, saying, Thus saith the Lord, the God of Israel; Go and seek to Zedekiah king of Judah, and tell him, Thus saith the Lord; Behold, I will give this city into the hand of the king of Babylon, and he will burn it with fire: And thou shalt not escape out of his hand, but shalt surely be taken, and delivered into his hand; and thine eyes shall behold the eyes of the king of Babylon, and he shall speak with thee mouth to mouth, and thou shalt go to Babylon. Yet hear the word of the Lord, O Zedekiah king of Judah; Thus saith the Lord of thee, Thou shalt not die by the sword: But thou shalt die in**

peace: and with the burnings of thy fathers, the former kings which were before thee, so shall they burn odours for thee, and they will lament thee, saying, Ah lord! for I have pronounced the word, saith the Lord. Then Jeremiah the prophet spake all these words unto Zedekiah king of Judah in Jerusalem, When the king of Babylon's army fought against Jerusalem, and against all the cities of Judah that were left, against Lachish and against Azekah: for these defensed cities remained of the cities of Judah (34:1-7).

v. 1. This is a time-identifying verse for the Lord's revelation—a word or verbal revelation—to Jeremiah. According to 2 Kings 25:1 the Chaldeans came against Jerusalem in Zedekiah's ninth year. The siege lasted for one year and six months. This message probably came near the beginning of the siege. Nebuchadnezzar's army consisted of Babylonian soldiers and doubtless from the various kingdoms or provinces he controlled at this time. Jerusalem and other Judean cities were the targets of the determined siege.

vs. 2,3. God's message to Jeremiah had king Zedekiah for its receptive object. Jeremiah is to tell the king very clearly, very cogently and very convincingly that Jehovah will surely deliver Jerusalem to Babylon and its destruction was to be a fiery one indeed. Escape is out of the question for Zedekiah. Jeremiah assured the besieged king that he would be taken, he would be delivered into Nebuchadnezzar's hand, that he would see the very eyes of the Chaldean conqueror and speak mouth-to-mouth (we would say face-to-face) with him. Without fail Zedekiah would go to Babylon. Ezekiel said Zedekiah would go to Babylon and would die there and yet would not see it (Ezekiel 12:13). The harmony of this is that Zedekiah's eyes would be put out at Riblah prior to his captive trip to Chaldea.

vs. 4,5. The stubborn monarch who had so long resisted sane, sensible counsel from Jeremiah is again charged to hear Jehovah's word. Zedekiah's Lord and God, whether the adamant king acknowledged the Almighty or not, made solemn promise that Zedekiah would not die by the sword, i. e., by the violence of war and bloodshed therein. He (Zedekiah) was promised a peaceful death which means he would die of natural causes and not from war and its ravishes. It was customary in that day that kings and men of distinguished careers have aromatic odors burned by way of extending them funeral honors. These would be accorded the king even though he would die far from home as a captive. His people will lament or mourn his passing much as we do a fallen leader though his character may be far from what it ought to be. God pronounced it would be this way and it would be fulfilled with surety.

vs. 6,7. Jeremiah spoke these words to the king at the hazard of his own life. Jeremiah feared God and then there were NO others worthy of fear. This message was given while the siege was going on. Cities had fallen to the Chaldean conqueror like hay before a modern mowing machine. Lachish and Azekah were cities of Judah with excellent defenses. They, along with Jerusalem, were holding out against the Chaldean siege but it was all to no avail. All three of these defensed citadels would soon collapse to the siege and be captured.

LIBERATED SLAVES—ENSLAVED AGAIN

Paragraph 2 of Jeremiah 34 reads,

> **This is the word that came unto Jeremiah from the Lord, after that the king Zedekiah had made a covenant with all the people which were at Jerusalem, to proclaim liberty unto them; That every man should let his manservant, and every man his maidservant, being an Hebrew or an Hebrewess, go free; that none should serve himself of them, to wit, of a Jew his brother. Now when all the princes, and all the people, which had entered into the covenant, heard that every one should let his manservant, and every one his maidservant, go free, that none should serve themselves of them any more, then they obeyed, and let them go. But afterward they turned, and caused the servants and the handmaids, whom they had let go free, to return, and brought them into subjection for servants and for handmaids (34:8-11).**

vs. 8-10. This is a revelation Jehovah gave Jeremiah. Probably, it was just a short time after the discourse given in the first paragraph of this chapter, vs. 1-7. Jeremiah identifies the time of the word revelation vouchsafed him from heaven. It was just subsequent to an agreement

Zedekiah made with his people in Jerusalem relative to a proclamation of liberty. In particular it concerned every slave holder. Each slave holder was to give liberty to any Hebrew manservant or Hebrewess maidservant. This was in perfect harmony with a Mosaic mandate that said any Israelite who held a fellow-Israelite in slavery should not do so beyond a specified period. According to Exodus 21:2 and Deuteronomy 15:12 this specified period was set at six years. The seventh year was to be the year of liberation. Both princes (rulers) and people had been made a party of this agreement. Upon hearing its contractual stipulations they obeyed. Freedom was granted to their former servants. Their obedience was a matter of action—they let them go. Retention of them would not have equaled obedience at all.

v. 11. Greed and power do strange things to people. After doing the right things in verses 8-10 they turned. The turning here is back to the wrong. They re-enslaved their former subjects again. Greed took precedence over God's law.

JEHOVAH'S REMONSTRANCE AT THIS SIGNAL DISOBEDIENCE

Paragraph 3 of Jeremiah 34 reads,

Therefore the word of the Lord came to Jeremiah from the Lord, saying, Thus saith the Lord, the God of Israel; I made a covenant with your fathers in the day that I brought them forth out of the land of Egypt, out of the house of bondmen, saying, At the end of seven years let ye go every man his brother an Hebrew, which hath been sold unto thee; and when he hath served thee six years, thou shalt let him go free from thee: but your fathers hearkened not unto me, neither inclined their ear. And ye were now turned, and had done right in my sight, in proclaiming liberty every man to his neighbour; and ye had made a covenant before me in the house which is called by my name: But ye turned and polluted my name, and caused every man his servant, and every man his handmaid, whom he had set at liberty at their pleasure, to return, and brought them into subjection, to be unto you for servants and for handmaids. Therefore thus saith the Lord; Ye have not hearkened unto me, in proclaiming

liberty, every one to his brother, and every man to his neighbour: behold, I proclaim a liberty for you, saith the Lord, to the sword, to the pestilence, and to the famine; and I will make you to be removed into all the kingdoms of the earth. And I will give the men that have transgressed my covenant, which have not performed the words of the covenant which they had made before me, when they cut the calf in twain, and passed between the parts thereof, The princes of Judah, and the princes of Jerusalem, the eunuchs, and the priests, and all the people of the land, which passed between the parts of the calf; I will even give them into the hand of their enemies, and into the hand of them that seek their life: and their dead bodies shall be for meat unto the fowls of the heaven, and to the beasts of the earth. And Zedekiah king of Judah and his princes will I give into the hand of their enemies, and into the hand of them that seek their life, and into the hand of the king of Babylon's army, which are gone up from you. Behold, I will command, saith the Lord; and cause them to return to this city; and they shall fight against it, and take it, and burn it with fire: and I will make the cities of Judah a desolation without an inhabitant (34:12-22).

vs. 12,13. This is another confirmation that Jeremiah's message was divinely-derived—not humanly originated. It was a word revelation; it was from Jehovah; it was given Jeremiah; it was given him to pass on to God's people. Reference is made to the Sinaitic covenant made with their forefathers nearly a full millennium earlier. It was made with Israel just subsequent to Jehovah's bringing them out of Egypt, out of the house of bondage. The Lord did not want them to forget that they had formerly been bondmen themselves.

vs. 14,15. Jehovah's law touching slave holders was crystal clear (Cf. Exodus 21:2ff; Deuteronomy 15:12ff). Six years was to be the full tenure of slave service. The seventh year was to be the year of granted liberty. The law was given; it was understood by Israelite subjects. They ignored it; they turned a deaf ear to it. In this present situation they temporarily had remembered and reverenced this slave-holding and slave-releasing ordinance. They had turned from spurning it toward submission thereunto. This they had done in Jehovah's sight and with His ardent approbation. This had been a public proclamation of their slave-release intents. They made a covenant, agreement, toward the release of their servants. It was made before Jehovah; it was made in Jehovah's very temple. A promise is a promise regardless of where made. But when people made such before God and in His very house of worship, they should have thought twice before its prompt violation. But how quickly they violated it shows their glaring, grievous depravity at that time of laxness and looseness. They were trucebreakers minus a single pang of conscience.

v. 16. Here is another turning. In verse 15 they turned toward right; in this verse they turned back to the wrong—their usual posture; their determined stance in sin. They polluted Jehovah's name by violating a promise made in His sight and even in His own temple. You gave your slaves their freedom but not permanently. You quickly reversed your liberty practice and brought them into slavery again. This was minus any and all justification on their hardened part. Greed had become their god; power had become their preferred priority.

v. 17. You have refused to honor me and your agreement in tendering liberty to your slaves. Now I proclaim a liberty to you that will be proportionate to the crime you have callously committed. Sin with its proper punishment is ever a burden of prophetic preaching. I will now extend liberty to sword, pestilence and famine to take their heavy toll upon you. No longer will the sword be sheathed; no longer will the pestilence be held in suspension; no longer will the famine be held at distance. All three will now be unleashed against you. From this goodly land you will be removed and will be taken to the various kingdoms of the earth.

vs. 18-22. The enormous nature of their sin is spelled out in verse 18. They are transgressors of Jehovah's covenant; they have not performed the words of the covenant or the agreement they made before me relative to the liberation of their slaves. Allusion is then made to the way covenants were solemnized in the ancient era. They took a calf and cut it into two equal sections from nose to rump. They laid the two original halves where there would be a passage way between. Each party of the contract would walk between the two halves—one beginning at the front and one at the back. They would meet in the middle. Then they would feast upon the slain animal when said covenant had been duly confirmed. It was a solemn occurrence and each, in essence, invited death if he should violate this contract that had been solemnly entered. Verse 19 names the violators. Guilty of this glaring violation were Judaean princes (rulers), Jerusalem princes (Judah was the province and Jerusalem the capital), the eunuchs, the priests (religious leaders) and the people of the land. They are the ones who had passed between the parts of the calf or entered this liberation of slaves agreement most solemnly. Verses 20-22 detail their sure-to-come punishment. They will be given into the hands of their enemies, the very ones who now seek their lives; their slain bodies will become food for preying fowls of the air and ravenous beasts of earth. The king and his princes will fall to the Chaldeans. The Babylonian army had recently retreated to meet and defeat the Egyptian army but this would be no permanent respite for the besieged monarch of Judah and his princes. Jehovah makes solemn promise that He will surely command a return of the Chaldean conqueror to Jerusalem. The siege will begin again. The city will fall to Nebuchadnezzar. His forces will burn the city. The neighboring cities of Judah will likewise become desolate and void of inhabitants.

A TREMENDOUS TRIBUTE TO
THE OBEDIENT RECHABITES

Paragraph 1 of Jeremiah 35 reads,

> **The word which came unto Jeremiah from the Lord in the days of Jehoiakim the son of Josiah king of Judah, saying, Go unto the house of the Rechabites, and speak unto them, and bring them into the house of the Lord, into one of the chambers, and give them wine to drink. Then I took Jaazaniah the son of Jeremiah, the son of Habaziniah, and his brethren, and all his sons, and the whole house of the Rechabites; And I brought them into the house of the Lord, into the chamber of the sons of Hanan, the son of Igdaliah, a man of God, which was by the chamber of the princes, which was above the chamber of Maaseiah the son of Shallum, the keeper of the door: And I set before the sons of the house of Rechabites pots full of wine, and cups, and I said unto them, Drink ye wine. But they said, We will drink no**

wine: for Jonadab the son of Rechab our father commanded us, saying, Ye shall drink no wine, neither ye, nor your sons for ever: Neither shall ye build house, nor sow seed, nor plant vineyard, nor have any: but all your days ye shall dwell in tents; that ye may live many days in the land where ye be strangers. Thus have we obeyed the voice of Jonadab the son of Rechab our father in all that he hath charged us, to drink no wine all our days, we, our wives, our sons, nor our daughters; Nor to build houses for us to dwell in: neither have we vineyard, nor field, nor seed: But we have dwelt in tents, and have obeyed, and done according to all that Jonadab our father commanded us. But it came to pass, when Nebuchadrezzar king of Babylon came up into the land, that we said, Come, and let us go to Jerusalem for fear of the army of the Chaldeans, and for fear of the army of the Syrians: so we dwell at Jerusalem (35:1-11).

vs. 1,2. In this chapter the prophet goes back several years—at least some fifteen or more. Its time setting, as indicated in verse 1, is in the time of Jehoiakim and perhaps around the year of 606 or 605 B. C. Jehovah directs Jeremiah to the house of the Rechabites. These were Kenites as we learn from 1 Chronicles 2:55. From such passages as Numbers 10:29-32; Judges 1:16 and 4:11 it appears very strongly that these people were descendants of Jethro, father-in-law to Moses. They worshipped and served Jehovah but were not descendants of Abraham, Isaac and Jacob as full-blooded Israelites and Judahites were. Jeremiah is directed to seek out the Rechabites, speak a message to them, bring them into one of the temple chambers and provide them wine to drink.

vs. 3,4. Jeremiah responds promptly and submissively—two great characteristics of this prophet observed throughout his distinguished life of service to Jehovah. He took Jaazaniah, son of Jeremiah (not the prophet who penned this book and who was forbidden to marry and have children—16:2), son of Habaziniah, his brethren, all his sons and the whole family of the Rechabites and brought them into one of the temple chambers. It was the chamber of Hanan, son of Igdaliah, a man of God, and whose chamber was of close proximity to the chamber of the princes. It was above the chamber of Masseiah, son of Shallum, keeper of the

289

door. These were chambers or meeting places for the ones herein named. Jeremiah's access to such surely shows that he still possessed great influence in the temple area and among its personnel.

v. 5. In full harmony with the directive that had been given him Jeremiah set pots and cups (bowls or goblets) full of wine before the assembled Rechabites in the temple chamber. Jeremiah's command is clear and concise—"Drink ye wine."

v. 6. Rechabite response is prompt and pointed. They had no intention of obeying the charge to drink the wine. Why? They refer back to a family directive given by Jonadab, son of Rechab our father, who charged us against such a practice by saying, "Ye shall drink no wine, neither ye, nor your sons for ever." Of special interest is the interval between Rechab and Jonadab and these Rechabites in Jeremiah's current company. Rechab and Jonadab were not RECENT or IMMEDIATE ancestors but very REMOTE ancestors. Jonadab was a faithful servant and zealous worshipper of God in King Jehu's era as we learn from 2 Kings 10:15ff. This was some three full centuries before this incident in the temple chamber in Jeremiah 35. What powerful testimony of parental example is set forth here. Jonadab set a tone and established a tenor of lifestyle that thrived with signal success for three centuries. They were not about to waver from it now. Nothing would have been wrong with grape juice usage but this directive also kept them away from fermented wine and its intoxicative powers. Does any reader think they, the marvelous Rechabites, had any social drinkers, any problem drinkers, any heavy drinkers, any drunkards or any alcoholics during these three centuries? They did not have as many as one of the foregoing. We would not have any of these today if people would remain totally aloof from every drink that has ANY alcoholic quality linked with it. What Herculean problems would be solved promptly by a world full of temperate people. The U. S. is filled with drinkers, drunkards and alcoholics with fully half of our adult population being alcoholic consumers in varying amounts. This is a sad commentary upon our so-called intelligence.

v. 7. Jonadab also desired them to maintain their nomadic lifestyle by building no houses, sowing no seed and planting no vineyards. They were to be tent dwellers and live off the produce of their livestock. They were to live in the land but count themselves as total strangers therein. He sought to shield them from the corruptible city life style that he saw in his day.

vs. 8-10. This trio of verses delineates just how loyal they had been across these three eventful centuries. (1) We have obeyed all that our father of old, Jonadab, has charged us. (2) We have strictly refrained from wine. We have done it as husbands and wives, as fathers and mothers and as sons and daughters. That is doing it family wise!! (3) We have built no permanent dwellings but have been nomadic tent dwellers. (4) We have not been vineyard planters or keepers. (5) We have not been sowers of fields. (6) We have obeyed all Jonadab charged upon us. The Rechabites had reverenced his word without deviation except in a recent decision which will be detailed in verse 11.

v. 11. The one exception is a recent contingency that faced us. When the Babylonian king came against this land we feared for our safety. Knowing the dangers that could come upon us by the Chaldean and Syrian armies in our residing places that were minus walls or buttresses of any kind, we left our nomadic tents and moved inside Jerusalem. Here we currently reside.

These eleven verses constitute one of the greatest cases of long term obedience in all the Bible. Jeremiah will make great use of it as he will contrast in the remnant of the chapter Rechabite obedience to an ancestor—Jonadab—and Jewish disobedience to one far greater than a Jonadab—the great Jehovah Himself.

A STINGING REBUKE TO DISOBEDIENT JUDAH

Paragraph 2 of Jeremiah 35 reads,

> **Then came the word of the Lord unto Jeremiah, saying, Thus saith the Lord of hosts, the God of Israel; Go and tell the men of Judah and the inhabitants of Jerusalem, Will ye not receive instruction to hearken to my words? saith the Lord. The words of Jonadab the son of Rechab, that he commanded his sons not to drink wine, are performed; for unto this day they drink none, but obey their father's commandment: notwithstanding I have spoken unto you, rising early and speaking; but ye hearkened not unto me. I have sent also unto you all my servants the prophets, rising up early and sending them, saying, Return ye now every man from his evil way, and amend your doings, and go not after other gods to serve**

them, and ye shall dwell in the land which I have given
to you and to your fathers: but ye have not inclined your
ear, nor hearkened unto me. Because the sons of Jonadab
the son of Rechab have performed the commandment
of their father, which he commanded them; but this
people hath not hearkened unto me: Therefore thus saith
the Lord God of hosts, the God of Israel; Behold, I will
bring upon Judah and upon all the inhabitants of
Jerusalem all the evil that I have pronounced against
them: because I have spoken unto them, but they have
not heard; and I have called unto them, but they have
not answered (35:12-17).

vs. 12,13. The divine derivation of God's word is again assured in verse 12. Jehovah is the source of the message; Jeremiah is the receptive mouthpiece, the faithful conveyor of the message. Jehovah refers to Himself as "Lord of hosts" which refers to His great power. His being the God of Israel shows the tender, intimate relationship between Him and His people. Jeremiah is charged to go and take a message to men of Judah and inhabitants of Jerusalem. The God-given message is prefaced with a query about whether Judah and Jerusalem possessed any inclination at all relative to instructional reception. Nothing was of deeper import to obstinate Judah and rebellious Jerusalem than a wonderful willingness to hearken and heed Jehovah's will. Thrice in these two verses there is a claim to inspiration. Jeremiah attributes his message as divinely derived nearly five hundred times in this prophetic product and in Lamentations.

vs. 14,15. It appears certain Jeremiah left the temple chamber where he and the Rechabites had conversed and went to the designated place God had in mind for Judah and Jerusalem to be addressed. It may well have been the case that all these Rechabites or at least representatives of those who met earlier with Jeremiah accompanied him. If so, the scene would be all that much more impressive. The Almighty condoned the full Rechabite report as being factual and accurate. Jehovah confirms that they had performed what their illustrious forefather had charged relative to no wine consumption. The Rechabites have been obedient to their father's command. Jonadab did not have to have a consecutive string of preaching prophets each generation to keep his descendants loyal and diligent. One message of few words was all that the Rechabites needed for century after century of amazing and remarkable submission. In marked contrast Jehovah had spoken frequently, forcefully and feelingly. Yet they would not hearken. The Rechabites were obedient to Jonadab—a man. The Israelites were rebellious toward Jehovah—the very God who made them, redeemed them and preserved them. With all the early rising and speaking that Jehovah had done Judah and Jerusalem had refused to hear and heed His message. Stubborn Judah and adamant Jerusalem are reminded of what Jehovah has done. Jehovah sent to these obstinate people His servants—the prophets. These prophets rose early and spoke with force, with fervency and with fearlessness. Their message was couched in the very language of clarity. They were charged to make a return to righteousness by forsaking their evil ways. They were to amend their lives by abandoning evil and doing good. They were warned against going after other gods and rendering them service. They were charged to dwell in the land a Gracious God had given them and their fathers. Toward these intense entreaties they inclined neither a ready ear nor a receptive heart. They were as adamant as stone.

vs. 16,17. The Rechabites have been obedient to Jonadab, their forefather. Judah has not been obedient to her Heavenly Father. Rechab's reward will be delineated in verses 18 and 19. Judah's punishment is spelled out in verse 17. All the punishment God intended to bring upon obstinate Judah is certain to come. None of it will be allayed or suspended. God had spoken; they refused to hear. Jehovah called; they met His call with deafening silence.

REWARDS FOR RECHABITES

Paragraph 3 of Jeremiah 35 reads,

And Jeremiah said unto the house of the Rechabites, Thus saith the Lord of hosts, the God of Israel; Because ye have obeyed the commandment of Jonadab your father, and kept all his precepts, and done according unto all that he hath commanded you: Therefore thus saith the Lord of hosts, the God of Israel; Jonadab the son of Rechab shall not want a man to stand before me for ever (35:18,19).

293

v. 18. This must have been a message of delight on Jeremiah's part. It differs from so many of the wrath-filled and punishment-oriented messages he had been constrained to give obstinate Judah and adamant Jerusalem throughout his prophetic ministry. To the Rechabites Jehovah is portrayed as the Lord of hosts (power) and the God of Israel. The reward to the Rechabites was based on their superb and stately spirit of submission. Note the threefold description that is given. (1) You have obeyed the commandment of Jonadab your father. (2) You have kept all his precepts. (3) You have done according to all he has commanded you. What a beautiful way to spell obedience!!

v. 19. This verse begins with "Therefore"—a connecting or linking term. Someone has well observed, and quite wisely, that when we see a "Therefore" in the Bible, we need to pause and see what it is "there" "for." Again, Jehovah portrays Himself as Lord of hosts (power) and the God of Israel. Perpetuity of the Rechabites is assured. Jonadab's family will continue. Of interest is a statement from Wolff, a nineteenth century missionary in the Middle East, who claims he found traces of these people still living in modern times. They still claim to be descendants of Jethro, Moses' father-in-law.

POINTS TO PONDER

(1) When we fear God there is no other worthy of whom we may fear and by whom to be intimidated.

(2) Trucebreakers are always a curse to all of human society.

(3) Totally sober ancestors is the best insurance against drinking, drunken, alcoholic descendants.

(4) The Rechabites preached a powerful and greatly needed lesson to adamant, wicked Judah.

(5) Judah's long-term ingratitude and disobedience to the God who had made them, loved them and blessed them so abundantly is positively minus any and all justification.

DISCUSSION QUESTIONS

1. What sad message of grievious weight was Jeremiah charged by Jehovah to convey to Zedekiah? Was he faithful in its deliverance?

2. Explain how Zedekiah would see Nebuchadnezzar face-to-face, be taken to Babylon, die there and yet never actually see the Chaldean capital.

3. Just how serious is a transgression of God's will?

4. Discuss the Rechabites as touching origin, lifestyle, obedience to ancestral charges and how they put to utter shame the disobedience of Jerusalem and Judah.

5. Why was Jonadab so interested in his descendants maintaining a nomadic lifestyle?

MULTIPLE-CHOICE: Underline correct answer

1. Nebuchadnezzar and Zedekiah were kings respectively of: (A) Egypt and Syria; (B) Edom and Lebanon; (C) Babylon and Judah; (D) Medo-Persia and Greece.
2. Lachish and Azekah were: (A) Babylonian cities; (B) Egyptian cities; (C) Arabian cities; (D) defensed cities of Judah.
3. Because of fear of Nebuchadnezzar and the Chaldean threat the Rechabites: (A) departed to Egypt; (B) surrendered promptly to Babylon; (C) sought out secret places in the desert; (D) came to Jerusalem, a walled city, for protection.
4. Rechab and Jonadab were: (A) recent ancestors; (B) remote ancestors; (C) contemporaries; (D) not related at all—to these Rechabites in Jeremiah 35.
5. Jehovah considered: (A) kings; (B) prophets; (C) priests; (D) apostles—as His servants sent to bring Judah and Jerusalem His word during this Old Testament period.

SCRIPTURAL FILL-IN: Each blank requires only one word

1. "Yet _____ the _____ of the _____ , O _____ king of _____ ; Thus _____ the _____ of thee, Thou shalt not _____ by the sword: . . ."

2. "But thou shalt _____ in _____ : and with the _____ of thy _____ , the former _____ which were before thee, so shall they _____ odours for thee; and they will _____ thee, saying, Ah _____ ! for I have _____ the _____ , saith the _____ ."

3. " _____ ye _____ ."

4. "Ye shall _____ no _____ , neither ye, nor your _____ for _____ ."

5. "But we have _____ in _____ , and have _____ , and done _____ to all that _____ our _____ commanded _____ ."

TRUE OR FALSE: Put either a "T" or "F" in the blanks

_____ 1. Babylon took Jerusalem in less than a week's time.

_____ 2. We have abundant proof throughout this book that God gave Jeremiah THOUGHT INSPIRATION and not WORD REVELATION at all.

_____ 3. Walking between equally cut halves of animals was a remote way of solemnizing ancient agreements or binding covenants.

_____ 4. Alcoholic consumption has NOTHING to do with social drinking, heavy drinking, outright drunkenness and alcoholic problems in society today.

_____ 5. Jehovah as "Lord of hosts" reflects His great power.

THOUGHT QUESTIONS

1. Why is it such a grievous sin to agree to do what is right and then rescind it later to do what is wrong?

2. Why should a promise-maker of that which is good be a promise-keeper of the same?

3. What great lessons of promptness and submission should we learn from Jeremiah and how could these improve all of us as Christians?

GRACE BAPTIST CHURCH LIBRARY

4. Discuss just how important and far-reaching a parental example can be for descendants down the line.

5. Discuss whether most of our society is more like the obedient Rechabites or disobedient Jews giving reasons for your answer.

CHAPTER SEVENTEEN

WICKED AND WAYWARD JEHOIAKIM: ANCIENT DESTROYER OF GOD'S WORD
Jeremiah 36

Attempted destruction of God's word is almost as old as the race. Satan, through serpentine agency in Genesis 3, sought to deny, descredit, and disparage God's word. Strict warnings are replete in Holy Writ against adding to or subtracting from the word of the Lord (Deuteronomy 4:2; 12:32; Proverbs 30:6; 22:18,19). There are always people who seek to make void God's law by the doctrines and commandments of men as per Mark 7:7-13. Truth is never safe among those determined to make merchandise of it (2 Corinthians 2:17). Every age has its irreverent men whose malicious major is to deal deceitfully with the Bible (2 Corinthians 4:2). Some men had rather pervert the gospel any day as to treat it reverently and practice it fervently and persistently (Galatians 1:6-9). Torturers of scripture did not all die in Peter's period (2 Peter 3:16). WOULD GOD THEY HAD!!

Marked attitudes toward God's word emerge in full, infamous fashion in this chapter of Jeremiah's prophetic product. Jeremiah and Baruch are faithful in their respective tasks of receiving and recording God's word; Jehoiakim and his motley crew of calloused, cruel colleagues are reckless and destructive of God's word. All Jehoiakims did not die in Jeremiah's era. The world is full of just such destroyers of God's word today. Yet they are in a work sure to fail for eternal is the word of our God (Isaiah 40:8) and puny man is never going to be successful in its destruction. This chapter is a marvelous must for all of us. It is an ancient picture in a modern setting with great lessons to learn from it.

BARUCH WRITES AND THEN READS PUBLICLY JEREMIAH'S INSPIRED WORDS

Paragraph 1 of Jeremiah 36 reads,

And it came to pass in the fourth year of Jehoiakim the son of Josiah king of Judah, that this word came unto Jeremiah from the Lord, saying, Take thee a roll of a book, and write therein all the words that I have spoken unto thee against Israel, and against Judah, and against all the nations, from the day I spake unto thee, from the days of Josiah, even unto this day. It may be that the house of Judah will hear all the evil which I purpose to do unto them; that they may return every man from his evil way; that I may forgive their iniquity and their sin. Then Jeremiah called Baruch the son of Neriah: and Baruch wrote from the mouth of Jeremiah all the words of the Lord, which he had spoken unto him, upon a roll of a book. And Jeremiah commanded Baruch, saying, I am shut up; I cannot go into the house of the Lord: Therefore go thou, and read in the roll, which thou hast written from my mouth, the words of the Lord in the ears of the people in the Lord's house upon the fasting day: and also thou shalt read them in the ears of all Judah that come out of their cities. It may be they will present their supplication before the Lord, and will return every one from his evil way: for great is the anger and the fury that the Lord hath pronounced against this people. And Baruch the son of Neriah did according to all that Jeremiah the prophet commanded him, reading in the book the words of the Lord in the Lord's house. And it came to pass in the fifth year of Jehoiakim the son of Josiah king of Judah, in the ninth month, that they proclaimed a fast before the Lord to all the people in Jerusalem, and to all the people that came from the cities of Judah into Jerusalem. Then read Baruch in the book the words of Jeremiah in the house of the Lord, in the chamber of Gemariah the son of Shaphan the scribe, in the higher court, at the entry of the new gate of the Lord's house, in the ears of all the people (36:1-10).

v. 1. The year is about 606 B. C. Jehoiakim, son of the just Josiah, was now in his fourth year as monarch of the land. God's word came to the faithful prophet. This is another of the hundreds of allusions in this prophetic product confirmatory of Jeremiah's inspiration.

vs. 2,3. Jeremiah is charged by Jehovah to take a role of a book wherein would be inscribed the divinely-derived message which soon would be read to the assembled nation. The writing material of that ancient era was parchment (vellum or sheepskins) strips stitched together and which could be extended with ease to provide space for the desired message. Upon rollers it could be rolled out for the initial writing and later the readings therefrom. The content of the inscribed message was to be a collection of all Jeremiah's messages against Israel, Judah and surrounding nations from day one of his prophetic ministry to the present. This would cover some twenty or more years of prophetic preaching. The why of this literary effort is then set forth. Jehovah desired to give adamant Judah another merciful opportunity to hear and heed His word. Great evil (severe punishment) hovered over these impious people of spiritual stubbornness. It would have pleased Jehovah immensely to see Judah repent of her grievous evils and return to the Gracious God they had forsaken in order that He might forgive their iniquity and pardon their sin.

vs. 4,5. Baruch (a man which means "blessed") has been mentioned earlier (32:13,16). Neriah was his father. He was a faithful associate to Jeremiah. He served as an amanuensis (writing secretary) to the faithful prophet. Jeremiah gave the message which he had received from the Lord; Baruch took it down faithfully. He inscribed it on the roll—the parchment strips stitched together. Jeremiah explains to his faithful literary secretary that he (Jeremiah) was shut up and thus unable to go to the temple. Jeremiah, at this time, was not imprisoned as per the record but there was evidently some restraining influence, details of which are unknown to us.

vs. 6,7. Baruch is charged by the prophet to go to the temple and read from the roll the message Jeremiah had him inscribe. It was to be read to assembled Judah. It was to be read at a time when the people were fasting. This was opportune since the people might be more religiously inclined under that circumstance. The assembly would doubtless be vast since people coming out of Judah's various cities would all be included. Jeremiah hopefully desired that the message to the people will receive a reverent hearing and will prompt the people to join fervent prayer to their fasting. Jeremiah longed for it to have the desired effect of turning them away from their evil lifestyles. He knew that Jehovah's anger and fury hovered over these people and would soon be discharged in great severity. The time was short; Jehovah's patience with these people was wearing thin indeed. Judgment had already been pronounced upon these people; soon it would be executed in fulness of fury.

v. 8. Baruch's faithfulness is exemplified in the prompt dispatch of the prophet's bidding. He went where directed and read there Jeremiah's message to the assembled masses. He read from the book "the words of the Lord in the Lord's house." Gospel preachers should realize that this is our pressing priority today—to read or quote from God's Book in His house (the church). This is what people most need to hear.

vs. 9,10. The message had been composed in the fourth year of Jehoakim's reign. Doubtless they waited till the time was opportune and the people of Jerusalem and Judah would be there en masse. This time came during the fifth year of the king's reign and in the ninth month. This corresponds to December of our calendar year. Recall that their year began about March-April—not in January—as with us. A fast was proclaimed. This evidently was a specially called one since the one fast legislated by Mosaic mandate was for the day of atonement— seventh month and tenth day. Both Jerusalem and the cities of Judah were included. Baruch read what Jeremiah requested in the temple area. His reading place was in the chamber of Gemariah, son of Shaphan the scribe. This Gemariah was doubtless the brother of Ahikam, mentioned in 26:24 and a supportive friend to Jeremiah. Gemariah doubtless shared the same friendship and sympathy for Jeremiah. Baruch read in the higher court and at the entry (door) of the new gate. Since he read the requested message in the words of all the people, it must have been an area that could accommodate a vast throng of people.

PROMPT EFFECTS OF READING JEREMIAH'S INSPIRED ROLL

Paragraph 2 of Jeremiah 36 reads,

> **When Michaiah the son of Gemariah, the son of Shaphan, had heard out of the book all the words of the Lord, Then he went down into the king's house, into the scribe's chamber: and, lo, all the princes sat there, even**

Elishama the scribe, and Delaiah the son of Shemaiah, and Elnathan the son of Achbor, and Gemariah the son of Shaphan, and Zedekiah the son of Hananiah, and all the princes. Then Michaiah declared unto them all the words that he had heard, when Baruch read the book in the ears of the people. Therefore all the princes sent Jehudi the son of Nethaniah, the son of Shelemiah, the son Cushi, unto Baruch, saying, Take in thine hand the roll wherein thou hast read in the ears of the people, and come. So Baruch the son of Neriah took the roll in his hand, and came unto them. And they said unto him, Sit down now, and read it in our ears. So Baruch read it in their ears. Now it came to pass, when they had heard all the words, they were afraid both one and other, and said unto Baruch, We will surely tell the king of all these words. And they asked Baruch, saying, Tell us now, How didst thou write all these words at his mouth? Then Baruch answered them, He pronounced all these words unto me with his mouth, and I wrote them with ink in the book. Then said the princes unto Baruch, Go, hide thee, thou and Jeremiah; and let no man know where ye be (36:11-19).

vs. 11,12. Upon hearing Jeremiah's roll read Michaiah felt that action was required and promptly. He was the son of Gemariah who had provided the very chamber in verse 10 for Baruch's reading of the roll to the people. Michaiah was grandson of Shaphan. Shaphan's son, Ahikam, earlier had exhibited sympathic support for the prophet and his work (26:24). So there was a certain concern in this family for the great prophet. Michaiah went down to the king's house (it was a descent from the elevated area where the temple was to the palace). There he met with certain ones who were in high places in the king's service. They are designated as princes. Present were Elishama the scribe, Delaiah, Elnathan, Gemariah, Zedekiah and a number of unnamed princes.

v. 13. With this assembled group of governmental dignitaries, Michaiah gave a report of what his ears had heard from Baruch's reading of Jeremiah's roll.

v. 14,15. The attentive princes are anything but indifferent at Michaiah's shocking report. In concert action they dispatched Jehudi to seek out Baruch. When found Baruch, with his prophetic roll, is to be summoned with rapidity into their presence. There is no hesitation on Baruch's part. With roll in hand he honored their request by coming promptly. When in their presence they gave him a twofold charge. He was to sit down and then read the roll in their ears. He did so promptly. This is another case of a great man of God reading God's word into the ears of people who desperately needed to hear it read.

v. 16. The response on their part was one of fear. They looked at each other and the glances were filled with fearful foreboding. Like Felix before Paul's bold preaching in Acts 24:24,25 fear and fright gripped their uneasy hearts. They knew the king must be told. There was no way it could be kept from him since there had already been a public reading of Jeremiah's roll in one of the temple courts.

vs. 17,18. They interrogate Baruch about the origin of the roll and its moving message. Just how was the message from Jeremiah delivered? Baruch is only too happy to explain the HOW of the literary message. Jeremiah pronounced these words with his mouth. My ear was open, my heart was receptive and my hand was busy in recording his dictation. Jeremiah was the human channel of the divine message; I but supplied hand, ink and writing material. He dictated the roll faithfully; I recorded the roll faithfully. Baruch answered with a weight of wonderful wisdom on his part.

v. 19. The princes knew the king well. They knew he would view the message with disdain—not with delight. Both Baruch the writer and Jeremiah the prophetic producer of the roll would be in danger. They counseled that Baruch and Jeremiah go promptly into hiding and leave concealed the place of their presence. This shows that Jeremiah, at this time, was not publicly imprisoned or even in a private prison from which he could not be moved. This was to be their shield of safety.

SCRIPTURES AND THE KING'S PENKNIFE

Paragraph 3 of Jeremiah 36 reads,

> **And they went in to the king into the court, but they laid up the roll in the chamber of Elishama the scribe, and told all the words in the ears of the king. So the king**

sent Jehudi to fetch the roll: and he took it out of Elishama the scribe's chamber. And Jehudi read it in the ears of the king, and in the ears of all the princes which stood beside the king. Now the king sat in the winterhouse in the ninth month: and there was a fire on the hearth burning before him. And it came to pass, that when Jehudi had read three or four leaves, he cut it with the penknife, and cast it into the fire that was on the hearth, until all the roll was consumed in the fire that was on the hearth. Yet they were not afraid, nor rent their garments, neither the king, nor any of his servants that heard all these words. Nevertheless Elnathan and Delaiah and Gemariah had made intercession to the king that he would not burn the roll: but he would not hear them. But the king commanded Jerahmeel the son of Hammelech, and Seraiah the son of Azriel, and Shelemiah the son of Abdeel, to take Baruch the scribe and Jeremiah the prophet: but the Lord hid them (36:20-26).

vs. 20,21. The princes who had just finished listening to Baruch's reading of Jeremiah's prophetic roll went promptly to the king. He was in one of the courts of his palace. Initially, they did not take the roll with them having left it secure in the chamber of Elishama, the scribe. They gave their own summary of what they had heard Baruch read from the roll. Jehudi, servant of Jehoiakim, was sent with dispatch to get the roll from Elishama's chamber. One wonders why Baruch was not sent for as reader since he wrote it and obviously could read it more intelligently than could Jehudi. A little later we see Jehoiakim's hatred of both Baruch and Jeremiah (v. 26). Jehudi read the roll in the ears of both the monarch and all his attending princes.

v. 22. Jehoiakim, at this time, sat in the winterhouse. Thomson, in his classic work, THE LAND AND THE BOOK, tells how that such houses in that era had a place where they stayed in summer and one in winter. The most airy place was the summerhouse; the warmest part was the winterhouse. The time is designated—the ninth month. This is not September—our ninth month—for their religious year began in March-April. Hence, this would be about December, a cold, rainy and stormy month in the Palestinian climate. There was something like a firepan or brazier burning on the hearth before him. This was designed to keep the room heated from the disagreeable cold outside.

v. 23. Jehudi had read only three or four leaves before Jehoiakim went into violent action. Leaves here would not be leaves such as we have in a modern book. Books, then, were unknown. Recall that the entire message had been inscribed on a roll. The margin of the ASV for leaves has columns and this is the correct picture we are to form. Baruch had written the entire roll in columns. The king became enraged at what he heard. Unlike his father Josiah he did not tremble at God's word (2 Kings 22:10ff). Even unlike wicked, notorious and abominable Ahab he was not temporarily moved for the better at hearing God's word (1 Kings 21:27ff). Jehoiakim was moved toward instant maliciousness. He took a penknife (used by scribes in shaping reeds for writing or making corrections in the parchment) and cut the written words to pieces. Then he cast the cut pieces into the fire for additional destruction. He was not satisfied until he had destroyed the whole roll of scripture. He hated God, His word and those who revealed and recorded it respectively—Jeremiah and Baruch.

v. 24. Insult is added to injury here as neither the king nor his attendant servants exhibited any fear or rent their garments—a usual occurrence when one trembled at God's word as did Josiah earlier (1 Kings 22:10ff). Jehoiakim was of a totally different bent of character than his godly father—Josiah. They were on different wave lengths!

v. 25. Elnathan, Delaiah and Gemariah showed far higher character than did any of the others. They pleaded with the king not to burn the roll. Their entreaty fell upon deaf ears and failed to penetrate the king's hardened heart.

v. 26. Jehoiakim was not content to destroy God's word. He would also destroy God's powerful prophet and the prophet's able amanuensis— Jeremiah and Baruch respectively. He gave charge to three of his servants—Hammelech, Seraiah and Shelemiah—to apprehend the prophet and the scribe. Had these two been present Jehoiakim would likely have killed them on the spot. With the same malicious ease he could have cut up their bodies and cast them into the fire just as he had done with God's Holy Word. Jehovah's providence is at work here. The Lord hid them. Doubtless diligent search was made for their whereabouts but to no avail.

THE DESTROYED ROLL TO BE REPRODUCED

Paragraph 4 of Jeremiah 36 reads,

> Then the word of the Lord came to Jeremiah, after that the king had burned the roll, and the words which Baruch wrote at the mouth of Jeremiah, saying, Take thee again another roll, and write in it all the former words that were in the first roll, which Jehoiakim the king of Judah hath burned. And thou shalt say to Jehoaikim king of Judah, Thus saith the Lord; Thou hast burned this roll, saying, Why hast thou written therein, saying, The king of Babylon shall certainly come and destroy this land, and shall cause to cease from thence man and beast? Therefore thus saith the Lord of Jehoiakim king of Judah; He shall have none to sit upon the throne of David: and his dead body shall be cast out in the day to the heat, and in the night to the frost. And I will punish him and his seed and his servants for their iniquity; and I will bring upon them, and upon the inhabitants of Jerusalem, and upon the men of Judah, all the evil that I have pronounced against them; but they hearkened not (36:27-31).

vs. 27-29. On the very heels of the destroyed roll by Jehoakim's penknife and the fire on his hearth Jehovah's word comes to Jeremiah. Heavenly charge is given that Jeremiah simply have another roll written. The new roll was to have the same message as the destroyed roll had contained. Jeremiah was not an eyewitness to the actual burning of the roll but Jehoiakim is to know that Jeremiah is very cognizant indeed of what had transpired. Jeremiah, likewise, was very cognizant of the king's motive in cutting and burning Jehovah's prophetic roll of Sacred Scriptures. The roll told by way of prediction Judah's and Jerusalem's destruction at the hands of Babylon. This, the king disliked and disdained. The destruction was to be vast—inclusive of both man and beast.

vs. 30,31. The newly produced roll will contain Jehoiakim's sad demise and the dishonorable way he would meet such. He shall have no successor on David's throne. Jehoiakim's son, Jehoiachin, ruled for just three short months but this is counted as nothing by way of succession. It constitutes no contradiction to this prediction at all. Zedekiah, the last ruler of Judah, was not of Jehoiakim's seed but was his own brother, being another son of Josiah. His own body at death will face the destructive and disintegrating forces of the day's heat and the night's frost. This means he would be denied an honorable burial. Jeremiah, earlier, had predicted the ignominious manner of Jehoiakim's death and that he would depart minus lamentation and would be buried with the burial of an ass being cast forth beyond Jerusalem's gates (22:18,19). Neither the account of Jehoiakim's death in 2 Kings 24:6 nor in 2 Chronicles 36:8 contradicts what Jeremiah was charged to write. The king, his children and his servants are all destined to be punished because all were guilty of iniquity. Without fail God fully intended to bring upon Jerusalem and Judah all the punishment He had predicted in the first roll and throughout this prophetic product of Jeremiah. Four very sad words, inexpressibly sad, end verse 31—"but they hearkened not." They were adamant and nothing could move them from wrongdoing back to right-doing. They were incorrigible. They were beyond any and all reclamation. Only a few more years were to be their respite before total destruction was experienced at the calloused, cruel hands of Babylonian hoardes.

THE FAITHFULNESS OF JEREMIAH AND BARUCH

Paragraph 5 of Jeremiah 36 reads,

> **Then took Jeremiah another roll, and gave it to Baruch the scribe, the son of Neriah; who wrote therein from the mouth of Jeremiah all the words of the book which Jehoiakim king of Judah had burned in the fire: and there were added besides unto them many like words (36:32).**

v. 32. The new roll was produced in similar fashion to the initial one. Jeremiah pronounced the words God gave him; Baruch recorded them down faithfully. In addition there were added "unto them many like words." Jehoiakim and his irreverent aides had just compounded the enormous nature of their daring and dastardly act. Matthew Henry is right on target in saying in his unique style, ". . .for, since they will yet **walk contrary to God,** he will **heat the furnace seven times hotter**" (Emphasis his).

POINTS TO PONDER

(1) The most serious of any and all literary crimes is the perversion of God's word and this crime has a mass of practitioners in our day. Heading the list are the makers and movers of perverted Bibles.

(2) Jeremiah is an excellent example of a how a concerned, sensitive and deeply-caring preacher should feel about people's repenting and obeying truth.

(3) Men who hate God and His word often take out their full fury against the messenger who simply echoes God's word.

(4) When a man hates God and His word as much as Jehoiakim did, there is no end to what he will do in destroying that despised message.

(5) Man only compounds his own sins when he seeks the fiery destruction of God's word.

DISCUSSION QUESTIONS

1. Give a brief history of various attempts to destroy God's word.

2. Discuss the writing material of that era and the type of the product when finished.

3. What great lesson should modern day preachers learn from Baruch?

4. Discuss Jeremiah's dictation and Baruch's faithful recording of the divinely-derived message as an excellent example of how heavenly truth was transmitted.

5. Discuss their summer houses and winter houses in that ancient era.

MULTIPLE-CHOICE: Underline correct answer

1. Jehoiakim: (A) defended Jeremiah as God's appointed prophet; (B) was equally inspired with Jeremiah; (C) made a turn for the better when Jeremiah's roll of Sacred Scripture was read to him; (D) hated God's word, cut it to pieces and brazenly burned it.
2. God's word is: (A) unimportant; (B) temporary; (C) eternal; (D) no higher in authority than is man's word.

3. Baruch was: (A) an avowed enemy of Jeremiah and truth; (B) Jehoiakim's right-hand man; (C) a high ranking official of Nebuchadnezzar in Babylon; (D) a good man and the faithful writing secretary to Jeremiah.

4. The one fast commanded of Israel by Mosaic law was: (A) at Passover; (B) the first day of each beginning religious year; (C) during the feast of weeks (Pentecost in the New Testament); (D) the day of atonement—seventh month and tenth day.

5. Baruch was: (A) irreverent; (B) indifferent; (C) faithful; (D) arrogant—in the reading of Jeremiah's words to the assembled people.

SCRIPTURAL FILL-IN: Only one word required in each blank

1. "Then _____ called _____ the son of _____ : and _____ wrote from the _____ of _____ all the _____ of the _____ , which he had _____ unto him, upon a _____ of a _____ ."

2. "And _____ the son of Neriah did according to all that _____ the _____ commanded him, _____ in the _____ the _____ of the _____ in the _____ house."

3. "And they asked _____ , saying, _____ us _____ , How didst thou _____ all these _____ at his _____ ?"

4. "Then _____ answered them, He _____ all these _____ unto me with his _____ , and _____ wrote them with _____ in the _____ ."

5. "And it came to _____ , that when _____ had _____ three or four _____ , he _____ it with the _____ , and _____ it into the _____ that was on the _____ , until all the _____ was _____ in the _____ that was on the _____ ."

TRUE OR FALSE: Put either a "T" or "F" in the blanks

_____ 1. Baruch doctored up Jeremiah's words before he read them to the assembled masses.

_____ 2. Jehoiakim was widely known as a hater and despiser of God's word.

_____ 3. Felix once trembled when he heard God's word from Paul but Jehoiakim was too hardened to tremble when Jeremiah's roll was read before him.

_____ 4. Jehudi was a much wiser choice to read Jeremiah's roll to the king than was Baruch since Baruch knew so little about the message of the roll.

_____ 5. Jehoaikim would die in disgrace and without weeping or wailing being made for him.

THOUGHT QUESTIONS

1. Why is it wise to choose a time to reach a person when he is more receptive in hearing and heeding truth?

2. What great lesson can gospel preachers today learn from Baruch's reading the Scriptures in God's temple?

3. Who are some of the modern Jehoiakim's today that cut up God's word with their modern penknives?

4. Contrast Josiah and Jehoiakim, a father and son respectively, relative to how each felt toward and reacted to God's word.

5. What in this chapter shows the indestructible nature of God's word?

310

CHAPTER EIGHTEEN

"IS THERE ANY WORD FROM THE LORD?"
Jeremiah 37, 38

The two previous chapters of this powerful, prophetic product, Jeremiah 35,36, had their setting in the first half of Jehoiakim's reign. In the two chapters we now contemplate, Jeremiah 37,38, we again return to the declining, disastrous days of wicked, wishy-washy Zedekiah. Much of these two chapters deals with communications between the despotic dictator and the just Jeremiah. The title of this chapter has been derived from a query the distraught monarch raised to the now imprisoned Jeremiah. Zedekiah desired to know if there is "any word from the Lord?" Jeremiah, in essence, declared in response, "There is but you are not going to like it." And he did not like it one bit when it was set forth.

ZEDEKIAH'S PLEA FOR JEREMIAH'S PRAYER

Paragraph 1 of Jeremiah 37 reads,

> **And king Zedekiah the son of Josiah reigned instead of Coniah the son of Jehoiakim, whom Nebuchadrezzar king of Babylon made king in the land of Judah. But neither he, nor his servants, nor the people of the land, did hearken unto the words of the Lord, which he spake by the prophet Jeremiah. And Zedekiah the king sent Jehucal the son of Shelemiah and Zephaniah the son of Maaseiah the priest to the prophet Jeremiah, saying, Pray now unto the Lord our God for us. Now Jeremiah came in and went out among the people: for they had not put him into prison. Then Pharaoh's army was come forth**

out of Egypt: and when the Chaldeans that besieged Jerusalem heard tidings of them, they departed from Jerusalem (37:1-5).

vs. 1,2. Four kings ruled Judah subsequent to the judicious Josiah, Judah's final king of righteousness. They were Jehoahaz, Jehoiakim, Coniah and Zedekiah. Three of these were sons of Josiah and the fourth, Coniah, was a grandson. Zedekiah was Judah's final ruler. He was made king by Nebuchadrezzar after the short, ineffective, inglorious reign of cruel Coniah, Jehoiakim's son. In a sweeping appraisal of the great wave of evil now overwhelming apostate Judah the prophetic pen delineates how that neither king, nor his servants, nor the people paid any attention to God's word. They refused to hear it; they refused to heed it. This was the Lord's word revealed by faithful, courageous Jeremiah. John Calvin summed such inexcusable behaviour as amazing stupidity in view of Coniah's recent punishment.

vs. 3,4. Zedekiah dispatched a couple of his deputies to Jeremiah. They were Jehucal whose true colors will reflect more in Jeremiah 38:1ff and Zephaniah—not to be confused with Zephaniah the Minor Prophet and who was an inspired book in the Minor Prophetic section of the Old Testament. Jeremiah is sought out for his prayerful help. How much better it would have been if the king had repented and then sent for Jeremiah to pray WITH him and NOT just FOR him. Jeremiah, at this time, was free. Imprisonment had been his lot earlier, 33:1, and would again later in this chapter (37:15).

v. 5. Portrayed here are two armies. The Chaldean army had been besieging Jerusalem. Zedekiah, though made king by Nebuchadrezzar, rebelled and made a secret agreement with Pharaoh in Egypt (Ezekiel 17:15). This would have been Pharaoh-hophra, son and successor of Pharaoh-necho against whom the just Josiah fought and lost his life in the skirmish (2 Kings 23:29ff). Pharaoh's army came up to relieve besieged Judah and to fight against the hated Chaldeans. Babylon heard of the coming of the invading Egyptians. They temporarily lifted the Jerusalem siege and went forth to meet Pharaoh-hophra and his army. Pharaoh was disastrously unsuccessful and the lifted siege against Jerusalem was very temporary. Any hopes in desperate Judah for a permanent lifting of the Babylonian siege were short-lived.

312

THE SURE RETURN BY CHALDEA
PREDICTED BY JEREMIAH

Paragraph 2 of Jeremiah 37 reads,

Then came the word of the Lord unto the prophet Jeremiah, saying, Thus saith the Lord, the God of Israel; Thus shall ye say to the king of Judah, that sent you unto me to enquire of me; Behold, Pharaoh's army, which is come forth to help you, shall return to Egypt into their own land. And the Chaldeans shall come again, and fight against this city, and take it, and burn it with fire. Thus saith the Lord; Deceive not yourselves, saying, The Chaldeans shall surely depart from us: for they shall not depart. For though ye had smitten the whole army of the Chaldeans that fight against you and there remained but wounded men among them, yet should they rise up every man in his tent, and burn this city with fire (37:6-10).

v. 6. Jehovah's word came promptly to Jeremiah in order that he might have proper words for the inquiring monarch.

v. 7,8. The message from God to Jeremiah for the desperate despot is crystal clear; it was not expressed in dark or mysterious signs at all. Place no confidence in Pharaoh's invading army. They will be defeated and will return to their homeland in humiliation. But the victorious Chaldeans over Egypt will not depart to their own homeland for a surety. They shall resume again the sure siege; they shall fight against this city; they shall take it; they shall burn it with fire.

vs. 9,10. Perhaps the false prophets, of which there were many, were feeding the desperate despot a message of false hope by assuring him that the lifted siege was permanent and Babylon would no longer be at Jerusalem's gates. The voice of deception said Chaldea would depart; Jehovah's voice of truth said they would not depart. How sure is the descending destruction upon doomed Jerusalem? Sure enough that if you were to smite the whole Chaldean army and there were left only grievously wounded or deeply pierced (thrust through—Hebrew) soldiers, they would rise up and burn this city with fire. These are strong words, as Adam Clarke says, but they show the surety of the city's impending collapse. Jerusalem will not survive; God had so willed and that settled that matter ONCE AND FOR ALL!

313

JEREMIAH FALSELY ACCUSED

Paragraph 3 of Jeremiah 37 reads,

> **And it came to pass, that when the army of the Chaldeans was broken up from Jerusalem for fear of Pharaoh's army, Then Jeremiah went forth out of Jerusalem to go into the land of Benjamin, to separate himself thence in the midst of the people. And when he was in the gate of Benjamin, a captain of the ward was there, whose name was Irijah, the son of Shelemiah, the son of Hananiah; and he took Jeremiah the prophet, saying, Thou fallest away to the Chaldeans. Then said Jeremiah, It is false; I fall not away to the Chaldeans. But he hearkened not to him: so Irijah took Jeremiah, and brought him to the princes. Wherefore the princes were wroth with Jeremiah, and smote him, and put him in prison in the house of Jonathan the scribe: for they had made that the prison (37:11-15).**

v. 11. There was a temporary lifting of the Chaldean siege due to the Egyptian invasion in an effort to aid the sagging cause of doomed Judah. Babylon made quick order of stopping cold the Egyptian threat. Jerusalem was given only a brief respite from the coming collapse at the sure hands of the Chaldean conquerors.

vs. 12,13. Jeremiah took advantage of the lifted siege to leave Jerusalem and go a few miles north into the territory of Benjamin. He was not abandoning the kingdom for Benjamin was of Judah's territory. Be it recalled that he was of Anathoth, a city of Benjamin, and had property there (Cf. Jeremiah 32). Doubtless, he went there on personal business. There could well be a share of the land's produce that he went to claim. Anathoth was a priestly city and Jeremiah was of the priestly family. Perhaps he went to claim what was his as a priest. It looked to the north and this was Jeremiah's direction of travel. Here he was apprehended and falsely accused by a captain of the ward—Irijah, son of Shelemiah and grandson of Hananiah. Be it recalled that Hananiah was a false prophet denounced by Jeremiah (Cf. Jeremiah 28). Irijah's action could well have been family vengeance paid back to Jeremiah. In the totally unjustified apprehension Irijah accused Jeremiah of falling away to the Chaldeans.

vs. 14,15. The accused prophet promptly denied the absurd accusation and baseless charge with twofold emphasis. (1) What you say is false. (2) I am not abandoning Judah for Chaldean favors extended. Irijah met the twofold denial with deaf ears and an adamant heart. He brought him to the princes. Earlier princes, still bearing the influence of just Josiah, had been friendly, favorable and supportive of Jeremiah. Doubtless, they had been taken in the 597 B. C. invasion by Nebuchadnezzar and were no longer around. A new breed of princes had taken their place. They were void of nobility and character. They met the apprehended prophet with wrath and malice. In their malice they smote (beat) the innocent prophet and imprisoned him in the house of Jonathan the scribe. Where this man (Jonathan) lived had become a prison. In ancient times prisons were often in the houses of such people. The houses thus afforded living quarters as well as prison facilities.

THE FACE-TO-FACE MEETING OF JEREMIAH AND ZEDEKIAH

Paragraph 4 of Jeremiah 37 reads,

When Jeremiah was entered into the dungeon, and into the cabins, and Jeremiah had remained there many days; Then Zedekiah the king sent, and took him out: and the king asked him secretly in his house, and said, Is there any word from the Lord? And Jeremiah said, There is: for, said he, thou shalt be delivered into the hand of the king of Babylon. Moreover Jeremiah said unto king Zedekiah, What have I offended against thee, or against thy servants, or against this people, that ye have put me in prison? Where are now your prophets which prophesied unto you, saying, The king of Babylon shall not come against you nor against this land? Therefore hear now, I pray thee, O my lord the king: let my suppliction, I pray thee, be accepted before thee; that thou cause me not to return to the house of Jonathan the scribe, lest I die there. Then Zedekiah the king commanded that they should commit Jeremiah into the court of the prison, and that they should give him daily a piece of bread out

of the bakers' street, until all the bread in the city were spent. Thus Jeremiah remained in the court of the prison (37:16-21).

vs. 16,17. The innocent and just Jeremiah is maliciously mistreated. The prison in which they placed him was a dungeon, i. e., a pit or cistern. The cabins were something like vaults or cells in which the prisoners were placed. It was not an overnight stay as Peter and John experienced in Acts 4 or that Paul and Silas endured at Philippi in Acts 16. It was for many days; it was longer than a little while. Zedekiah sent for him. The audience was private, kept in close secrecy and occurred in the monarch's palace. Babylon no doubt had again placed the city under siege after making short order of interfering Egypt. The king is in a strait or hard place. He inquires if there is word from Jehovah? There is, Jeremiah affirms, and you are not going to like it one bit when I tell you. And, sure enough, he did not like it when the clarion message was conveyed. Babylon will be victorious in this siege and you, Zedekiah, will be delivered into the hands of the Chaldean conquerors.

vs. 18,19. Jeremiah seized the occasion to protest the gross miscarriage of justice he was experiencing. He had committed NO offense worthy of imprisonment. It was unclear in the preceding paragraph as touching whether the king joined the princes in Jeremiah's imprisonment. He was an accessory according to it as per verse 18. Jeremiah says, ''that **ye** have put me in prison.'' (Emphasis supplied). Jeremiah chides, and justly so, as to the whereabout of his smooth speaking prophets who shortly before had denied any Chaldean invasion of Judah and Jerusalem. They lied to you, Jeremiah avers, and yet you believed them and rejected my prophetic predictions which came straight from Jehovah.

vs. 20,21. Jeremiah presents an impassioned plea for himself. Do not return me to the dungeon that belongs to Jonathan. My life is in peril in that darkened dungeon. Zedekiah does not release him as pure justice demanded. However, he did change prison locations and made provisions for Jeremiah to receive a piece of bread (usually circular in nature and considered the "staff of life") daily from the bakers' street as long as the food supply in Jerusalem lasted. This would imply that the siege by Babylon was in full force again. Bakers' street is of interest. In Oriental lands of that day those of the same craft or skill shared the same city location. It is still that way in many modern cities where merchants of similar goods and services are frequently of close proximity. Jeremiah thus remained for the time being "in the court of the prison." He was not given deserved liberty, but at least his conditions were noticeably improved.

PERSISTENT MALICE AGAINST JEREMIAH FROM JUDEAN PRINCES

Paragraph 1 of Jeremiah 38 reads,

> **Then Shephatiah the son of Mattan, and Gedaliah the son of Pashur, and Jucal the son of Shelemiah, and Pashur the son of Malchiah, heard the words that Jeremiah had spoken unto all the people, saying, Thus saith the Lord, He that remaineth in this city shall die by the sword, by the famine, and by the pestilence: but he that goeth forth to the Chaldeans shall live; for he shall have his life for a prey, and shall live. Thus saith the Lord, This city shall surely be given into the hand of the king of Babylon's army, which shall take it. Therefore the princes said unto the king, We beseech thee, let this man be put to death: for thus he weakeneth the hands of the men of war that remain in this city, and the hands of all the people, in speaking such words unto them: for this man seeketh not the welfare of this people, but the hurt. Then Zedekiah the king said, Behold, he is in your hand: for the king is not he that can do any thing against you. Then took they Jeremiah, and cast him into the dungeon of Malchiah the son of Hamelech, that was in the court of the prison: and they let down Jeremiah with cords. And in the dungeon there was no water, but mire: so Jeremiah sunk in the mire (38:1-6).**

v.1. A quartet of men is herein portrayed with intense infamy properly belonging to each one. An ancient writer by the name of Dabler once called them the "antitheocratic faction." They opposed God's true theocracy or government over them and greatly hated Jehovah's prophetic representative—Jeremiah. They heard what Jeremiah had been preaching and in subsequent verses they go into prompt action.

317

vs. 2,3. In this duet of verses a short summary of Jeremiah's plain preaching is given. (1) To remain in this city and be adamant against the Chaldeans is to invite sure destruction in the form of death by sword, famine and pestilence. (2) Surrender to the Chaldeans is the only option if one wishes to live. (3) The Lord has already decreed that this city shall fall to the Babylonians; they are going to conquer this city without failure.

v. 4. The princes, haters of Jeremiah, place great pressure on the weak, vacillating king to put Jeremiah to death. They hated the man and his message. They accused him of treason weakening the hands of our army and the people and being totally oblivious to the welfare of the people. They said Jeremiah's only intent was to injure the oppressed and besieged city. Jeremiah was the nation's greatest patriot and they portrayed him as a national traitor. How blind of heart his detractors were.

v. 5. No verse in all Jeremiah pictures more graphically what a weak, unprincipled, vacillating man Zedekiah was. He dared not buck his princes though he was their superior in the sway of governmental power. In essence he said the power was in THEIR hands—not his!! Unlike former President Truman, he did not think the buck stopped with him and his office!

v. 6. The king had just given them permission to do with despised Jeremiah whatever they desired. To another dungeon, perhaps the closest one available, they now hurled him minus mercy and void of any sensitive sympathy. It evidently was a deep cistern for they lowered him by cords. Later, it required thirty men to retrieve him (v. 10). The water was gone from the cistern but it was not dry. Jeremiah sank down in the mire. Josephus, the first century (A. D.) Jewish historian, says he sank down with only head above the mire. Their calloused intention was to kill him slowly and painfully and yet VERY surely. Cruelty found a sure personification in them.

A MUCH NEEDED FRIEND—EBEDMELECH—
TO THE PROPHET'S RESCUE

Paragraph 2 of Jeremiah 38 reads,

Now when Ebedmelech the Ethiopian, one of the eunuchs which was in the king's house, heard that they had put Jeremiah in the dungeon; the king then sitting in the gate

318

of Benjamin; Ebedmelech went forth out of the king's house, and spake to the king, saying, My lord the king, these men have done evil in all that they have done to Jeremiah the prophet, whom they have cast into the dungeon, and he is like to die for hunger in the place where he is: for there is no more bread in the city. Then the king commanded Ebedmelech the Ethiopian saying, Take from hence thirty men with thee, and take up Jeremiah the prophet out of the dungeon, before he die. So Ebedmelech took the men with him, and went into the house of the king under the treasury, and took thence old cast clouts and old rotten rags, and let them down by cords into the dungeon to Jeremiah. And Ebedmelech the Ethiopian said unto Jeremiah, Put now these old cast clouts and rotten rags under thine armholes under the cords. And Jeremiah did so. So they drew up Jeremiah with cords, and took him up out of the dungeon: and Jeremiah remained in the court of the prison (38:7-13).

v. 7. Three things are told us relative to the man introduced in this verse. (1) We have his name—Ebedmelech. It only occurs in this chapter and the subsequent one. His name means servant or slave of the king. It is a Hebrew name which means, in all probability, that he changed it from an Ethiopian designation to a Hebrew appellation. This says much for the man. (2) By nationality he was an Ethiopian. Nobility characterized him even as a well-known Ethiopian in Acts 8:26ff. (3) He was an eunuch in Zedekiah's palace. Eunuchs frequently were in charge of the king's harem. This may or may not have been his assigned task. Being an eunuch meant that his powers of procreation were non-existent. He could never marry in the fullest sense of that term; he could never father children. Yet this great deprivation had not embittered him or made him sour on the world. Ebedmelech learned of Jeremiah's imprisonment in the dungeon. The king was then situated at the gate of Benjamin, a gate that faced the north.

vs. 8,9. Ebedmelech was a person of promptness. He went to the king with a plain and pointed message. He was fearless; he spoke it in public. He addressed the king, his superior, politely and respectfully. He labeled what the evil princes had done to Jeremiah as a grievous wrong. He

319

knew the prophet's life was in great peril being in the miry dungeon. Starvation faced the prophet. No bread is now available in the city.

vs. 10,11. For once in his life as king Zedekiah acted decisively. He decreed that interceding Ebedmelech take thirty men and draw up Jeremiah out of the miry dungeon. This was to be done promptly before the mistreated Seer die. Why take thirty men? Some commentators say there is an error here and the number is more likely three. Some even say thirty men could not be spared from the city's defense. Their arguments are all flimsy and far from conclusive. Zedekiah sent enough men to ward off any hindrance if the wicked princes sought to thwart their mission as well they might. Ebedmelech prosecutes the mission quickly. Castaway garments are used to retrieve Jeremiah from the miry dungeon. They are lowered by means of cords to where the prophet lay mired.

vs. 12,13. Ebedmelech calls down orders on what Jeremiah should do. The old cast clouts (ragged remains of torn garments) and rotten rags would be soft enough that no injury would be inflicted on Jeremiah as they drew him out. Jeremiah acted as commanded. It would be no little task to draw a man who was deeply mired in the deep dungeon. The task is soon completed. Jeremiah is now where he had been earlier—the court of the prison. His circumstances, thanks to his Ethiopian benefactor, were much improved. Here he would remain until the city was taken (Cf. 38:28).

ANOTHER PRIVATE AUDIENCE BETWEEN ZEDEKIAH AND JEREMIAH

Paragraph 3 of Jeremiah 38 reads,

> **Then Zedekiah the king sent, and took Jeremiah the prophet unto him into the third entry that is in the house of the Lord: and the king said unto Jeremiah, I will ask thee a thing; hide nothing from me. Then Jeremiah said unto Zedekiah, If I declare it unto thee, wilt thou not surely put me to death? and if I give thee counsel, wilt thou not hearken unto me? So Zedekiah the king sware secretly unto Jeremiah, saying, As the Lord liveth, that made us this soul, I will not put thee to death, neither will I give thee into the hand of these men that seek thy**

life. Then said Jeremiah unto Zedekiah, Thus saith the Lord, the God of hosts, the God of Israel; If thou wilt assuredly go forth unto the king of Babylon's princes, then thy soul shall live, and this city shall not be burned with fire; and thou shalt live, and thine house: But if thou wilt not go forth to the king of Babylon's princes, then shall this city be given into the hand of the Chaldeans, and they shall burn it with fire, and thou shalt not escape out of their hand. And Zedekiah the king said unto Jeremiah, I am afraid of the Jews that are fallen to the Chaldeans, lest they deliver me into their hand, and they mock me. But Jeremiah said, They shall not deliver thee. Obey, I beseech thee, the voice of the Lord, which I speak unto thee: so it shall be well unto thee, and thy soul shall live. But if thou refuse to go forth, this is the word that the Lord hath shewed me: And, behold, all the women that are left in the king of Judah's house shall be brought forth to the king of Babylon's princes, and those shall say, Thy friends have set thee on, and have prevailed against thee: thy feet are sunk in the mire, and they are turned away back. So they shall bring out all thy wives and thy children to the Chaldeans: and thou shalt not escape out of their hand, but shalt be taken by the hand of the king of Babylon: and thou shalt cause this city to be burned with fire (38:14-23).

vs. 14,15. Desperate Zedekiah arranges for another secret meeting with Jeremiah just subsequent to his release from the miry dungeon. The private audience occurred in the third entry in the Lord's house. This possibly was the entrance into the temple from the king's palace that the king usually used. It afforded a place for the secret meeting. The desperate monarch made a request and charged the prophet that nothing be hidden. He should have known Jeremiah better than this. Jeremiah NEVER concealed from the king what he (the king) needed to hear and heed. Jeremiah prefaces his pronouncements with two observations—if I tell you what you desire to know, will not the death penalty hang over my head and will it not be as uniformly before—you will not heed my message at all? Zedekiah's weak, wicked character was an open book to the astute Seer.

v. 16. Zedekiah only responded to one of these leaving untouched and uncommitted the other. He swore that Jeremiah's life would be spared. He made no promise as to whether he would heed the divine will or not. Down deep he knew that he would pursue his own way—not Jehovah's way. Note that he swore by the very soul (life) the living Jehovah had bequeathed them. Clarke says this is the first time anyone ever employed "the profane custom of swearing by the soul.;;

vs. 17,18. Jeremiah makes triply sure that the requesting monarch knows the origin of the prophetic message. (1) The message is the Lord's. (2) He is the God of hosts (power, authority). (3) He is the God of Israel (ownership established). Surrender is the only wise counsel. A threefold promise is given the king if he accepts this counsel. (1) You shall live; (2) Jerusalem will be spared a fiery destruction; and (3) your house shall live. Rebellion to this counsel on the king's part calls for a threefold consequence. (1) This city will be given to the Chaldeans; (2) it will then be burned with fire; and (3) you shall not escape out of their land, i. e., you shall be counted a captive of war.

v. 19. The real, weak, indecisive and vacillating Zedekiah appears in this verse. He is fearful—not of the coming, conquering Chaldeans—but of the Jews who have already fallen to the Chaldeans. He feared their treachery and the mocking that surely would be his.

vs. 20,21. Obedience to God's will on your part will surely avert what you hear and will result in your own betterment. Refusal on your part will compound the problems you face. These are spelled out in the two subsequent verses.

vs. 22,23. A distinction is to be made in the women of verse 22 and those of verse 23. The former would be his harem or concubines (secondary wives). They shall be brought forth to the Babylonian princes (who doubtless would relish them as objects of sexual satisfaction) and would taunt their former king by saying that his friends (false prophets and conniving princes) have betrayed him and prevailed against him. His feet are sunk in the mire. He will reap what he allowed Jeremiah to face (v. 6). We surely reap what we sow, yea far more than we sow (Cf. Galatians 6:7,8; Hosea 8:7). These are the very types of people, counsellors and aides, in which the foolish king had earlier placed his confidence. They were the very ones he feared coming under their displeasure. The latter women would be his main wives or the ones who had given him children. It is likely that the women in verse 22 were childless, younger and far more desirable to the lusty Babylonian leaders than those women portrayed in verse 23. Your wives will be taken; your children will be taken; you shall not escape Chaldean hands but shall surely become a captive to Babylon's king; and your wilful rebellion will cause this city to be burned. The message was not what the king desired to hear. There WAS word from the Lord and he did not like it one bit! The wicked seldom ever consider unpleasant truth in any other fashion than in deeply despising it and him who delivers it. Unwelcome is ALWAYS the sign they project toward what is unpleasant for them.

ZEDEKIAH'S REQUEST OF JEREMIAH

Paragraph 4 of Jeremiah 38 reads,

> **Then said Zedekiah unto Jeremiah, Let no man know of these words, and thou shalt not die. But if the princes hear that I have talked with thee, and they come unto thee, and say unto thee, Declare unto us now what thou hast said unto the king, hide it not from us, and we will not put thee to death; also what the king said unto thee: Then thou shalt say unto them, I presented my supplication before the king, that he would not cause me to return to Jonathan's house, to die there. Then came all the princes unto Jeremiah, and asked him: and he told them according to all these words that the king had commanded. So they left off speaking with him; for the matter was not perceived. So Jeremiah abode in the court of the prison until the day that Jerusalem was taken: and he was there when Jerusalem was taken (38:24-28).**

vs. 24-26. The king knew well the wicked princes in his court. In view of such he suggested a precaution to Jeremiah relative to keeping secret their conference. If these princes come to you and ask of the nature of our conversation, simply relate that you (Jeremiah) requested of me (Zedekiah) not to be returned to Jonathan's house to die there. Jeremiah had made such a request of the king in 37:20 and it could well have been repeated in this current conversation though unrecorded.

323

v. 27. The princes did come just as Zedekiah predicted they might and asked exactly what the king thought they would. Jeremiah related what the king had suggested and it satisfied the snooping princes. Did Jeremiah do wrong here? Some have contended that he did. He did not tell them anything but what had transpired between him and the king. What he told was truth and nothing but truth. He just did not tell ALL that had transpired and it was not essential that he do so unless one feels that a person is obligated to tell a group of murderers everything they want to know!! This is not a case of situation ethics as some have contended. Sometime back I was conducting an Open Forum in a Texas Lectureship and this very question on this very text came up. The querest desired to know if this was not a case of situation ethics and was not Jeremiah in the wrong. I answered it then about like I have answered it in these comments.

v. 28. Jeremiah was not taken back to the miry dungeon. Zedekiah at least kept that much of his promise. He abode in the court of the prison till the very day Jerusalem fell to Babylon, the thrust of chapter 39.

POINT TO PONDER

(1) There is as much difference between devout Jeremiah and the despotic Zedekiah as there is between good and evil, between righteousness and unrighteousness.

(2) Prayer is impotent when unaccompanied by repentance and amendment of life.

(3) Ebedmelech, as a breath of fresh air, stands out as a man of remarkable nobility.

(4) Matthew Henry, old English commentator, once wrote of Jeremiah's great benefactor, "Ebedmelech lived in a wicked court and in a corrupt degenerate age, and yet he had a great sense of equity and piety."

(5) Zedekiah is an example of a man determined to pursue his own way even at the peril of his own life and those whom he led.

DISCUSSION QUESTIONS

1. Summarize introductory remarks.

2. How widespread was evil in the last days of Judah?

3. What request did the imprisoned Jeremiah make of Zedekiah and what was its outcome?

4. What shows Zedekiah's weak, vacillating character when certain of his subjects approached him relative to Jeremiah?

5. Discuss in some detail this remarkable man Ebedmelech.

MULTIPLE-CHOICE: Underline correct answer

1. The four kings who succeeded Josiah in Judah were: (A) Saul, David, Solomon and Rehoboam; (B) Jeroboam, Ormi, Ahab and Jehu; (C) Asa, Jehoshaphat; Jehoram and Ahaz; (D) Jehoahaz, Jehoiakim, Coniah and Zedekiah.
2. Shephatiah, Gedaliah, Jucal and Pashur have been rightly called: (A) "the fearless foursome for Jeremiah's defense;" (B) "counsellors who urged surrender to Babylon;" (C) "faithful prophets of Jehovah;" (D) "the antitheocratic faction."
3. Anathoth was primarily a city of: (A) prophets; (B) priests; (C) kings; (D) potter workers.
4. Zedekiah was a man who believed in: (A) seizing; (B) abdicating; (C) honoring; (D) using fully—his authority as king of Judah.
5. Zedekiah, in conversation with Jeremiah, swore by his own: (A) soul; (B) silver; (C) palace; (D) family.

SCRIPTURAL FILL-IN: Each blank requires only one word

1. "It _____ false; I _____ not _____ to the _____ ."
2. "_____ there any _____ from the _____ ?"
3. "This _____ shall _____ be _____ into the _____ of the _____ of _____ army, which shall _____ it."
4. "My _____ the _____ , these _____ have done _____ in _____ that they have _____ to _____ the _____ , whom they have _____ into the _____ ; and _____

325

is _____ to _____ for _____ in the
_____ where he _____ : for there is no more
_____ in the _____ ."
5. "_____ , I _____ thee, the _____ of
the _____ , which I _____ unto
thee: so it shall be _____ unto thee, and thy
_____ shall _____ ."

TRUE OR FALSE: Put either a "T" or "F" in each blank

_____ 1. Pharaoh-hophra of Egypt was very successful in repelling permanently the Babylonian threat to Jerusalem.
_____ 2. Irijah proved to be a friend indeed to the frequently persecuted Jeremiah.
_____ 3. Jeremiah was Jerusalem's and Judah's greatest patriot in his era.
_____ 4. Rebellion to God's counsel always compounds man's problems.
_____ 5. Jerusalem's future lay in the hands of Zedekiah and how he responded to Jeremiah's counsel.

THOUGHT QUESTIONS

1. How sure was coming Babylonian destruction to Jerusalem and what lesson about the sure punishment for our sins can we learn from this?

2. What vital questions did Zedekiah ask of Jeremiah, what response did the king give the answer and what important lesson can we derive from such?

3. How does the case of Zedekiah prove that a man reaps what he sows?

4. Deal with whether Jeremiah practiced wrong or situation ethics in the latter part of Jeremiah 38.

5. In what ways might we face similar situations and yet not have to resort to so-called situation ethics? Tell why situation ethics is never acceptable deportment for God's children?

CHAPTER NINETEEN

JERUSALEM'S FALL AND THE AFTERMATH
Jeremiah 39, 40, 41

Jeremiah 39 delineates the fall of Jerusalem, the binding of Zedekiah, his being taken to Babylon, the captivity of those yet in the collapsed capital, the poor remnant allowed to remain and the message to Ebedmelech. Jeremiah 40 portrays the freedom extended Jeremiah and a generous choice given him for the future, his return to Gedaliah the newly appointed governor, the remnant left in the land, Gedaliah's counsel to them and the revealed conspiracy against the new governor by Ishmael. Jeremiah 41 depicts the treacherous slaying of Gedaliah by the iniquitous Ishmael, the calloused murders of others by Ishmael and the courageous recovery of the captives by the valiant Johanan.

JERUSALEM'S SIEGE AND FALL

Paragraph 1 of Jeremiah 39 reads,

In the ninth year of Zedekiah king of Judah, in the tenth month, came Nebuchadrezzar king of Babylon and all his army against Jerusalem, and they besieged it. And in the eleventh year of Zedekiah, in the fourth month, the ninth day of the month, the city was broken up. And all the princes of the king of Babylon came in, and sat in the middle gate, even Nergalsharezer, Samgarnebo, Sarsechim, Rabsaris, Nergalsharezer, Rabmag, with all the residue of the princes of the king of Babylon (39:1-3).

vs. 1,2. These two verses tell of the duration of the Babylonian siege. It was begun in Zedekiah's ninth year as king and in the tenth month which is Tebeth. This is our January. The siege lasted for eighteen months. The city fell in the eleventh year of Zedekiah's reign and in the fourth month which was Thammuz and corresponds to our July. The city walls were finally breached by the determined Babylonians.

v. 2,3. Some Babylonian princes or leaders are named in this verse with only general allusion made to others left nameless. They sat in the middle gate. This was possibly the gate that divided the Upper City (Zion) from the lower city (that which lay to the north). This but emphasizes their complete control of the captured capital, the now fallen citadel of Jewish pride.

FLEEING ZEDEKIAH APPREHENDED AND THEN BLINDED

Paragraph 2 of Jeremiah 39 reads,

> **And it came to pass, that when Zedekiah the king of Judah saw them, and all the men of war, then they fled, and went forth out of the city by night, by the way of the king's garden, by the gate betwixt the two walls: and he went out the way of the plain. But the Chaldeans' army pursued after them, and overtook Zedekiah in the plains of Jericho: and when they had taken him, they brought him up to Nebuchadnezzar king of Babylon to Riblah in the land of Hamath, where he gave judgment upon him. Then the king of Babylon slew the sons of Zedekiah in Riblah before his eyes: also the king of Babylon slew all the nobles of Judah. Moreover he put out Zedekiah's eyes, and bound him with chains, to carry him to Babylon (39:4-7).**

vs. 4,5. Zedekiah realized any further defense of the now conquered capital was hopeless. He and his men of war fled the conquered metropolis. They chose to leave under cover of darkness. Ezekiel, already in Babylon, predicted that the king would choose the night for his hasty exit (12:12). The exit route may have been to the south of the city. The conquerors had invaded from the north which was of lower altitude than the south (sometimes called the upper city). Clarke says there were two commonly traveled routes from Jerusalem to Jericho—across Olivet and the way of the plain. He chose the latter it appears. His escape was not hidden from the Chaldean conquerors. They promptly pursued him

328

overtaking him in the Jericho plains. This would be part of the famed Jordan Valley. They promptly took him to Riblah, headquarters of Nebuchadnezzar. Riblah was on the frontier of Northern Palestine. This would be Syrian territory. The fierce Babylonian ruler passed judgment upon one he considered to be a rebel to his crown of world-wide power (2 Kings 24:20). Nebuchadnezzar earlier made him king (2 Kings 24:17).

vs. 6,7. Zedekiah's first judgment was a cruel one indeed. His very sons were slain before his very eyes. Did the king not recall Jeremiah's words and how such could have been averted? (38:17-23). Surely, he must have!! Zedekiah was twenty-one years old when he began to reign (2 Kings 24:18). Now he is only thirty-two. His children were likely only teenagers at this time and maybe not even this old. The cruel Babylonian ruler also slew all Judah's nobles. This appears to have been done before Zedekiah's eyes also. Again, did he not remember Jeremiah's counsel again and again on how all this could have been averted? Surely, he must have!! Then came another severe judgment upon the rebellious Zedekiah. They put out his eyes or literally "dugged" them out. This passage explains and harmonizes perfectly Jeremiah 32:4 that says Zedekiah would see eye-to-eye Nebuchadnezzar and Ezekiel 12:13 that he would go to Babylon, die there and yet never SEE it. He saw the Chaldean conqueror before they blinded him; he was taken to Babylon where he died and yet blindness kept him from ever surveying the city with his sight. How beautifully harmonious are all the Scriptures when the whole of them is considered. The blinded, humiliated king is placed in chains (brazen, bronze chains, fetters, manicles—margin) and led to Babylon. A chained king always signified a defeated city or nation by the victorious monarch or general of the army.

THE FIERY FATE OF JERUSALEM
AND CAPTIVITY OF HER PEOPLE

Paragraph 3 of Jeremiah 39 reads,

And the Chaldeans burned the king's house, and the houses of the people, with fire, and brake down the walls of Jerusalem. Then Nebuzaradan the captain of the guard carried away captive into Babylon the remnant of the people that remained in the city, and those that fell away, that fell to him, with the rest of the people that remained.

329

But Nebuzaradan the captain of the guard left of the poor of the people, which had nothing, in the land of Judah, and gave them vineyards and fields at the same time (39:8-10).

v. 8. Jeremiah here does not relate that nearly one month passes between the fall of the city and the fiery destruction depicted in this verse. The city was broken up the fourth month and ninth day of Zedekiah's eleventh year; according to 2 Kings 25:8 the burning of the city occurred the fifth month and the seventh day. During the interval the king and his men are taken to Riblah and judgment passed on and executed relative to Zedekiah. Perhaps during this time Nebuchadnezzar made the final decision as to Jerusalem's destiny. This verse carried out the king's wishes as the Chaldeans burned the king's palaces, the houses of the people and finished breaking down the walls of Jerusalem.

vs. 9,10. The account in 2 Kings 25:8ff tells of Nebuzaradan's coming to Jerusalem. Brother DeHoff, and with excellency of reason, calls him the "chief executioner or field marshall of the king of Babylon." He chose the ones still left in the city to be taken into captivity and the ones to be left. The poorest of the people were left. Evidently, Babylon felt such people could be of no benefit to them, only liabilities. They were left with vineyards and fields—the very possessions long denied them due to their extreme poverty and the constant oppression they suffered at the unhold hands of greedy landowners. There seems to be a real measure of reaped justice here for those long denied such property possession.

NEBUCHADNEZZAR'S MERCIFUL TREATMENT
OF JEREMIAH

Paragraph 4 of Jeremiah 39 reads,

Now Nebuchadrezzar king of Babylon gave charge concerning Jeremiah to Nebuzaradan the captain of the guard, saying, Take him, and look well to him, and do him no harm; but do unto him even as he shall say unto thee. So Nebuzaradan the captain of the guard sent, and Nebushasban, Rabsaris, and Nergalsharezer, Rabmag, and all the king of Babylon's princes; Even they sent, and took Jeremiah out of the court of the prison, and com-

mitted him unto Gedaliah the son of Ahikam the son of Shaphan, that he should carry him home: so he dwelt among the people (39:11-14).

vs. 11,12. The Babylonian king had doubtless heard of Jeremiah's persistent teaching that Zedekiah not rebel against Babylon and he was favorably impressed. Four merciful and sensitive orders are given relative to the faithful prophet. (1) He is to be taken; (2) what is well for him is to be done without fail; (3) no harm is to be inflicted on him; and (4) give him a choice as touching his future. God remembered and fulfilled His promise, as He ALWAYS does, of 15:11. What a contrast between the way a pagan monarch felt toward Jeremiah and the way Zedekiah, supposedly a religious man, felt toward the persecuted prophet from Anathoth. Another great contrast is seen in the way Zedekiah was treated by the Chaldeans and the way Jeremiah fared.

vs. 13,14. Nebuzaradan filtered the king's orders to those under him and carefully executed them in Jeremiah's regard. Zedekiah had imprisoned Jeremiah very unjustly; the Babylonians set him free. The prophet is committed into the careful keeping of Gedaliah, the newly appointed governor over Judah, who was to provide lodging for Jeremiah and give him freedom. Evidently, it was Jeremiah's choice to remain in Judah with the small remnant allowed to stay there. Additional details of this are given in 40:1ff. There is no contradiction but simply some details contained in 40:1ff are not here set out.

Paragraph 5 of Jeremiah 39 reads,

Now the word of the Lord came unto Jeremiah, while he was shut up in the court of the prison, saying, Go and speak to Ebedmelech the Ethiopian, saying, Thus saith the Lord of hosts, the God of Israel; Behold, I will bring my words upon this city for evil, and not for good; and they shall be accomplished in that day before thee. But I will deliver thee in that day, saith the Lord: and thou shalt not be given into the hand of the men of whom thou art afraid. For I will surely deliver thee, and thou shalt not fall by the sword, but thy life shall be for a prey unto thee: because thou hast put thy trust in me, saith the Lord (39:15-18).

vs. 15,16. It appears this message had come earlier to Jeremiah but related here so as not to break the sequence of events the prophet was depicting. The message touched the excellent Ebedmelech, the Ethiopian eunuch who had courageously delivered Jeremiah from the perilous pit of mire in 38:7-13. The prophet's message to Ebedmelech assures the Ethiopian that God's words will surely experience exacting fulfillment. This would assure Ebedmelech that Jeremiah was Jehovah's faithful prophet.

vs. 17,18. When Jerusalem is conquered and pillaged by the Chaldean conquerors, Ebedmelech's life will be spared. He will not be delivered into the hands of the men he feared; he would not die by the sword. The why of this gracious promise is simply stated, "because thou hast put thy trust in me, saith the Lord."

A GRACIOUS BABYLONIAN OFFER MADE TO JEREMIAH

Paragraph 1 of Jeremiah 40 reads,

> **The word that came to Jeremiah from the Lord, after that Nebuzaradan the captain of the guard had let him go from Ramah, when he had taken him being bound in chains among all that were carried away captive of Jerusalem and Judah, which were carried away captive unto Babylon. And the captain of the guard took Jeremiah, and said unto him, The Lord thy God hath pronounced this evil upon this place. Now the Lord hath brought it, and done according as he hath said: because ye have sinned against the Lord, and have not obeyed his voice, therefore this thing is come upon you. And now, behold, I loose thee this day from the chains which were upon thine hand. If it seem good unto thee to come with me into Babylon, come; and I will look well unto thee: but if it seem ill unto thee to come with me into Babylon, forbear: behold, all the land is before thee: whither it seemeth good and convenient for thee to go, thither go. Now while he was not yet gone back, he said, Go back also to Gedaliah the son of Ahikam the son of Shaphan, whom the king of Babylon hath made governor over the cities of Judah, and dwell with him among the people:**

or go wheresoever it seemeth convenient unto thee to go. So the captain of the guard gave him victuals and a reward, and let him go. Then went Jeremiah unto Gedaliah the son of Ahikam to Mizpah; and dwelt with him among the people that were left in the land (40:1-6).

v. 1. As affirmed hundreds of times earlier in this prophetic product, Jeremiah is inspired. Numerous commentators have remarked at this point that we have here no immediate prophetic pronouncement from Jeremiah. The solution is a simple one. Jeremiah gives an account, an inspired one at that, of what occurs beginning in this chapter and it all serves to pave the way for statements he will begin to make from Jehovah in chapters 42 and 43. Commentators frequently create problems where none exists except in their own dense and frequently unenlightened minds created by too little homework before their pens of commentary begin to function. Though given freedom from the court of the prison in 39:14 and there committed to Gedaliah's protective security yet there are some interval happenings noted by way of supplement set forth here and not covered in the extremely brief account of 39:14. There is NO contradiction but just a more detailed account than in the previous chapter. Jeremiah, along with other captives from Jerusalem, was taken bound to Ramah, a city of Benjamin located five miles north of Jerusalem. Here the processing plans were to occur prior to their being taken to Babylon. Jeremiah was indiscrimately placed in chains and led the short distance north to Ramah, headquarters at this time for Nebuzaradan, Nebuchadnezzar's captain of the guard or his field marshall.

vs. 2-4. Very promptly Jeremiah is distinguished out from the captive throngs of Jews in chains. Nebuzaradan, in someway, had learned that he and his Babylonian warrriors had become Jehovah's chastening rods of desperately needed discipline to adamant, rebellious Judah. He informs Jeremiah that the Lord had pronounced this punishment upon Judah and it has been executed in harmony with His (Jehovah's) wishes. The Babylonian captain explains positively and negatively (making it a complete description) as touching the why of Judah's fall. (1) This nation has sinned against the Lord (positive explanation) and (2) this nation has failed, flagrantly failed (negative explanation), to obey Jehovah's voice. This is why national collapse has materialized against this degenerate, depraved nation. Jeremiah is then released from the fetters placed earlier

333

upon him prior to deportation to Ramah. A merciful and very generous choice is then bequeathed to him by the Chaldean captain of the guard. (1) You (Jeremiah) may come with me to Babylon and very generous will be your welfare and security there. (2) If you decide against this, you may remain right here in Palestine. Do what your wisdom suggests. Make the decision in full view of your better interests.

vs. 5,6. Jeremiah is very hesitant about the feasibility of the Babylonian choice for his future. Nebuzaradan discerns reluctance on the part of the slow-to-respond Jeremiah and beckons him to go to Gedaliah, newly appointed governor by Nebuchadnezzar over captured Judah and Jerusalem or wherever it might be convenient. Generously and graciously, the Babylonian conqueror and captain gave him victuals (food and other needs) and a reward (a present or gift). He allowed the now freed Jeremiah to leave Ramah. Jeremiah retires to the protective shield of Gedaliah. He goes to nearly Mizpah, just southwest of Ramah and five miles northwest of Jerusalem. Here he would be near his hometown of Anathoth. By choice he dwelt among the poor remnant (Cf. 39:10) of the land. This proves his great patriotism for both his native land and his people—a point his lifelong enemies persistently failed to grasp. Jeremiah was one of the most misunderstood men who ever lived. In this he was like the Misunderstood Jesus six centuries later would be.

THE PEOPLE COME TO THE NEW GOVERNOR

Paragraph 2 of Jeremiah 40 reads,

> **Now when all the captains of the forces which were in the fields, even they and their men, heard that the king of Babylon had made Gedaliah the son of Ahikam governor in the land, and had committed unto him, men, and women, and children, and of the poor of the land, of them that were not carried away captive to Babylon. Then they came to Gedaliah to Mizpah, even Ishmael the son of Nethaniah, and Johanan and Jonathan the sons of Kareah, and Seraiah the son of Tanhumeth, and the sons of Ephai the Netophathite, and Jezaniah the son of a Maachathite, they and their men. And Gedaliah the son of Ahikam the son of Shaphan sware unto them and to their men, saying, Fear not to serve the Chaldeans:**

dwell in the land, and serve the king of Babylon, and it shall be well with you. As for me, behold, I will dwell at Mizpah to serve the Chaldeans, which will come unto us: but ye, gather ye wine, and summer fruits, and oil, and put them in your vessels, and dwell in your cities that ye have taken. Likewise when all the Jews that were in Moab, and among the Ammonites, and in Edom, and that were in all the countries, heard that they king of Babylon had left a remnant of Judah, and that he had set over them Gedaliah the son of Ahikam the son of Shaphan; Even all the Jews returned out of all places whither they were driven, and came to the land of Judah, to Gedaliah, unto Mizpah, and gathered wine and summer fruits very much (40:7-12).

vs. 7,8. Captains of the forces referred to former war leaders of Judah who had fled Jerusalem during the Chaldean siege and resided in places where they would be secure from Chaldean dangers. News of the appointment of Gedaliah as new governor came to these dispersed leaders and their men. They heard of the provisions that had been made for the remnant left in the land. Buoyed by such news and the hope it reflected they came to Gedaliah at Mizpah, his headquarters. Ishmael is mentioned first and he may have been their recognized leader. He proves later to be anything but honorable as he rose up and murdered the goodly Gedaliah (Cf. 41:2). Other names then follow. Some are left nameless.

vs. 9,10. Gedaliah, son of Ahikam who earlier aided Jeremiah (26:24), responds with wisdom, goodness, gentleness, assurance and with measured leadership ability. (1) He dispels any and all fears they may have of serving the Babylonians. (2) Dwell peacefully in the land and serve faithfully Babylon's king and well will be your continued lot. (3) He outlines what his protective duties of shielding them will be as he would deal with any directives that came from the Chaldeans. (4) You may major in providing for your needs by gathering wine, summer fruits and oil placed in your vessels. Note that the wine is to be gathered. It was then in the cluster. It was not then intoxicative. This is one of a number of passages in the Bible that speak of wine while yet in the grape hull. Hence, the word is NOT uniformly intoxicative in connotation. Context decides such—not an arbitary ruling from moderns who wish

335

to read into the Bible scriptural sanction for their notorious intake of alcoholic beverages. (5) You may dwell in the cities you have taken. People in ancient times lived in the cities as a rule and went forth to tend the land or shepherd their sheep.

vs. 11,12. Some of the Jews had even fled the land of Judah and sought asylum in neighboring lands of Moab, Ammon and Edom, lands east, southeast and south of Palestinian territories. News now came to them of the recent changes in Judah. They came also to Gedaliah in Mizpah. They followed his earlier counsel, doubtless given them also upon their return, in gathering an abundance of wine and summer fruits. These they would need for the coming winter. The Chaldean siege had ended around August.

GEDALIAH RECEIVES A DEATH WARNING THREAT BUT DISCOUNTS ITS POTENTIAL DANGER

Paragraph 3 of Jeremiah 40 reads,

> **Moreover Johanan the son of Kareah, and all the captains of the forces that were in the fields, came to Gedaliah to Mizpah, And said unto him, Dost thou certainly know that Baalis the king of the Ammonites hath sent Ishmael the son of Nethaniah to slay thee? But Gedaliah the son of Ahikam believed them not. Then Johanan the son of Kareah spake to Gedaliah in Mizpah secretly, saying, Let me go, I pray thee, and I will slay Ishmael the son of Nethaniah, and no man shall know it: wherefore should he slay thee, that all the Jews which are gathered unto thee should be scattered, and the remnant in Judah perish? But Gedaliah the son of Ahikam said unto Johanan the son of Kareah, Thou shalt not do this thing: for thou speakest falsely of Ishmael (40:13-16).**

vs. 13,14. Johanan had been mentioned earlier in this chapter (v. 8). Here he and a number of his associates left their working posts in the fields and came to Mizpah with a message of tremendous urgency for Governor Gedaliah. As assassination attempt was now in the planning stages and would soon be executed. Johanan and his concerned colleages learned of this death plot. They inquired if the Governor knew of it.

The planner of the assassination was Baalis (derived from the idol god-Baal) king of Ammon. The hit man, as we would express it in modern parlance, was Ishmael. It is a bit difficult to pinpoint the precise why of Baalis' motives in this assassination plot of a ruling neighbor to the west. Some think he may have possessed political aspirations of removing an able ruler in order that he might invade, conquer and control his nearby neighboring nation to the west. It may have been due to a thirst of revenge. Recall that Gedaliah was the son of Ahikam. In Jeremiah 26 Ahikam was a loyal friend of Jeremiah. In the very next chapter Jeremiah received a message of coming subjection to Babylon inclusive of several nations. Ammon was of that doomed group (26:1-8). This may have been a long, smoldering hatred and hostility toward Jeremiah and the family of Ahikam who befriended and defended the prophet. With Ishmael's motives we can be somewhat more certain. Doubtless he was envious. He was of the seed royal (David's family) and doubtless resented his being passed over in this top political post and one outside David's seed being chosen as the new governor. Envy and malice are of close kin. Both are Satanic offspring. Gedaliah was a good man himself and evidently thought others were of the same disposition. He rejected the death threat. He must have thought, "Surely, Ishmael will not be of such a base, diabolical disposition to slay a man who only wishes well for the remnant remaining in Judah." How little he knew of Ishmael will be revealed subsequently.

vs. 15,16. Johanan persists in determined attempts to save Gedaliah's life. Secretly, he agrees to kill Ishmael and keep closely concealed who did it. Johanan reminded the new governor of the rapid chaos that would envelop desperate Judah were he (Gedaliah) assassinated. In your absence, we shall be scattered hopelessly. Gedaliah still refused to believe the threat and even accused Johanan of bringing a false report against Ishmael. Johanan was not whistling in the dark; he was not crying wolf when no danger was hovering nearby. The next chapter will portray how wrong Gedaliah was in labeling the threat as false.

GEDALIAH AND MANY OTHERS SLAIN
BY INFAMOUS ISHMAEL

Paragraph 1 of Jeremiah 41 reads,

Now it came to pass in the seventh month, that Ishmael the son of Nethaniah the son of Elishama, of the seed

royal, and the princes of the king, even ten men with him, came unto Gedaliah the son of Ahikam to Mizpah; and there they did eat bread tobether in Mizpah. Then arose Ishmael the son of Nethaniah, and the ten men that were with him, and smote Gedaliah the son of Ahikam the son of Shaphan with the sword, and slew him, whom the king of Babylon had made governor over the land. Ishmael also slew all the Jews that were with him, even with Gedaliah, at Mizpah, and the Chaldeans that were found there, and the men of war. And it came to pass the second day after he had slain Gedaliah, and no man knew it, That there came certain from Shechem, from Shiloh, and from Samaria, even fourscore men, having their beards shaven, and their clothes rent, and having cut themselves, with offerings and incense in their hand, to bring them to the house of the Lord. And Ishmael the son of Nethaniah went forth from Mizpah to meet them, weeping all along as he went: and it came to pass, as he met them, he said unto them, Come to Gedaliah the son of Ahikam. And it was so, when they came into the midst of the city, that Ishmael the son of Nethaniah slew them, and cast them into the midst of the pit, he, and the men that were with him. But ten men were found among them that said unto Ishmael, Slay us not: for we have treasures in the field, of wheat, and of barley, and of oil, and of honey. So he forbare, and slew them not among their brethren. Now the pit wherein Ishmael had cast all the dead bodies of the men, whom he had slain because of Gedaliah, was it which Asa the king had made for fear of Baasha king of Israel: and Ishmael the son of Nethaniah filled it with them that were slain. Then Ishmael carried away captive all the residue of the people that were in Mizpah, even the king's daughters, and all the people that remained in Mizpah, whom Nebuzaradan the captain of the guard had committed to Gedaliah the son of Ahikam: and Ishmael the son of Nethaniah carried them away captive, and departed to go over to the Ammonites (41:1-10).

Matthew Henry prefaces his comments on this chapter with these words of weight,

> **Such base, barbarous, bloody work is here done by men who by their birth should have been men of honour, by their religion just men, and this done upon those of their own nation, their own religion, and their brethren in affliction, upon no provocation—all done in cold blood (Matthew Henry's ONE VOLUME COMMENTARY, p. 1008).**

vs. 1,2. The seventh month corresponds to our September-October. Ishmael and his assassins came to Gedaliah. They came as supposed friends and even enjoyed a meal together—courtesy of Gedaliah's generosity. In that culture people who ate together were friends and enjoyed mutual fellowship. Base and infamous Ishmael showed how little he was in character. He and his assassins slew with sword the goodly Gedaliah, the very appointee of Babylon to govern the land.

v. 3. His bloodthirsty ways were insatiable. He slew all the Jews that were there. He even slew the Chaldeans who were men of war and possibly served as a bodyguard for the new governor. Those slain probably were at ease thinking Gedaliah was entertaining warm and loyal friends of longstanding at a banquet.

vs. 4,5. More murderous activity is on the way. These two verses give the background of others soon to feel the wrath of infamous, iniquitous Ishmael. The time was the second day after Gedaliah had been slain. Secrecy still covered that enormous assassination. Some eighty men came from central Canaan headed for the Jerusalem area. They came from Shechem, area where Abraham first came into the land and near where Jacob's well was located, from Shiloh, an earlier site of the tabernacle during the Judges and from Samaria, recent capital of the Northern Kingdom. They were men in mourning as touching what had happened to Jerusalem and their beloved temple. Shaved beards, rent clothes and self-mutilation were signs of deep mourning and genuine sadness. They had offerings (bloodless no doubt) and incense they intended to offer on the ashes of what once constituted their beloved temple. It no longer stood but at its remains they deemed that holy ground was still theirs to tread.

vs. 6,7. Alert Ishmael hears of this traveling group. His iniquitous ear does not miss a trick as we would express it in modern parlance. He joined them as a pretender to great piety. He met them as a fellow weeper. He requested that these eighty pious men all come to Gedaliah at Mizpah. When the group arrived in Mizpah, Ishmael and his henchmen fell upon them and slew them. They threw them into a pit or cistern. This refers to a cistern first built by Asa, an earlier king of Judah, as we learn later in this context.

vs. 8,9. It appears that only seventy of the eighty were killed. Ten saw a way to bribe their safety at Ishmael's hands. They offered him treasures they had hidden if he would let them live. Covetous Ishmael saw an instant way to enrich himself and he left them alive. Dead men could not have taken him to these coveted treasures. One is made to wonder relative to their continued welfare as soon as wicked Ishmael had the promised treasures in hand. Further information is given of where the mass of bodies were buried. It was in a pit or cistern made many years earlier by Asa of Judah who was fearful of Baasha of Israel. Ishmael filled the pit with the innocents he had slain in such infamy. Wickedness was personified in Ishmael.

v. 10. Further infamy is pictured of iniquitous Ishmael. Ishmael emptied Mizpah of the remaining people, the king's daughters and all that the Babylonians had committed into the care and keeping of Gedaliah. He carried them as captives and headed for the land of Ammon. Recall that it was Baalis, the Ammonite king, who had put Ishmael up to all this mass homicide. The lot of these captives among the calloused and cruel Ammonites would be anything but pleasant. Quite possibly they faced being sold as slaves with Baalis, Ishmael or both sharing in the slave traffic profits.

BRAVE AND BOLD JOHANAN RECOVERS THESE CAPTIVES

Paragraph 2 of Jeremiah 41 reads,

> **But when Johanan the son of Kareah, and all the captains of the forces that were with him, heard of all the evil that Ishmael the son of Nethaniah had done, Then they took all the men, and went to fight with Ishmael the son of Nethaniah, and found him by the great waters that are in Gibeon. Now it came to pass, that when all the people**

which were with Ishmael saw Johanan the son of Kareah, and all the captains of the forces that were with him, then they were glad. So all the people that Ishmael had carried away captive from Mizpah cast about and returned, and went unto Johanan the son of Kareah. But Ishmael the son of Nethaniah escaped from Johanan with eight men, and went to the Ammonites. Then took Johanan the son of Kareah, and all the captains of the forces that were with him, all the remnant of the people whom he had recovered from Ishmael the son of Nethaniah, from Mizpah, after that he had slain Gedaliah the son of Ahikam, even mighty men of war, and the women, and the children, and the eunuchs, whom he had brought again from Gibeon: And they departed, and dwelt in the habitation of Chimham, which is by Bethlehem, to go to enter into Egypt, Because of the Chaldeans: for they were afraid of them, because Ishmael the son of Nethaniah, had slain Gedaliah the son of Ahikam, whom the king of Babylon made governor in the land (41:11-18).

vs. 11,12. Be it recalled that Johanan earlier had warned Gedaliah of impending danger at Ishmael's evil hands but Gedaliah refused to honor the warning. News now reached Johanan and his warriors of what infamy Ishmael had done. Promptly, they went into military action. Gathering their armed forces together they pursued infamous Ishmael overtaking him at the waters of Gibeon. Gibeon, it is said, was some two miles north of Mizpah, scene of Ishmael's slaying of Gedaliah and his forces. Gibeon had been the bloody scene of a battle between Abner's men and Joab's men in 2 Samuel 2:12ff.

vs. 13,14. The captives that had been taken by Ishmael were filled with grateful gladness when they beheld the coming of their victorious deliverers. They managed to break away from Ishmael and came under the protection of Johanan.

v. 15. Ishmael is not so brave now. Outnumbered and on the brink of embarrassing defeat he sought out a sure route of escape. Eight of his men joined him in the quick exit. Since he had ten men originally (v. 2) two must have abandoned him or perhaps were killed in the conflict. He went to the Ammonites—his former allies in all the crimes he had perpetrated in recent days. Jeremiah makes no further mention of him beyond this chapter. His name last occurs in 41:18. Inspiration mentions nothing worthwhile relative to him. One great Bible scholar mentions him as a VILE character and he surely fits that diabolical designation.

vs. 16-18. Johanan took all that were with him, military captains, remnant of the people, mighty men of war, women, children, eunuchs and left the Mizpah-Gibeon area. They departed to a more southern point—Chimham near Bethlehem. This would be about six miles south of Jerusalem. See 2 Samuel 19:31-40 for further information about Chimham. Johanan evidently felt secure here until he could complete his plans of fleeing into Egypt. They feared reprisals from the Chaldeans who might blame all Jews for not protecting sufficiently the newly appointed governor—Gedaliah. Babylon also might be well offended at their allowing Ishmael, Gedaliah's murderer, to escape without proper punishment of the infamous Ishmael. A number of factors may have produced the fears that tugged at their heartstrings.

POINTS TO PONDER

(1) Ebedmelech the Ethiopian is a great case showing the great wisdom of putting one's trust in God.

(2) In Ishmael we see what envy, jealousy and murderous thoughts can ultimately do to the man who harbors such emotional hazards as these.

(3) Jeremiah once said man's heart is deceitful above things and desperately wicked (Jeremiah 17:9). Ishmael was a living personification of that sad, yet true, observation.

(4) Ishmael was one of the vilest men who ever lived.

(5) King Zedekiah paid dearly for his crimes against Jehovah, Jehovah's law and the just Jeremiah.

DISCUSSION QUESTIONS

1. Summarize introduction.

2. What cruel indemnities were done Zedekiah by the victorious Chaldeans?

3. What positive and negative explanation did the Babylonian captain of the guard give for Judah's defeat at Chaldean hands?

4. How did Matthew Henry describe the murderous men of Jeremiah 41?

5. What may have prompted Johanan and those under him to go to the Bethlehem area?

MULTIPLE-CHOICE: Underline correct answer

1. The time it took Babylon to capture Jerusalem was: (A) one month; (B) six months; (C) ten years; (D) eighteen months.
2. Nebuzaradan was: (A) a field marshal; (B) an enemy; (C) an occult adviser; (D) the superior—of Nebuchadnezzar during the Jerusalem siege.
3. At the siege's end Jeremiah: (A) decided to go to Babylon; (B) chose to remain in Judah; (C) was executed by the Chaldeans; (D) was promptly executed by rebellious Jews who despised him.
4. Gedaliah was: (A) an Egyptian envoy to Jerusalem; (B) a captain in the Chaldean army; (C) the newly appointed governor of Judah; (D) a spy for Jerusalem and sent among the Chaldeans.
5. Ishmael, at heart, was a: (A) murderer; (B) good man; (C) great supporter of Governor Gedaliah; (D) person totally void of envy and jealousy.

SCRIPTURAL FILL-IN: One word is required for each blank

1. "Then the _____ of _____ slew the sons of _____ in _____ before his _____ : also the _____ of _____ slew all the _____ of _____ ."

2. "_____ he put out Zedekiah's _____ , and _____ him with _____ , to _____ him to _____ ."

3. "For I will _____ deliver thee, and thou shalt not _____ by the _____ , but thy _____

343

shall be for a _____ unto thee: _____ thou hast
_____ thy _____ in _____ , saith the
_____ ."

4. "Then went _____ unto _____ the son
_____ to _____ ; and dwelt with him among the
_____ that were _____ in the _____."

5. "_____ not to _____ the _____ : dwell
in the _____ , and serve the _____ of
_____ , and it _____ be _____ with
you."

TRUE OR FALSE: Put either a "T" or "F" in the blanks

_____ 1. King Zedekiah was very successful in his escape plans to elude capture by the Chaldeans.
_____ 2. Nebuchadnezzar and Nebuzaradan both dealt very cruelly and harshly with Jeremiah subsequent to the Chaldean capture of the city.
_____ 3. Gedaliah possessed the necessary qualities of a good leader.
_____ 4. Ishmael was insatiable in his bloodthirsty ways.
_____ 5. Sin has a sure way sooner or later in catching up with the iniquitous Ishmaels of the world.

THOUGHT QUESTIONS

1. Explain the harmony of the Biblical declarations that Zedekiah would be taken to Babylon yet would never see the city.

2. Contrast the way pagan Chaldea treated Jeremiah and the way so-called religious Jerusalem had treated him for some twenty-five years of his prophetic ministry.

3. In what ways were Jeremiah and Jesus both misunderstood men by their peers in their respective ages?

4. What is said of wine in this lesson that proves the term does not ALWAYS refer to an intoxicant?

344

5. What may have motivated Baalis, Ammonite king, to conspire with Ishmael for the death of Governor Gedaliah?

CHAPTER TWENTY

JEREMIAH AND THE OBSTINATE REMNANT
Jeremiah 42, 43

Men frequently desire to do the Lord's will but only IF Deity rubber stamps what they have already decided they intend to do. This duet of chapters surely depicts that very adamancy of mankind. The remnant request of Jeremiah to give them God's word relative to their future. They promise an obedient disposition to what God spoke by Jeremiah. All the time they knew that they were going to exit Judah for Egypt. When the Lord spoke through Jeremiah against their going to Egypt and what sure punishment awaited them there, they promptly denied Jeremiah's inspiration and laid plans to migrate to the Land of the Nile with all speed. They take Jeremiah with them. Jeremiah promptly gives a prophecy that Babylon will surely invade and conquer Pharaoh's land. Jeremiah gives his prophecy in a very graphic way as the latter part of this chapter will unfold.

THE PEOPLE'S REQUEST OF JEREMIAH
AND HIS PROMPT RESPONSE

Paragraph 1 of Jeremiah 42 reads,

> **Then all the captains of the forces, and Johanan the son of Kareah, and Jezaniah the son of Hoshaiah, and all the people from the least even unto the greatest, came near, And said unto Jeremiah the prophet, Let, we beseech thee, our supplication be accepted before thee, and pray for us unto the Lord thy God, even for all this remnant; (for we are left but a few of many, as thine eyes do behold us:) That the Lord thy God may shew us the**

way wherein we may walk, and the thing that we may do. Then Jeremiah the prophet said unto them, I have heard you; behold, I will pray unto the Lord your God according to your words; and it shall come to pass, that whatsoever thing the Lord shall answer you, I will declare it unto you; I will keep nothing back from you. Then they said to Jeremiah, The Lord be a true and faithful witness between us, if we do not even according to all things for the which the Lord thy God shall send thee to us. Whether it be good, or whether it be evil, we will obey the voice of the Lord our God, to whom we send thee: that it may be well with us, when we obey the voice of the Lord our God (42:1-6).

vs. 1-3. The captains of the forces would be the various leaders over the people who had been greatly scattered due to the siege and fall to the city. Johanan and Jezaniah are named in particular. The people, from the least to the greatest, are gathered together to seek counsel from Jeremiah. They request that he pray to the Lord for them. They remind the veteran and faithful prophet that they are but a remnant, a few of the former many, even as Jeremiah could tell by looking. They desire to know what way God would have them go—how He would have them walk—what He would have them do. How noteworthy this request would have been had it only been from the heart and made in sincerity. But alas, it was not as the sad sequel reveals very clearly!

v. 4. Jeremiah here reminds us of Samuel who had been slighted by his generation and yet would not sin in a refusal to pray for them (Cf. 1 Samuel 12:20-25). Though they had rejected Jeremiah for nearly all his prophetic ministry, yet he does not now retaliate by a resounding refusal to pray for them and to seek the desired counsel from the Lord. Jeremiah told them that he would convey back to them exactly what God told him. He vowed to declare to them God's whole counsel; he would keep back nothing from them. Paul speaks a similar sentiment in Acts 20:20,26,27.

vs. 5,6. They make a sworn appeal to the Lord and a solemn agreement with Jeremiah that they will accept faithfully and completely whatever message Jeremiah brings them. They solemnly aver that they will accept God's will in this desired matter whether it be good or evil. Since the

Lord is NEVER the author of any evil, then this should be understood as whether it be pleasant or unpleasant, whether it be easy or difficult. They voiced the sentiment that it might be well with them when they obeyed God's voice. They did not preface any of this with a condition already ingrained in their hearts—provided the Lord rubber stamps our already established intention of vacating Judah for Egypt.

JEHOVAH ANSWERS JEREMIAH TEN DAYS LATER

Paragraph 2 of Jeremiah 42 reads,

> **And it came to pass after ten days, that the word of the Lord came unto Jeremiah. Then called he Johanan the son of Kareah, and all the captains of the forces which were with him, and all the people from the least even to the greatest, And said unto them, Thus saith the Lord, the God of Israel, unto whom ye sent me to present your supplication before him; If ye will still abide in this land, then will I build you, and not pull you down, and I will plant you, and not pluck you up: for I repent me of the evil that I have done unto you. Be not afraid of the king of Babylon, of whom ye are afraid; be not afraid of him, saith the Lord: for I am with you to save you, and to deliver you from his hand. And I will shew mercies unto you, that he may have mercy upon you, and cause you to return to your own land (42:7-12).**

vs. 7-9. Jeremiah did not receive any word from the Lord immediately but had to wait ten days for the requested revelation. This would give the inquirers sufficient time to weigh with deliberate calmness the strong, obedient response they had just proposed to Jeremiah. When the message did come, Jeremiah called for Johanan, the captains of the forces and all the people from the least to the greatest. He desired them in aggregate to be present. He prefaced his message with an affirmation that it was God's word he was about to deliver. He would not be speaking Jeremiah's mind; he would be speaking Jehovah's mind. He wisely reminds them that THEY had been the very ones who had requested this revelation of God's will. Hence, heavenly authority will punctuate every syllable he speaks.

vs. 10-12. Abide in this land and the following blessings of beauty will be yours. (1) I will build you up; (2) I will not pull you down; (3) I will plant you; (4) I will not pluck you up; (5) I have done sufficient punishing of you and there will be no more of this if you are ready to submit to me; (6) there is no need of your being afraid of Babylon's king; (7) I, one who is far greater than the Babylonian monarch, will be with you; (8) I will save you; (9) I will deliver you from any danger he may pose; (10) my extended mercies will be bequeathed you; (11) the Babylonian king will see that I am on your side and his land will be yours in returning to claim it, maintain it and delight in it.

A STIFF WARNING IF THEY REJECT JEHOVAH'S COUNSEL

Paragraph 3 of Jeremiah 42 reads,

> **But if ye say, We will not dwell in this land, neither obey the voice of the Lord your God, Saying, No; but we will go into the land of Egypt, where we shall see no war, nor hear the sound of the trumpet, nor have hunger of bread; and there will we dwell: And now therefore hear the word of the Lord, ye remnant of Judah; Thus saith the Lord of hosts, the God of Israel; If ye wholly set your faces to enter into Egypt, and go to sojourn there; Then it shall come to pass, that the sword, which ye feared, shall overtake you there in the land of Egypt, and the famine, whereof ye were afraid, shall follow close after you there in Egypt; and there ye shall die. So shall it be with all the men that set their faces to go into Egypt to sojourn there; they shall die by the sword, by the famine, and by the pestilence: and none of them shall remain or escape from the evil that I will bring upon them. For thus saith the Lord of hosts, the God of Israel; As mine anger and my fury hath been poured forth upon the inhabitants of Jerusalem; so shall my fury be poured forth upon you, when ye shall enter into Egypt: and ye shall be an execration, and an astonishment, and a curse, and a reproach; and ye shall see this place no more (42:13-18).**

vs. 13-16. Jehovah knew these people with precise perfection. He knew in their hearts that they had every intent to defy Him and migrate to

Egypt regardless of His prohibition to the contrary. On the condition that you decide against dwelling in this land and obeying my voice by saying that we are Egypt-bound where no war will afflict us, no trumpet sound of coming battle will pierce our ears and no hunger pains will be ours again, be assured that such dreams of peace and prosperity will NOT materialize for you in Pharaoh's land. Set your faces to flee into Egypt and here is what you will face. (1) The lethal sword you feared in Palestine will overtake you in Egypt. You cannot outrun it. (2) The famine or lack of food that you imagine will be your lot in Judah will, without fail, be your SURE lot in Egypt. It will be at your heels every step you take. (3) The death reality you think you will escape by fleeing Judah will engulf you in the Land of the Nile.

vs. 17,18. This shall be the sure punishment of every man who sets his face toward Egypt. Death will come in a threefold manner. (1) Some shall die by the lethal sword; (2) Some shall die by the famine; they will starve. (3) Some shall die by pestilence, i. e., by sickness, disease, etc. There will be NO escape from these sure penalties to be imposed on you as you defiantly enter Egypt. Death is on the door of Egyptian entrance. Jehovah reminds the adamant, defiant and rebellious remnant bent on an Egyptian migration that just as He poured out His anger and fury on obstinate Jerusalem, the same anger and fury will be hurled upon them in Egypt. Five consequences would be theirs for this rebellious migration into Egypt. (1) They would be an execration. They would be hated and abhorred by those who would afflict them till they died. (2) They would be an astonishment. It would even amaze their enemies at the enormity of their punishment. (3) They would be a curse. In contempt and ignominy would they be held. None would feel an obligation to befriend or defend them. (4) They will be a reproach. People will mock them, sneer at them and make their end one of anguish, embarrassment and humiliation. (5) Judah's land they will NOT see again. Egypt will be your tomb, your cemetery.

JEREMIAH'S POIGNANT EPILOGUE

Paragraph 4 of Jeremiah 42 reads,

> **The Lord hath said concerning you, O ye remnant of Judah; Go ye not into Egypt: know certainly that I have admonished you this day. For ye dissembled in your**

hearts, when ye sent me unto the Lord your God, saying, Pray for us unto the Lord our God; and according unto all that the Lord our God shall say, so declare unto us, and we will do it. And now I have this day declared it to you; but ye have not obeyed the voice of the Lord your God, nor any thing for the which he hath sent me unto you. Now therefore know certainly that ye shall die by the sword, by the famine, and by the pestilence, in the place whither ye desire to go and to sojourn (42:19-22).

vs. 19,20. The remnant of Judah would be those who survived Jerusalem's fall, who were not among the captives headed for far-off Babylon but were left in Judah. They were a small group by their own admission (Cf. 42:2). The Lord's will which He had communicated to them was crystal clear. They were forbidden to go into Egypt. Jeremiah had admonished them that very day to table all intentions for the proposed Egyptian migration. They were dissemblers, i. e., hypocrites. You sent me to the Lord for His word on this venture. You requested that I pray to Jehovah relative to this matter. You solemnly averred you would honor His word when I received it and conveyed it to you.

vs. 21,22. I have delivered fully and forcefully what Jehovah's will is. You have defied my message from beginning to end. You never intended to honor His will unless His will had coincided fully with yours. Egypt is your determined destination. It will be your cemetery. There you will die by sword, by starvation and by sickness. You have an adamant desire to go there. You anticipate it as just a sojourn, i. e., that one day you will leave it and come back to Judah. NOT SO!! Egypt will be your graveyard for defying my God and His will for your lives.

JEREMIAH ACCUSED OF BEING A FALSE PROPHET

Paragraph 1 of Jeremiah 43 reads,

And it came to pass, that when Jeremiah had made an end of speaking unto all the people all the words of the Lord their God, for which the Lord their God had sent him to them, even all these words, Then spake Azariah the son of Hoshaiah, and Johanan the son of Kareah, and all the proud men, saying unto Jeremiah, Thou speakest falsely: the Lord our God hath not sent thee to

351

say, **Go not into Egypt to sojourn there: But Baruch the son of Neriah setteth thee on against us, for to deliver us into the hand of the Chaldeans, that they might put us to death, and carry us away captives into Babylon. So Johanan the son of Kareah, and all the captains of the forces, and all the people, obeyed not the voice of the Lord, to dwell in the land of Judah. But Johanan the son of Kareah, and all the captains of the forces, took all the remnant of Judah, that were returned from all nations, whither they had been driven, to dwell in the land of Judah; Even men, and women, and children, and the king's daughters, and every person that Nebuzaradan the captain of the guard had left with Gedaliah the son of Ahikam the son of Shaphan, and Jeremiah the prophet, and Baruch the son of Neriah. So they came into the land of Egypt: for they obeyed not the voice of the Lord: thus came they even to Tahpanhes (43:1-7).**

v. 1. Jeremiah, in total faithfulness, had done what they requested. He had gone to the Lord in their behalf. The Lord had given him the needed revelation. Jeremiah had given them the revelation in full. He had withheld no word from Jehovah from them.

vs. 2,3. The Azariah here is doubtless the same as Jezaniah in 42:1. Hoshaiah is mentioned as father in both verses. Johanan is also specified. We are deeply disappointed to see a reversal of roles for Johanan. Earlier chapters had depicted him on the side of good and right. Now he has abandoned that saintly side and has gone to the sinful side of the rebels against both Jehovah and Jeremiah. This defiant duet is joined by men of like character and designated by Inspiration as proud men. Proud men are so full of their own supreme importance that they have no room in heart for Heaven's will, for Jehovah's wishes. Bluntly and blasphemously, they accuse Jeremiah of maliciously manufacturing this whole matter. They accused him of speaking falsely. This is strange because for more than forty years now he has told them nothing but truth in his prophetic proclamations. From such a stately standard he had never wavered—as much as a compromising inch! They deny that God has issued any prohibition at all about their going to Egypt. God has neither sent you nor said what you say He said. Desperately needing a scapegoat they atrociously accuse Baruch, Jeremiah's faithful secretary and a God-fearing man second only to Jeremiah in all Judah, of fabricating the whole affair. Baruch has turned you (Jeremiah) against us and our desire to migrate to Egypt. Baruch, they aver, has a clever plan to deliver us into Chaldean hands, into hands that will kill us and carry us captives to Chaldea. Such was a bold, blasphemous lie in all its fabricating facets.

v. 4. These defiant and proud rebels obeyed not Jehovah's voice. Heavenly counsel called for their staying in Judah. To Egypt they were determined to go. Nothing was going to impede their going.

vs. 5,6. This proud, dictatorial element in the leadership took those who had returned to Judah from other places and headed them toward Egypt. Included in the aggregate of those compelled to go were men, women and children. Taken also were the king's daughters. These would have been Zedekiah's daughters and doubtless by his harem of concubines. His sons had been killed earlier (Cf. 39:6). Babylon left these daughters of the king possibly because they posed no threat to Chaldea. Taken were all that Nebuzaradan, captain of the Chaldean guard, had left as remnant in the demolished land. Jeremiah and Baruch were taken. There seems little doubt but what they were FORCED to go. Knowing both of these godly men as we do, there can be no doubt they WILLINGLY would flaunt God's will and thwart His wishes. They knew it was God's will that this preserved remnant NOT go into the Land of the Nile.

v. 7. In coming into Egypt they clearly violated God's crystal clear command. He said NOT GO; they WENT nevertheless! In coming to Tahpanhes, they were at the northeast border of Egypt. This was possibly the first Egyptian city they approached. Verse 9 corroborates this observation.

ANOTHER REVELATION FROM JEHOVAH TO JEREMIAH

Paragraph 2 of Jeremiah 43 reads,

> **Then came the word of the Lord unto Jeremiah in Tahpanhes, saying, Take great stones in thine hand, and hide them in the clay in the brickkiln, which is at the entry of Pharaoh's house in Tahpanhes, in the sight of the men of Judah; And say unto them, Thus saith the Lord of hosts, the God of Israel; Behold, I will send and**

take Nebuchadrezzar the king of Babylon, my servant, and will set his throne upon these stones that I have hid; and he shall spread his royal pavilion over them. And when he cometh, he shall smite the land of Egypt, and deliver such as are for death to death; and such as are for captivity to captivity; and such as are for the sword to the sword. And I will kindle a fire in the houses of the gods of Egypt; and he shall burn them, and carry them away captives: and he shall array himself with the land of Egypt, as a shepherd putteth on his garment; and he shall go forth from thence in peace. He shall break also the images of Bethshemesh, that is in the land of Egypt; and the houses of the gods of the Egyptians shall he burn with fire (43:8-13).

vs. 8,9. Jeremiah is still Jehovah's prophet even though, by constraint, he has been deported into Egypt. Jehovah could speak to Jeremiah in Egypt with the same ease as he formerly did in Judah. The Lord's word came to Jeremiah in Tahpanhes. Brother DeHoff says this "was a fortress in the Nile delta on the highway that leads from Egypt to Palestine." This prophecy and its execution are punctuated with graphic plainness and vivid forcefulness. The addressed prophet is to take great stones in hand, probably as large as he could carry and hide them in the clay (in the mortar as we would express the matter) in the brickkiln—the place where they burned or dried their bricks. In Egypt this was usually done by placing them under the burning sun. This was at the entry of Pharaoh's house in this fortress city. Jeremiah was not to do this silently but in sight of Judah's men. It had special and sad significance to them.

vs. 10,11. Actions permeate verse 10. The revelation to Judah begins in verse 10. The message is God's. Jeremiah affirms such nearly five hundred times, by my personal count, in his prophetic writings. Nebuchadrezzar is here referred to as Jehovah's servant. Jehovah often used pagan, idolatrous rulers to carry out His will. This is the sense in which Nebuchadrezzar is Jehovah's servant. The Babylonian monarch will surely invade Egypt as he had successfully done at Jerusalem just about one year earlier. Significance of these set stones in mortar now becomes evident. Nebuchadrezzar will set his very throne on these set stones; his royal pavilion (canopy or covering) will be draped over his throne at this very spot. Men of Judah should have been stunned with the impact of this plain, prophetic pronouncement. The Chaldean monarch will not be making just a social call. He will come as conqueror, as devourer of Egypt, as smiter of the Land of the Nile. Three classes are next depicted. (1) Those destined to die, probably with plagues and pestilences in mind, will surely die. (2) Those destined to be taken captive shall surely go into captivity. (3) Those destined to die by sword shall surely perish by sword. Men of Judah thought they would surely escape such by coming to Egypt. They could have escaped such by obeying Jehovah and remaining in Judah (Cf. 42:7-22). Now what they hoped to avert will surely be visited upon them for sure.

vs. 12,13. Though a pagan and idolater himself yet the avenging Babylonian monarch will smite Egyptian idolatry where it will hurt the most—in the very temples or houses of their gods. As God's avenging agent, he will set fire to these temples housing Egyptian deities. Some of these gods he would burn with fire. These would be made of perishable ingredients. Those of metal—silver, gold, etc.,—he will carry away as spoils of his devastating victory. The prophet is very graphic in the next prophetic pronouncement. With the same ease and assurance that a shepherd drapes his body with his garment just that easy will be Egyptian capture by a determined Nebuchadrezzar. Nothing will impede or interrupt his victorious exit from Egypt. Bethshemish, an Egyptian city filled with idols and their temples, was the same as Heliopolis, as called by the Greeks, or On, as called by the Egyptians. This city lay east of the Nile and just north of ancient Memphis. Nebuchadrezzar shall be a smasher of Bethshemish idols and images and shall destroy by fire temples that housed Egyptians gods.

POINTS TO PONDER

(1) Jeremiah's great character is seen in his prompt willingness to pray for the very people who long had persecuted and rejected him.

(2) Great rewards always abide us when we obey implicitly God's counsel for our lives.

(3) It is tragic for a man to pursue right for a part of his life as Johanan did and reverse that role for evil as later he did.

(4) Jeremiah's whole life had been spent in being FAITHFUL to Jehovah and HELPFUL to Judah.

(5) Nebuchadrezzar was Jehovah's servant due to his role as God's avenging rod to punish and punish severely rebellious Judah, Jerusalem and Egypt.

DISCUSSION QUESTIONS

1. Summarize introduction.

2. What was basically wrong with their prayer proposal to Jeremiah?

3. How careful was Jeremiah in prefacing the God-given revelation he was about to deliver to the inquiring remnant?

4. List and discuss the eleven blessings Jeremiah promised the inquiring remnant.

5. How is Johanan such a major disappointment to us in Jeremiah 42,43?

MULTIPLE-CHOICE: Underline each correct answer

1. The people look to Jeremiah as: (A) "the king"; (B) "the prophet"; (C) "the deliverer"; (D) "the liason" to Nebuchadrezzar.
2. In his quick willingness to pray for those who had frequently rejected him, Jeremiah reminds us of another great Old Testament character who was: (A) Samuel; (B) Solomon; (C) Isaac; (D) Jacob.
3. The requested revelation to Jeremiah came: (A) the next day; (B) ten days later; (C) five days later; (D) one month later.
4. Johanan was: (A) determined to keep the remnant in Judah; (B) ready to lead the remnant to Babylon; (C) adamant in his plans to lead the remnant to Egypt; (D) a man who honored his word and kept his promises.
5. Jeremiah and Baruch were: (A) left in Jerusalem; (B) sent off to Babylon; (C) taken to Egypt; (D) banished to Arabia.

SCRIPTURAL FILL-IN: Each blank requires only one word

1. "_____ will _____ nothing _____ from _____ ."

2. "And _____ I have this day _____ it to you; but ye have not _____ the _____ of the _____ your _____ , nor any _____ for the _____ he hath _____ me unto you."

3. "So they _____ into the _____ of _____ : for they _____ not the _____ of the _____ : thus came _____ even to _____ ."

4. "_____ , I will _____ and take _____ the _____ of _____ , my _____ , and will _____ his _____ upon these _____ that I have _____ ; and he shall _____ his _____ pavilion _____ them."

5. "And _____ he _____ , he shall _____ the _____ of _____ , and _____ such as are for _____ to _____ ; and such as are for _____ to _____ ; and such as are for the _____ to the _____ ."

TRUE OR FALSE: Put either a "T" or "F" in the blanks

_____ 1. Evil, as used relative to God's will, does not mean wrongdoing but that which is difficult or unpleasant.

_____ 2. It was Jehovah's will for this remnant to migrate to Egypt with prompt rapidity.

_____ 3. Egypt would surely become the cemetery for this determined remnant.

_____ 4. Proud men filled with egotistical arrogance are always an abomination to God.

_____ 5. The rebellious remnant spoke glowingly about Baruch, Jeremiah's faithful and competent secretary.

THOUGHT QUESTIONS

1. Show the striking similarity between Jeremiah 42:4 and Acts 20:20,26,27.

2. What is so very repulsive about insincerity and a pretension toward prayer?

3. How does the material in this chapter show the heavy price tag attached to sin?

4. Prove that Jeremiah and Baruch were FORCED to migrate into Egypt with the rebellious remnant and did not go FREELY.

5. Why is it the utmost folly for man to defy the clearly revealed will of Heaven's great Jehovah?

CHAPTER TWENTY-ONE

DESERVED PUNISHMENT IN EGYPT
Jeremiah 44, 45

The gravely serious sins of an adamant people are depicted with force and finality in the material composing Jeremiah 44. We see precisely how concerned Jehovah was with their sins and how glibly unconcerned they were. Their fondness for idols and total trust in them are set forth in Jeremiah 44. Sure punishment of a grievous nature was on their threshold. Jeremiah 45 is a short chapter in which Baruch is given assurance and comfort. It bears no close literary kinship to the main points of Jeremiah 44 at all. It is of much closer, literary kinship to Jeremiah 36.

JEWISH OBSTINACY TOWARD IDOLATROUS SIN PROVOKES JEHOVAH'S WRATH

Paragraph 1 of Jeremiah 44 reads,

> **The word that came to Jeremiah concerning all the Jews which dwell in the land of Egypt, which dwell at Migdol, and at Tahpanhes, and at Noph, and in the country of Pathros, saying, Thus saith the Lord of hosts, the God of Israel; Ye have seen all the evil that I have brought upon Jerusalem, and upon all the cities of Judah; and, behold, this day they are a desolation, and no man dwelleth therein. Because of their wickedness which they have committed to provoke me to anger, in that they went to burn incense, and to serve other gods, whom they knew not, neither they, ye, nor your fathers. Howbeit I sent unto you all my servants the prophets, rising early and**

sending them, saying, Oh, do not this abominable thing that I hate. But they hearkened not, nor inclined their ear to turn from their wickedness, to burn no incense unto other gods. Wherefore my fury and mine anger was poured forth, and was kindled in the cities of Judah and in the streets of Jerusalem; and they are wasted and desolate, as at this day. Therefore now thus saith the Lord, the God of hosts, the God of Israel; Wherefore commit ye this great evil against your souls, to cut off from you man and woman, child and suckling, out of Judah, to leave you none to remain; In that ye provoke me unto wrath with the works of your hands, burning incense unto other gods in the land of Egypt, whither ye be gone to dwell, that ye might cut yourselves off, and that ye might be a curse and a reproach among all the nations of the earth? Have ye forgotten the wickedness of your fathers, and the wickedness of the kings of Judah, and the wickedness of their wives, and your own wickedness, and the wickedness of your wives, which they have committed in the land of Judah, and in the streets of Jerusalem? They are not humbled even unto this day, neither have they feared, nor walked in my law, nor in my statutes, that I set before you and before your fathers (44:1-10).

vs. 1-3. Jeremiah is now an aged man but yet very faithful to the Lord and fervent for His Cause. Here is another word revelation that comes to Him. The recipients of the hard-hitting message were the aggregate of all Jews in Egypt. By now the Jews were pretty well scattered throughout the main parts of Pharaoh's domain. Migdol and Tanpanhes were in northern Egypt (called Lower Egypt). Noph (ancient Memphis and now where modern Cairo stands) and Pathros were in the more southern parts of Egypt (called Upper Egypt). The origin of the message is clearly identifiable. It is from the Lord of hosts. This reflects His power. It is from the God of Israel. This reflects His ownership of them— an ownership they disdained and had long rejected. Evil in verse 2 does not refer to moral or unethical evil that God brought upon them for He ALWAYS does right—NEVER wrong. It refers to the unpleasant punishment He visited upon them due to their grievous sins, especially

360

the capital crime of idolatry. This severe devastating punishment had been brought upon both Jerusalem and the cities of Judah. How complete or comprehensive was it? It was now a desolate land, a depopulated land. For their unmitigated sins against the pure, righteous and ever fair Jehovah they were now paying a very high price in reaped consequences. Sin always pays a wage and it is always high (See Romans 6:23). Their wickedness is spelled out in verse 3. It was such a deep-seated wickedness as to provoke God to anger. They burned incense to other gods—foreign gods whom neither they nor their fathers had known. Idolatry had become their priority. It, in turn, always triggers all other kinds of sins.

vs. 4-6. Jehovah was concerned; He entreated for a reversal of their grievous sins. He sent His servants—Hebrew prophets—as voices of urgency. They arose early to give their messages which portrays the most serious of urgent pleading. God pleaded through prophets for them not to engage in such. The plea was on the basis that it is an abomination; it is a thing I hate. That Jehovah hated it seemingly made them even more adamant toward its continuation. They would not bend a listening ear of concern to the heavenly entreaty. They neither backed off from their wickedness in general nor from the burning of incense to other gods in particular. Burning of incense represents the full allegiance and service they rendered these worthless and lifeless deities. Due to such atrocious adamacy, Jehovah poured out upon their obstinate heads the fulness of His fury and an avalanche of His aroused anger. God's weighty wrath was visited upon both Jerusalem and Judah. Now that once prosperous city and that once affluent province lie in waste and desolation. What a powerful reminder of what sin can do to a once highly blessed people.

vs. 7,8. You people here in Egypt are not one whit better. You are sinning against your very souls. You are sowing the seeds of your own destruction. Your very remnant faces sure destruction. Verse 8 is filled with stinging rebukes. (1) You provoke me (God) to wrath with your unlawful works. (2) You defy me in burning incense to other gods. You defy me in burning incense to others god right here in Egypt which you have chosen as your deliberate dwelling place. (3) By your adamant transgressions you are cutting yourselves off. (4) You will be a curse and reproach among all nations of the earth. You will be held in the depths of contempt and will face the heights of disdain and despite.

vs. 9,10. In verse 9 the weighty word wickedness occurs five times! Note its emphatic repetition. (1) Have you forgotten the wickedness of your fathers? (2) Have you forgotten the wickedness of Judah's kings? (3) Have you forgotten the wickedness of their wives or queens (from Solomon to Zedekiah)? (4) Have you forgotten you own wickedness? (5) Have your forgotten the wickedness of your own wives? Wickedness was a family matter in which all majored. An ever increasing wave of wickedness permeated all Judah and each street of Jerusalem. Have you learned nothing till this very day? Not that first thing? (1) You are not yet humbled; (2) you still do not fear me; (3) you still do not walk in my law; (4) you reject my statutes. These laws and statutes have been set before you even as they were your fathers. You reject them just as did they.

SURE AND COMPLETE PUNISHMENT FORETOLD

Paragraph 2 of Jeremiah 44 reads,

> **Therefore thus saith the Lord of hosts, the God of Israel; Behold, I will set my face against you for evil, and to cut off all Judah. And I will take the remnant of Judah, that have set their faces to go into the land of Egypt to sojourn there, and they shall all be consumed, and fall in the land of Egypt; they shall even be consumed by the sword and by the famine: they shall die, from the least even unto the greatest, by the sword and by the famine: and they shall be an execration, and an astonishment, and a curse, and a reproach. For I will punish them that dwell in the land of Egypt, as I have punished Jerusalem, by the sword, by the famine, and by the pestilence: So that none of the remnant of Judah, which are gone into the land of Egypt to sojourn there, shall escape or remain, that they should return into the land of Judah, to the which they have a desire to return to dwell there: for none shall return but such as shall escape (44:11-14).**

vs. 11,12. The powerful Lord is the speaker; he is the God of Israel. "Behold" is an attention gainer; something of intense impact follows it. Jehovah makes solemn promise that His face will be AGAINST them—not FOR them. They would not have Him as shield as their more

362

fortunate fathers had in earlier centuries. Jehovah proposes to cut off Judah. This is limited for He surely had no intention of cutting off ALL Judah for then the Abrahamic promises would fail. Shiloh (the Messiah) shall descend from Judah, Jacob affirmed in Genesis 49:8-10. Also there would be a remnant return from Babylon under Cyrus' decree in the book of Ezra. Even in Egypt there would be a small number that would escape as this very chapter later depicts (v. 28). By cutting off Judah the Lord must have had in mind those who had willingly gone to Egypt and there had become more settled than ever in idolatrous fascinations and forms. The evil Jehovah pronounces against them is forthcoming punishment—not any moral or unethical evil He would trigger for the Judge of the earth will ALWAYS do right (Cf. Genesis 18:25). Verse 12 confirms that God has in mind those whose faces had been set to come to Egypt. Their faces had been set for the Egyptian migration; God's face was set against them after they were situated in Pharaoh's land of the Nile. They were the ones determined to sojourn there; they were the ones who later would be consumed; their fall is a certainty and nothing will impede it. The lethal sword will claim some of them; famine and starvation will claim others. Death will claim the arrogant leaders. Sword and famine are mentioned a second time. The repetition of these lethal devices makes it even more certain. Four terms describe their coming fate. (1) They shall be an execration (worthy of being cursed). (2) They shall be an astonishment. Their enemies will hiss at them. (3) They shall be a curse (it will surely fall on them). (4) They shall be a reproach. They will become a by-word, a people of unparalleled contempt by all beholders.

vs. 13,14. Punishment is surely destined for these proud rebels in Egypt. It will be similar to the punishment visited upon Jerusalem. (1) The sword shall devour. (2) Starvation, triggered by famine, will devour. (3) Pestilence—sickness and disease—will destroy. Of the ones God planned to punish, the rebels, not any of them shall escape. They have gone to sojourn thinking surely they could return, at will, to Judah. Their later desires to return shall not materialize. Only a very few would escape (v. 28). Their adamant determination to plan a temporary sojourn in Egypt paid an exceedingly high wage of reaped punishment.

THE ADAMANT ANSWER FROM THE PROUD REBELS

Paragraph 3 of Jeremiah 44 reads,

**Then all the men which knew that their wives had burned
incense unto other gods, and all the women that stood
by, a great multitude, even all the people that dwelt in
the land of Egypt, in Pathros, answered Jeremiah, saying,
As for the word that thou hast spoken unto us in the name
of the Lord, we will not hearken unto thee. But we will
certainly do whatsoever thing goeth forth out of our own
mouth, to burn incense unto the queen of heaven, and
to pour out drink offerings unto her, as we have done,
we, and our fathers, our kings, and our princes, in the
cities of Judah, and in the streets of Jerusalem: for then
had we plenty of victuals, and were well, and saw no evil.
But since we left off to burn incense to the queen of
heaven, and to pour out drink offerings unto her, we have
wanted all things, and have been consumed by the sword
and by the famine. And when we burned incense to the
queen of heaven, and poured out drink offerings unto
her, did we make her cakes to worship her, and pour
out drink offerings unto her without our men? (44:15-19).**

vs. 15-17. Jeremiah had struck a sensitive spot indeed. The women
were disturbed, the men were mad in having to defend their wives due
to Jeremiah's remonstrance of their idolatrous proclivities. The occasion
may well have been a festival in honor to the queen of heaven (the moon).
Moon-worship is much more likely than an allusion to sun-worship
which would have been the King of heaven. A great multitude has
congregated—both men and women en masse. In the aggregate they
answer angrily. Jeremiah seemingly was in the minority and may have
been the only one who championed truth that day. This would have been
no new position for him for he frequently had been in this lonely, isolated
source. In the aggregate, they informed him that they were not going
to give ANY heed to his God-sent message of prophetic revelation. To
the contrary we will do what we want to do; we shall honor the vows
we have made to our cherished queen of heaven in burning incense to
her and in pouring out drink offerings to her. We have done it; our
ancestors did it; our kings did it; our princes did it; we did it openly
in both Judah's cities and the streets of Jerusalem. When we did so we
were blessed with food and all our needs. We were well in those days

and faced no calamities at all. Matthew Henry, in essence, has these interesting observations on their rebellious answer to the inspired prophet. (1) Antiquity is pleaded; this was ancestral practice. (2) Authority is pleaded; kings and princes have led us in this. (3) Unity is pleaded; they did it en masse. (4) Universality is pleaded; cities of Judah and streets of Jerusalem witnessed our worship of Heaven's Queen. (5) Visibility is pleaded; they had done this openly in Judaean cities or on Jerusalem streets—not in secret or darkened places. (6) Prosperity is pleaded; they said they had plenty then. In their naive thinking and dense reasoning, they were totally unaware of WHO really gave them every good and perfect gift. The Maker of the moon—not the moon— had blessed them. Even the evil and righteous reap God's showers and enjoy His sunshine. This trio of verses is filled with self-will in whole and no room for Jehovah's will at all. How utterly pathetic; how immeasurably sad!

vs. 18,19. They attribute all tribulations and persecutions to their failure to continue in worshipping and serving Heaven's Queen. Such calamities came and were triggered when we left off our moon-worship. The women are prominently portrayed in this whole defense of their idolatrous worship to the moon. Such worship is delineated. (1) They burned incense to her; (2) they poured out drink-offerings to her; (3) they made cakes to worship her; (4) they did it all with the full approbation of their husbands. The cakes they made for moon worship may well have been crescent-shaped and to remind them of the various appearances of the moon throughout each month. The men, our husbands, approved it. Why should you, Jeremiah, object? Today, we have women who want to do everything in church functions as do men—teach mixed adult classes, lead such in prayers, preach, lead singing, serve as elders, be in business meetings and help in all decisions made, serve as deacons, be public evangelists, etc. They plead the same—we have the approbation of the men, the elders, etc. It is as flimsy and sinful today to plead such for an authoritative stance as it was 2,600 years ago in Jeremiah's apostate era. And this is precisely what such erroneous practices will trigger today—another apostate era on us!!!

JEREMIAH'S COURAGEOUS, UNCOMPROMISING REPLY

Paragraph 4 of Jeremiah 44 reads,

Then Jeremiah said unto all the people, to the men, and to the women, and to all the people which had given him that answer, saying, The incense that ye burned in the cities of Judah, and in the streets of Jerusalem, ye, and your fathers, your kings, and your princes, and the people of the land, did not the Lord remember them, and came it not into his mind? So that the Lord could no longer bear, because of the evil of your doings, and because of the abominations which ye have committed; therefore is your land a desolation, and an astonishment, and a curse, without an inhabitant, as at this day. Because ye have burned incense, and because ye have sinned against the Lord, and have not obeyed the voice of the Lord, nor walked in his law, nor in his statutes, nor in his testimonies; therefore this evil is happened unto you, as at this day. Moreover Jeremiah said unto all the people, and to all the women, Hear the word of the Lord, all Judah that are in the land of Egypt: Thus saith the Lord of hosts, the God of Israel, saying; Ye and your wives have both spoken with your mouths, and fulfilled with your hand, saying, We will surely perform our vows that we have vowed, to burn incense to the queen of heaven, and to pour our drink offerings unto her: ye will surely accomplish your vows, and surely perform your vows. Therefore hear ye the word of the Lord, all Judah that dwell in the land of Egypt; Behold, I have sworn by my great name, saith the Lord, that my name shall no more be named in the mouth of any man of Judah in all the land of Egypt, saying, The Lord God liveth, Behold, I will watch over them for evil, and not for good: and all the men of Judah that are in the land of Egypt shall be consumed by the sword and by the famine, until there be an end of them. Yet a small number that escape the sword shall return out of the land of Egypt into the land of Judah, and all the remnant of Judah, that are gone into the land of Egypt to sojourn there, shall know whose words shall stand, mine, or theirs (44:20-28).

vs. 20,21. The veteran, uncompromising prophet spoke his inspired reply to all the people inclusive of the men, the women and all who had given him the foregoing answer of such defiance and rebellion. Their burning of incense would include all the worship and service they gave to the lifeless deities of their era. They had done it publicly both in Judah and in Jerusalem and God had called such highhanded actions to remembrance. He was perfectly in the know; it escaped not His All-Seeing Eye and All-Knowing Mind for as much as a fleeting moment of time.

vs. 22,23. You have gravely misread matters. You think all calamities came upon you because you had left off your idolatrous practices toward Heaven's queen—the moon. NOT SO!! Jehovah was longsuffering with you and blessed you for a period of time even when you were so engaged. You mistook these as blessings bequeathed by your preferred idol. When His patience wore thin due to your increasing evils and your abounding abominations, the Lord visited your sins in severity. Your land, Judah, became desolate, an astonishment, a curse and minus inhabitants. Judah is that way till this very day, Jeremiah avers. The calamities came not because you ceased for awhile to burn incense to your moon-god. The calamities came because: (1) you sinned against the Lord; (2) you have not obeyed His voice; (3) you have not walked in His law; (4) you have not honored His statutes; (5) you have not been submissive to His testimonies. Law, statutes, and testimonies would be inclusive of all the Mosaic mandates, all of Sinai's commandments whether pertaining to moral mandates or ceremonial commandments. Your rejection of God and His law has triggered all this—not any displeasure by a so-called moon god!

vs. 24-26. Jeremiah charges all Jews, men and women, in Egypt to hear his inspired message. Your sins have not been spur-of-moment occurrences. To the contrary, they have been premeditated. Your intentions were first oral or spoken; then you executed them with your hands. You were in gross error to make vows about burning incense and pouring out drink-offerings to Heaven's queen. You have but compounded your sin by translating these rash and sinful vows to idolatrous reality. You seem to think that since you made such idolatrous vows that you are totally justified in executing them. Jeremiah thunders forth a message of strict severity for them. They are charged to hear the prophetic warning. God intended to remove once and for all their glib lip

367

pronouncements that God lives and yet in their hearts and by their hands they were wedded to their idols. Such glaring inconsistencies would soon cease.

vs. 27,28. God's watchfulness over them will not be as a fountain of blessing and a shield of security. He will make absolutely sure that the appropriate punishment He plans for them will come with certainty. It WILL NOT be averted; it CANNOT be averted. These rebellious Jews in Egypt who are determined to pursue their own way will be comprehensively consumed either by the lethal sword or the slower way of death—starvation by famine. Only a small number shall escape these sure decrees. They, as a small remnant, shall leave Egypt and go back to Canaan. It will then be clear as to whose words shall stand—God's or theirs. It would NOT be theirs!

A SURE SIGN

Paragraph 5 of Jeremiah 44 reads,

> **And this shall be a sign unto you, saith the Lord, that I will punish you in this place, that ye may know that my words shall surely stand against you for evil: Thus saith the Lord; Behold, I will give Pharaoh-hophra king of Egypt into the hand of his enemies, and into the hand of them that seek his life; as I gave Zedekiah king of Judah into the hand of Nebuchadrezzar king of Babylon, his enemy, and that sought his life (44:29,30).**

v. 29. Jehovah promises them a sign of great certainty in order that they might have no doubts about their own forthcoming punishment.

v. 30. Pharaoh-hophra or Apries, the then reigning king of Egypt and the very person you think will befriend and aid you, is facing a deposing of office himself. I will deliver him into the hands of his enemies. He became Pharaoh the year before Jerusalem fell. God solemnly promised that it would be the same for Pharaoh-hophra as it had been for Zedekiah. One of Pharaoh's own generals turned against him and was quickly acknowledged as new king in the Land of the Nile. Hophra had to flee. Later he was defeated and strangled in his own palace. Due to this civil conflict greatly weakening the whole Land of the Nile, Nebuchadrezzar took the land with ease and left as his viceroy the successful general—

Amasis. Jeremiah's prophecy was fulfilled with striking precision and in absolute detail.

BARUCH'S DEEP SORROW AND GRIEF PORTRAYED

Paragraph 1 of Jeremiah 45 reads,

> **The word that Jeremiah the prophet spake unto Baruch the son of Neriah, when he had written these words in a book at the mouth of Jeremiah, in the fourth year of Jehoaikim the son of Josiah king of Judah, saying, Thus saith the Lord, the God of Israel, unto thee, O Baruch; Thou didst say, Woe is me now! for the Lord hath added grief to my sorrow; I fainted in my sighing, and I find no rest (45:1-3).**

Jeremiah 45 is the shortest chapter of this prophetic product consisting of but five verses. It has its literary link with Jeremiah 36. It would be well for the student to go back and review this chapter again. The writer of these notes has just done this before penning any comments on each of these five verses.

Numerous writers have called attention to the link it has with chapter 36. One commentator referred to its placement between chapters 44 and 46 as "shameless transposition." But there are some things commentators forget. (1) Jeremiah 36 was for a public reading; Jeremiah 45 is addressed to a private individual—Baruch. (2) Baruch was filled with sorrow over what was predicted for his people in Jeremiah 36. But be it recalled that he was with Jeremiah in Egypt (Cf. 43:6). Jeremiah has just finished revealing some very deep and severe punishments to come upon Jews in Egypt. Baruch, if still the prophet's secretary, may have needed comfort in view of these forthcoming punishments. Doubtless, he was far more able now to understand all these than as a younger man eighteen or more years earlier in Jeremiah 36. (3) Biblical writers, as a rule, were not as chronologically conscious as some of their critics today think they should have been. The critics are really the ones on trial—not Biblical scribes. I have no problem with the placement of Jeremiah 45 here and not as an appendage to Jeremiah 36.

v. 1. Here Jeremiah has a word revelation not for the nations in general or even Judah in particular as true with nearly every other chapter in this prophetic product. It is intended especially for Baruch's admonition,

369

profit, comfort and assurance. The time is given—the fourth year of Jehoiakim. This was about eighteen years before the city fell or about 604 B. C.

v. 2. Jeremiah is but the conveyor of the word revelation. Jehovah is the source of the message; Baruch is its intended recipient. Note how very singular it is—"unto thee, O Baruch."

v. 3. This verse portrays the depths of Baruch's despondency and discouragement. We would say he had reached bottom's end. (1) He felt a personal woe; (2) grief had been added to his personally-felt sorrow; (3) he was on the threshold of fainting in his sighing; (4) nowhere could he turn for rest. He had too much of Baruch in the poignant picture and insufficient place for Jehovah's purpose in the chastisement he was bringing on rebellious Judah and defiant Jerusalem. Baruch needed the word of the Lord to establish his proper prospective again. He was overburdened with personal grief and sorrow relative to this soon-to-come punishment.

JEHOVAH'S MESSAGE OF COMFORT AND ADMONITION

Paragraph 2 of Jeremiah 45 reads,

> **Thus shalt thou say unto him, The Lord saith thus; Behold, that which I have built will I break down, and that which I have planted I will pluck up, even this whole land. And seekest thou great things for thyself? seek them not: for, behold, I will bring evil upon all flesh, saith the Lord: but thy life will I give unto thee for a prey in all places whither thou goest (45:4,5).**

v. 4. Jehovah desires the forlorn Baruch to recognize that God was in charge. Jehovah—not Baruch—had built the land (Judah). He—not Baruch—was to break it by this forthcoming chastisement upon it. Jehovah—not Baruch—had planted this people; He—not Baruch—was to do the plucking up by way of punishment. Though God was concerned with Baruch the individual, yet His comprehensive concern was much wider than just one man. He had the whole land, its ultimate good and His ultimate plan before Him. These were above and beyond Baruch—a man.

v. 5. Baruch had too much personal ambition. Jehovah sought to thwart that. Heavenly counsel is given that he push these personal ambitions

370

to the background. NO LONGER was he to seek such. Baruch needed to see the whole picture—not just what concerned himself. God was going to bring with surety this punishment upon these rebellious people. Baruch need not expect this nation to amend until they had been refined in the fires of Chaldean chastisement. This was to be a needed chapter in the future book of these people and the place God intended them to play in His overall cause. Comfort and assurance are given Baruch by God's grace and goodness. Baruch's life would be spared. This meant that he would not die by the sword, by famine or by pestilence—the three lethal forces designed to take prematurely the masses of this rebellious people. The sparing of his life would be the prey or the spoils he would enjoy. The imagery is of a conquering warrior who takes spoils in a war—objects he considers to be of great value. Baruch was to receive solace in that wherever he went and into whatever vicissitudes of life he may be hurled that God would grant him preservation of life till the time for him to go the way of all the earth.

POINTS TO PONDER

(1) The high cost of sin is fully reflected in Jeremiah 44.

(2) It is immeasurably tragic when adamant men hate what Almighty God loves and love what He hates.

(3) The continuing Abrahamic promises are tremendously involved in this chapter.

(4) Self-will—not God's will—has always been a besetting sin to adamant, defiant, rebellious humanity.

(5) Commentators would greatly enhance their role if they would give us an able and accurate analysis of the passages they cover instead of setting themselves up as critics of God's inspired penmen.

DISCUSSION QUESTIONS

1. Give a short summation of Jeremiah 44 and 45.

2. List and discuss the stinging rebukes of Jeremiah 44:8.

3. Discuss the marked contrast between God's face AGAINST them and not FOR them.

4. What interesting comments are made by Matthew Henry on Jeremiah 44:15-17?

5. Discuss the message to Baruch in Jeremiah 45.

MULTIPLE-CHOICE: Underline correct answer

1. Jehovah through Jeremiah sends a message to His people who were dwelling in: (A) Babylon; (B) Assyria; (C) Egypt; (D) Arabia.
2. Northern Egypt was known as: (A) Upper Egypt; (B) Lower Egypt; (C) Mountainous Egypt; (D) Desolate Egypt.
3. Modern Cairo, Egypt, now stands where ancient: (A) Migdal; (B) Tahpanhes; (C)Noph; (D) Pathros—once stood as a great Egyptian city.
4. The Queen of heaven likely refers to the worship of: (A) clouds; (B) moon; (C) stars; (D) the sun.
5. (A) Rameses; (B) Necho; (C) Hophra; (D) Amasis—was Pharaoh of Egypt in Jeremiah's final era and to whom the Jews looked for great aid against Babylon.

SCRIPTURAL FILL-IN: Only one word required in each blank

1. "_____ I _____ unto you all my _____ the _____ , rising _____ and _____ them, saying, Oh, _____ not this _____ thing that I _____ ."

2. "As for the _____ that thou hast _____ unto _____ in the _____ of the _____ , _____ will not _____ unto _____ ."

3. "_____ the _____ of the _____ , all _____ that are in the _____ of _____ ."

4. "_____ is _____ now! for the _____ hath _____ grief to my _____ ; I _____ in my _____ , and I _____ no _____ ."

5. "_____ , that which I have _____ will I
    _____ down, and that which _____ have
    _____ I will _____ up, even this _____
land."

TRUE OR FALSE: Put either a "T" or "F" in the blanks

_____ 1. "Lord of hosts" reflects Jehovah's great power.
_____ 2. Jews of Jeremiah's era NEVER had any problems with
         idolatrous worship and service.
_____ 3. Severe calamities descended upon Judah and Jerusalem because
         of their determined defiance of God's law.
_____ 4. Burning of incense to their idols was of little concern to
         Jehovah.
_____ 5. Baruch greatly needed the comfort, sympathy, promises,
         reprimands and information of Jeremiah 45.

THOUGHT QUESTIONS

1. How do we know that the word evil in Jeremiah 44:2 does not
    refer to wrongdoing on Jehovah's part?

2. In what senses should Christians be voices of urgency in the current
    proclamation of God's glorious gospel?

3. Why is wickedness such a tragic thing when it becomes an entire
    family matter?

4. How are certain rebellious, defiant women in the church today very
    much like rebellious, defiant women in Jeremiah's era?

5. Why is the placement of Jeremiah 45 in its present location not
    "shameless transposition" at all?

CHAPTER TWENTY-TWO

VENGEANCE VISITED ON NEIGHBORING NATIONS (NO. 1)
Jeremiah 46, 47, 48

In these three chapters we have the prophetic thrust aimed at Egypt, the Philistines and the land of Moab. Those who think there is no wrath in the character of Jehovah have never studied with any care these three chapters.

THE FIRST OVERTHROW OF PHARAOH'S ARMY

Paragraph 1 of Jeremiah 46 reads,

The word of the Lord which came to Jeremiah the prophet against the Gentiles; Against Egypt, against the army of Pharaoh-necho king of Egypt, which was by the river Euphrates in Carchemish, which Nebuchadrezzar king of Babylon smote in the fourth year of Jehoiakim the son of Josiah king of Judah. Order ye the buckler and shield, and draw near to battle. Harness the horses; and get up, ye horsemen, and stand forth with your helmets; furbish the spears, and put on the brigandines. Wherefore have I seen them dismayed and turned away back? and their mighty ones are beaten down, and are fled apace, and look not back: for fear was round about, saith the Lord. Let not the swift flee away, nor the mighty man escape; they shall stumble, and fall toward the north by the river Euphrates. Who is this that cometh up as a flood, whose waters are moved as the rivers? Egypt

riseth up like a flood, and his waters are moved like the rivers; and he saith, I will go up, and will cover the earth; I will destroy the city and the inhabitants thereof. Come up, ye horses; and rage, ye chariots; and let the mighty men come forth; the Ethiopians and the Libyans, that handle the shield, and the Lydians, that handle and bend the bow. For this is the day of the Lord God of hosts, a day of vengeance, that he may avenge him of his adversaries; and the sword shall devour, and it shall be satiate and made drunk with their blood: for the Lord God of hosts hath a sacrifice in the north country by the river Euphrates. Go up into Gilead, and take balm, O virgin, the daughter of Egypt: in vain shall thou use many medicines; for thou shalt not be cured. The nations have heard of thy shame, and thy cry hath filled the land: for the mighty man hath stumbled against the mighty, and they are fallen both together (45:1-12).

v. 1. This begins a word revelation given Jeremiah from Jehovah the prophetic thrust of which will not be Jerusalem and Judah but the Gentiles. In this and subsequent chapters, the prophet will touch a number of nearby and more distant neighbors. Egypt will be first; Babylon will be the final one. Be it recalled that Jeremiah was to be a prophet to the nations (1:5,10).

v. 2. This verse lists the nation to be defeated, the victorious nation, the two opposing leaders, the location of the defeat and the time element. Earlier, Necho of Egypt had met and defeated the Babylonians at Carchemish. The just Josiah had been slain by Necho at this time (Cf. 2 Kings 23:29,30; 2 Chronicles 35:20-24). Necho returned home. Babylon did not take this defeat lightly. They made prompt preparations to engage Egypt in another battle and in the same area. This time Nebuchadrezzar defeated Necho. It was in the fourth year of Jehoiakim or about 604 B. C.

vs. 3-6. Egypt is given charge for the battle that soon will ensue. Buckler and shield respectively were used to protect the soldier. The former was smaller and the latter was sufficiently large to protect the entire body. They were to draw nigh for the ensuing battle. The horses were to be harnessed to the chariots. Egypt was long famous for its

army of chariots. The horsemen were to be ready. Helmets (protectors of the head) were to be donned; spears were to be furbished (polished and sharpened); brigadines (coats of mail or armor) were to be donned. Defeat and dismay were soon to be before them. Soldiers of might were beaten down. They fled with no backward glances. Fear enveloped them from all side. Yet the fleet of foot and mighty in strength would discover no successful escape. To the north and at the Euphrates, they had been summoned to do battle and yet would taste of humiliating defeat there.

vs. 7-9. The description of the Egyptian army is graphic indeed. They come from the Lord of the Nile—a sacred stream to them that overflowed annually and covered with water all in its torrential path. They expected to defeat the Chaldeans at Carchemish and in quick order. With the Nile overflow as the employed imagery, they came to Carchemish like a flood; they expected to move to instant victory with nothing to impede or hinder similar to the flooded Nile that sweeps everything in its watery path as it marches rampantly toward the Mediterranean Sea. Egypt expected to destroy the enemy with stunning surety. The Egyptian stallions are charged to come; the mighty chariots are invited to rage. The men of might are told to come. All the mercenary armies are invited to come—Ethiopians, Libyans and Lydians. These were African neighbors of the Egyptians. Some of these would be in the forefront of the emerging battle; others would back them up; others would be in the hinder part with bows and arrows.

vs. 10-12. The day of the Lord in the Old Testament was a day of wrath, of defeat for His enemies, of vengeance to those who long had opposed Him. Vengeance would come to Egypt for all their many evils. Egypt had slain Jewish people including righteous Josiah. Now the sword shall kill them in mass form. The sword will slay so many that it will be filled and made drunk with blood. Egypt will fall as a sacrifice to God's avenging hand by the Euphrates. Gilead was noted for its balm or medicine of great healing powers. Gilead's balm would not heal what Egypt would face from the Chaldeans. Egypt is called a virgin due to her former power and independence. Now she would lose that power and become an assaulted nation thus losing her national virginity. Usage of many medicines would work no cure at all for her. Her defeat at Chaldean hands would be filled with shame, embarrassment and humiliation of the deepest dye. Their cry of defeat filled the land. In the frustration of total discomfiture and defeat, the mighty men of their vast army will fight against each other and fall together in a defeat that would be amazing to behold.

COMPLETE CHALDEAN DEFEAT OF EGYPT
IN EGYPT'S OWN BACKYARD

Paragraph 2 of Jeremiah 46 reads,

The word that the Lord spake to Jeremiah the prophet, how Nebuchadrezzar king of Babylon should come and smite the land of Egypt. Declare ye in Egypt and publish in Migdol, and publish in Noph and in Tahpanhes: say ye, Stand fast, and prepare thee; for the sword shall devour round about thee. Why are thy valiant men swept away? they stood not, because the Lord did drive them. He made many to fall, yea, one fell upon another: and they said, Arise, and let us go again to our own people, and to the land of our nativity, from the oppressing sword. They did cry there, Pharaoh king of Egypt is but a noise; he hath passed the time appointed. As I live, saith the King, whose name is the Lord of hosts. Surely as Tabor is among the mountains, and as Carmel by the sea, so shall he come. O thou daughter dwelling in Egypt, furnish thyself to go into captivity: for Noph shall be waste and desolate without an inhabitant. Egypt is like a very fair heifer, but destruction cometh; it cometh out of the north. Also her hired men are in the midst of her like fatted bullocks; for they also are turned back, and are fled away together: they did not stand, because the day of their calamity was come upon them, and the time of their visitation. The voice thereof shall go like a serpent; for they shall march with an army, and come against her with axes, as hewers of wood. They shall cut down her forest, saith the Lord, though it cannot be searched; because they are more than the grasshoppers, and are innumerable. The daughter of Egypt shall be confounded; she shall be delivered into the hand of the people of the north. The Lord of hosts, the God of Israel, saith; Behold, I will punish the multitude of No, and Pharaoh, and

Egypt, with their gods, and their kings; even Pharaoh, and all them that trust in him: And I will deliver them into the hand of those that seek their lives, and into the hand of Nebuchadrezzar king of Babylon, and into the hand of his servants: and afterward it shall be inhabited, as in the days of old, saith the Lord (46:13-26).

vs. 13. Jeremiah receives the word revelation Jehovah desires him to convey. It touches the soon-to-occur invasion of Egypt by Babylon. Without fail Nebuchadrezzar will invade and smite doomed Egypt. It is generally believed, and with good reason, that this occurred subsequent to his long thirteen year siege of Tyre. The Egyptian invasion by Babylon would have been some sixteen years following Jerusalem's fall or about 570 B. C.

vs. 14-16. The prophetic message is to be declared in the whole country (Egypt) and in such prominent Egyptian cities as Migdol, Noph and Tahpanhes (cities of north, east and south Egypt). Western Egypt is not mentioned due to Babylon's failure to penetrate that far. They are charged to be ready for the devouring sword approaches with lethal force. Men of valiancy will not be able to stand; they will be swept away. The Lord is directing the destiny of the battle. Masses will fall in the ensuing battle. They will fall by the hands of each other. Their mercenary soldiers (hired fighters) will be bereft of any patriotic loyalty and will flee the scene with a spineless resolution that all is hopeless and let us go to our respective homes. The oppressing sword made them forgetful of an agreement to fight for Egyptian security.

vs. 17-19. These fleeing soldiers partly justified their hasty departure due to Pharaoh's impotency in reigning power. Doubtless he had promised to come to them with a well equipped army. It was all just empty chatter; it was sound minus any substance. It is now past the time when he was to arrive. Jehovah, the powerful and living King, is put into marked contrast with the impotent Pharaoh. God was not just sound or noise minus substance and action. Tabor rises above its neighboring mountains and Carmel, rugged mountain range in Western Canaan, stands majestically above the Great Sea to its west. Nebuchadrezzar, when he comes, will be just as high and superior to his Egyptian enemies as Tabor and Carmel are in towering over smaller hills and the Sea below them. Egypt is addressed as daughter as in verse 11. Egypt is charged by the prophetic message to make adequate preparation for coming captivity. Noph (Memphis) would be left waste and void of inhabitant. Though a great and renowned city her destruction would be similar to Jerusalem's—thorough and devastating.

vs. 20,21. Egypt is compared to a fair heifer—ready to be devoured. The imagery may well have been used due so much to her idolatry being calf-centered. Egypt is ripe for widespread destruction. The destroyer will be from the north. Babylon lay to the northeast and the approach would be from the north as well. Mercenary or hired soldiers had become like fatted animals. In heat of battle they turned and fled. They felt no patriotic loyalty to the land that hired them to fight. When calamity struck and the time of military visitation descended they quickly exited Egypt.

vs. 22-24. The voice alluded to here is that of the besieged and attacked Egyptians. About all they can do is hiss as a snake that has been marked for destruction and has no exit of escape available. The enemies will march against Egypt as with an army. Like wooded areas fall quickly before axemen and their axes, Egypt will fall before its destroyers. These Chaldean destroyers will cut down her forest though that forest appeared to be indestructible. The size of the invading Chaldean army is likened to grasshoppers; they are beyond human calculation as touching numbers. Again Egypt is referred to as daughter. She will be confounded or thoroughly confused; she will not know which way to turn. Without fail Egypt is destined to fall to the invincible invaders from the north.

vs. 25,26. Jehovah is Lord of hosts; this reflects His power. He is the God of Israel. Israel still has a strategic role to play in his developing cause which ultimately will bring the Messiah into the world. God's wrath is unfurled here. His punishment will come to No (ancient Thebes) with its masses. Pharaoh and Egypt will feel the weight of His wrath. Egyptian gods and kings will come under that exhibited wrath. All who have trusted in Pharaoh will come to naught. God surely planned to give the Egyptians into the hands of their avowed enemies. Egypt shall not be a permanently desolate land; it would be inhabited again as in days of old. The Lord spoke it; He would see to its sure accomplishment.

COMFORTING REASSURANCE GIVEN ISRAEL

Paragraph 3 of Jeremiah 46 reads,

> **But fear not thou, O my servant Jacob, and be not dismayed, O Israel: for, behold, I will save thee from afar**

off, and thy seed from the land of their captivity; and Jacob shall return, and be in rest and at ease, and none shall make him afraid. Fear thou not, O Jacob my servant, saith the Lord: for I am with thee; for I will make a full end of all the nations whither I have driven thee: but I will not make a full end of thee, but correct thee in measure; yet will I not leave thee wholly unpunished (46:27,28).

v. 27. The Bible is filled with "fear nots" such as we have here and directed to God's people. In the very midst of prophetic pronouncements aimed at neighboring nations Jehovah has comfort, solace and assurance for His people. Israel need not be dismayed into thinking her end was at hand. It was not!! Note the particulars of God's promise. (1) I will save thee from afar off; (2) thy captivity will not prove to be thy end; (3) there will be a return of Jacob (his descendants) from captivity; (4) rest and ease will again be his; (5) there will be none to make him afraid.

v. 28. Another "fear not" prefaces the remarks of this verse. Jacob is Jehovah's servant and that is what really matters. Jehovah promises to be with His people. A contrast is then drawn. God revealed that the nations to whom they were driven would experience a national end; they would become extinct as nations. But there would be NO full end of Jacob. Correction, discipline and proper punishment would be meted out but there would be no full end. This is a remarkable prophecy and its fulfillment is evident to every unprejudicial beholder. Frederich the Great, Prussian leader, once asked of a religious adviser to give him in short answer evidence of Biblical inspiration. The religious counsellor said concisely, "The Jews." This was an excellent answer; it was as powerful as it was accurate.

PHILISTINE DESTRUCTION PROPHETICALLY PORTRAYED

Jeremiah 47 is not divided into paragraphs. It is a very short chapter. It reads,

The word of the Lord that came to Jeremiah the prophet against the Philistines, before that Pharaoh smote Gaza. Thus saith the Lord; Behold, waters rise up out of the north, and shall be an overflowing flood, and shall overflow the land, and all that is therein; the city, and them

that dwell therein: then the men shall cry and all in the inhabitants of the land shall howl. At the noise of the stamping of the hoofs of his strong horses, at the rushing of his chariots, and at the rumbling of his wheels, the fathers shall not look back to their children for feebleness of hands; Because of the day that cometh to spoil all the Philistines, and to cut off from Tyrus and Zidon every helper that remaineth: for the Lord will spoil the Philistines, the remnant of the country of Caphtor. Baldness is come upon Gaza; Ashkelon is cut off with the remnant of their valley: how long wilt thou cut thyself? O thou sword of the Lord, how long will it be ere thou be quiet, put up thyself into thy scabbard, rest, and be still. How can it be quiet, seeing the Lord hath given it a charge against Ashkelon, and against the sea shore? there hath he appointed it (47:1-7).

vs. 1,2. It is a bit difficult to tell just when this prophecy was written but it had to be before Pharaoh smote Gaza. Gaza was one of the five main Philistine cities. The other four were Ashdod, Gath, Ashkelon and Ekron. The Pharaoh would have been either Necho or Hophra with the former more likely. The Philistines, proverbial enemies of Israel especially in the times of Samson, Samuel, Saul and David, are the objects of this chapter's prophecies. The Lord speaks articulately and authoritatively. Waters rising out of the north refer to the coming Chaldeans. Like waters inundate the land before them, the conquering Chaldeans would overwhelm everything in their path. Reference to the city may refer to Gaza since it is mentioned in verse 1. Widespread destruction will prevail throughout all the Philistine land. Cries and howls shall spring from the lips of these persecuted Philistines.

vs. 3,4. Stamping of the hoofs, chariots rushing and wheels rumbling are deeply graphic reminders of the relentless approach of the fierce enemy. It will produce such a time of desperation that parents will forget natural affections and think only of their own security. They will cast no backward looks relative to how their children are faring. They will be too feeble of hands to provide such security. Coming is a severe day of judgment upon the proverbially base and idolatrous Philistines. Tyre and Sidon, helpers from the north, will be cut off and will be in no position to aid the besieged Philistines. The Philistines will be spoiled. Controversy exists relative to Caphtor but apparently has a link with the Philistines either as helper or place where they lived.

vs. 5-7. Baldness upon Gaza refers to anguish, dismay and how barren this warfare with the Chaldeans would leave them. Arrogant Ashkelon would be cut off due to the misfortunes that would surely come to afflict her. The Lord's avenging hand is personified as His sword. The sword was a lethal weapon. There would be so much bloodshed for this sword to accomplish that the Philistines inquire how long it would be before the sword would cease its lethal work. They beg for it to be sheathed again into the scabbard, to be at rest, to be quiet. Response is given promptly. How can it be quiet seeing the Lord has given it an avenging charge against Ashkelon and the seashore—representative of the whole Philistine land. God has so appointed it and they could not repeal the appointed vengeance of which the Philistines were so worthy. Payday for all their countless crimes and cruelties was now at hand and money would not allow their averting it.

MOAB SINGLED OUT FOR DESTRUCTION

Paragraph 1 of Jeremiah 48 reads,

> **Against Moab thus saith the Lord of hosts, the God of Israel; Woe unto Nebo! for it is spoiled: Kiriathaim is confounded and taken: Misgab is confounded and dismayed. There shall be no more praise of Moab: in Heshbon they have devised evil against it; come, and let us cut it off from being a nation. Also they shalt be cut down, O Madmen; the sword shall pursue thee. A voice of crying shall be from Horonaim, spoiling and great destruction. Moab is destroyed; her little ones have caused a cry to be heard. For in the going up of Luhith continual weeping shall go up; for in the going down of Horonaim the enemies have heard a cry of destruction. Flee, save your lives, and be like the heath in the wilderness (48:1-6).**

vs. 1,2. The Moabites were descendants of that incestuous union between a drunken Lot and his firstborn, conniving, corrupt daughter (Cf. Genesis 19:31ff). Relations between Moab and Israel were almost always strained and frequently warlike. Powerful Jehovah, Israel's God

382

pronounces a weighty woe upon the Moabites. Nebo (not the mountain where Moses died but a city) was to be conquered and spoiled of its worth and wealth. Kiriathaim and Misgab, a duet of other Moabite cities, were likewise to be conquered, confounded and left in dismay. Moab's glory is past. Nothing shall remain worthy of her boasting. Hesbon, perhaps her main city, shall become a plot-house wherein evil against her will be devised. Her national demise will be the punch line of the plotting. Madmen, heap, was another Moabite city destined to be cut down, destined to have a pursuing sword hovering over it.

vs. 3-6. Horonaim, another Moabite city, will weep and wail due to the great spoiling and utter destruction to be visited upon her. Moab, the entire country, is marked for national destruction. Bitter cries of little ones will fill the air. Luhith, another Moabite city, will know a weeping minus abatement. Horonaim is mentioned a second time in these verses and again in a framework of deep anguish. Physical salvation can only come from fleers of great rapidity. Heath in the wilderness reflects a wasteland—the very thing to come upon once mighty Moab.

WIDESPREAD DESTRUCTION DEPICTED

Paragraph 2 of Jeremiah 48 reads,

For because thou hast trusted in thy works and in thy treasures, thou shalt also be taken: and Chemosh shall go forth into captivity with his priests and his princes together. And the spoiler shall come upon every city, and no city shall escape: the valley also shall perish, and the plain shall be destroyed, as the Lord hath spoken. Give wings unto Moab, that it may flee and get away: for the cities thereof shall be desolate, without any to dwell therein. Cursed be he that doeth the work of the Lord deceitfully, and cursed be he that keepeth back his sword from blood (48:7-10).

vs. 7,8. Moab's trust had not been in Deity but in the works of their own hands. This doubtless includes their fortifications, their idolatrous system, their proficiency as a nation, etc. Their treasures were earthly—not heavenly—and in these they reposed their perilous trust. All these shall fail in the hour of invasion. Chemosh was their national god (Cf. Numbers 21:29; Judges 11:24). Lifeless Chemosh would be no deterrent to the enemy at all. Chemosh would be taken into captivity. Ancient conquerors took not only the spoils of wealth and people but also their gods. This always showed the TOTAL defeat of their enemies. Priests and princes who worshipped and served Chemosh will be taken into captivity. The spoiler would be Chaldea—God's rod of chastisement for wicked Moab. Every city will be targeted for destruction; no city will know escape. Valleys and plains will perish and know total devastation.

vs. 9,10. Moab could only escape if given the wings of a bird. These would not be given and hence national destruction is on her sad threshold. Desolation awaits once mighty Moab. How devoted is Jehovah to her defeat? God would curse Chaldea if she did only a half-way job on Moab or did the avenging in negligent fashion. The sword belongs to the destroyer and Chaldea was not to hold back this lethal weapon for the ripened destruction of this doomed country.

THE END OF MOABITE EASE

Paragraph 3 of Jeremiah 48 reads,

> **Moab hath been at ease from his youth, and he hath settled on his lees, and hath not been emptied from vessel to vessel, neither hath he gone into captivity: therefore his taste remained in him, and his scent is not changed. Therefore, behold, the days come, saith the Lord, that I will send unto him wanderers, that shall cause him to wander, and shall empty his vessels, and break their bottles. And Moab shall be ashamed of Chemosh, as the house of Israel was ashamed of Bethel their confidence (48:11-13).**

v. 11. Moab was a land of vineyards and the imagery here is drawn from grapes and wine-making. Moab has been at ease from youth. No power has disturbed her by removing her into captivity. She is settled on her lees much like the wine allowed to settle on its lees or sediments, and not disturbed from being changed from vessel to vessel. Moab is like such wine—settled, no change, etc.

v. 12. These former times of little or no disturbing are at an end. Wanderers will come from Chaldea. In turn they shall make Moab wander. His vessels will be emptied; his bottles broken. These graphically depict her sure-to-come destruction.

v. 13. Chemosh will no longer be Moab's patron god. Shame and embarrassment will replace what once was awe, worship, service and admiration. It will be much like Israel who found out in a hurry that Bethel's calf was no deterrent at all to the Assyrians who plundered her land, murdered her citizens minus mercy and conquered the God-forsaken kingdom. Confidence placed in an idol, whether ancient or modern, is always misplaced!

A DYNAMIC DEPICTION OF MOABITE CALAMITY

Paragraph 4 of Jeremiah 48 reads,

> **How say ye, We are mighty and strong men for the war? Moab is spoiled, and gone up out of her cities, and his chosen young men are gone down to the slaughter, saith the King, whose name is the Lord of hosts. The calamity of Moab is near to come, and his affliction hasteth fast. All ye that are about him, bemoan him; and all ye that know his name, say, How is the strong staff broken, and the beautiful rod! Thou daughter that dost inhabit Dibon, come down from thy glory, and sit in thirst; for the spoiler of Moab shall come upon thee, and he shall destroy thy strong holds. O inhabitant of Aroer, stand by the way, and espy; ask them that fleeth, and her that escapeth, and say, What is done? Moab is confounded; for it is broken down: howl and cry; tell ye it in Arnon, that Moab is spoiled, And judgment is come upon the plain country; upon Holon, and upon Jahazah, and upon Mephaath, And upon Dibon, and upon Nebo, and upon Bethdiblathaim, And upon Kiriathaim, and upon Bethgamul, and upon Bethmeon, And upon Kerioth, and upon Bozrah, and upon all the cities of the land of Moab, far or near. The horn of Moab is cut off, and his arm is broken, saith the Lord (48:14-25).**

vs. 14-17. Moab had long trusted in its great men of military might—heroes who were strong and courageous in warfare. Yet Moab is to be plundered or spoiled. Her cities, citadels of her trust, are destined to go UP in destruction while her choice young warriors are to go DOWN to slaughter. Who has said this? Not Chemosh, their chief god but the living Lord, the reigning and strong Jehovah. Moab's calamity is near; the destined affliction comes with great rapidity. So stunning and complete will be Moab's defeat that neighboring nations will mourn in human sympathy and empathy. Moab had a name of might feared by one and all. Yet the strong staff (military might) and rod (scepter of Moabite beauty) shall be broken and marred. Such sudden destruction will amaze all beholders.

vs. 18-20. Daughter refers to people of a city or country. Dibon, a Moabite city of prominence, power and plenty, will lose her once prized glory and will sit in thirst. This is very graphic for she was built in a well-watered area and not far from the Arnon stream of water. Moab's spoiler or destroyer is Chaldea. Chaldea will destroy the Moabite strongholds; her fortifications will not withstand the Chaldean invasion. When Dibon fell Aroer, another Moabite city, would be next. Aroer was charged to stand by and espy. Espy means to look, see or watch. Inquiry is to be made by those fleeing or escaping with the question, ''What is done?'' The answer is anything but comforting or reassuring. Moab is confounded; she is confused; she is put to shame; she has had to swallow her once sinful pride; she is a broken or collapsed power. Howl and crying are appropriate for vocal expressions. Moab's spoil is to be told in Arnon. Arnon was a prominent stream that watered northern Moab. The river is personified to reflect the sorrowful tragedy of Moab's calamity and fall to the Chaldean conquerors, the Babylonian plunderers.

vs. 21-24. Coming catastrophe from Chaldean conquerors will hit the plain country; it will descend with surety upon Moabite cities such as Holon, Jahazah, Mephaath, Dibon, Nebo, Bethdiblathaim, Kiriathaim, Bethgamul, Bethmeon, Kerioth and Bozrah. These are cities specificially delineated. All Moabite cities, far and near, will feel the cruel, avenging hand of Babylon's unleashed power and Chaldea's unfurled fury. Destruction will be complete and widespread; it will be devastating to a once proud and mighty people.

v. 25. Horn and arm in this passage symbolized power or might. Moabite power is cut off or destroyed; she is totally broken as a nation of might. With striking imagery the Lord portrays her crushing collapse, her fatal fall as a nation.

SEVERE JUDGMENT UPON MOAB
DUE TO HER DISDAIN FOR GOD

Paragraph 5 of Jeremiah 48 reads,

Make ye him drunken: for he magnified himself against the Lord: Moab also shall wallow in his vomit, and he also shall be in derision. For was not Israel a derision unto thee? was he found among thieves? for since thou spakest of him, thou skippedst for joy. O ye that dwell in Moab, leave the cities, and dwell in the rock, and be like the dove that maketh her nest in the sides of the hole's mouth. We have heard the pride of Moab, (he is exceeding proud) his loftiness, and his arrogancy, and his pride, and the haughtiness of his heart. I know his wrath, saith the Lord; but it shall not be so; his lies shall not so effect it. Therefore will I howl for Moab, and I will cry out for all Moab; mine heart shall mourn for the men of Kirheres. O vine of Sibmah, I will weep for thee with the weeping of Jazer: thy plants are gone over the sea, they reach even to the sea of Jazer: the spoiler is fallen upon thy summer fruits and upon thy vintage. And joy and gladness is taken from the plentiful field, and from the land of Moab; and I have caused wine to fail from the winepresses: none shall tread with shouting; their shouting shall be no shouting. From the cry of Heshbon even unto Elealeh, and even unto Jahaz, have they uttered their voice, from Zoar even unto Horonaim, as an heifer of three years old: for the waters also of Nimrim shall be desolate. Moreover I will cause to cease in Moab, saith the Lord, him that offereth in the high places, and him that burneth incense to his gods. Therefore mine heart shall sound for Moab like pipes, and mine heart shall sound like pipes for the men of Kirheres: because the riches that he hath gotten are perished. For every head shall be bald, and every beard clipped: upon all the hands shall be cuttings, and upon the loins sackcloth. There shall be lamentation generally upon all the housetops of Moab, and in the streets thereof: for I have broken Moab like a vessel wherein is no pleasure, saith the Lord. They shall howl, saying, How is it broken down! how hath Moab turned the back with shame! so shall Moab be a derision and a dismaying to all them about him. For thus saith the Lord; Behold, he shall fly as an eagle, and shall spread his wings over Moab. Kerioth is taken, and the strong holds are surprised, and the mighty men's hearts in Moab at that day shall be as the heart of a woman in her pangs. And Moab shall be destroyed from being a people, because he hath magnified himself against the Lord. Fear, and the pit, and the snare, shall be upon thee, O inhabitant of Moab, saith the Lord. He that fleeth from the fear shall fall into the pit; and he that getteth up out of the pit shall be taken in the snare: for I will bring upon it, even upon Moab, the year of their visitation, saith the Lord. They that fled stood under the shadow of Heshbon because of the force: but a fire shall come forth out of Heshbon, and a flame from the midst of Sihon, and shall devour the corner of Moab, and the crown of the head of the tumultuous ones. Woe be unto thee, O Moab! the people of Chemosh perisheth: for thy sons are taken captives, and thy daughters captives (48:26-46).

vs. 26,27. Drunken here is used figuratively. Soon Moab would be drinking the cup of the wine of Jehovah's wrath. Moab was a proud, haughty and arrogant people. Over a century earlier Isaiah had said Moab was "very proud" (16:6). Pride goes before destruction and a haughty spirit precedes a fall (Proverbs 16:18). In his arrogancy and pride, Moab had even magnified himself against Jehovah. Man is really full of himself when he does this. Moab is destined to wallow in his own vomit. This continues the graphic imagery of a man who has drunk too much, begins to vomit it up and is so senseless that he does not realize he is wallowing in it. Moab faces derision himself. He had treated God's people with great derision in their previous fall to Babylonian hoardes. Moab skipped for joy (was highly elated) at what had happened to Judah and Jerusalem.

vs. 28,29. Moabites who had lived in cities were charged to leave these doomed, targeted cities for great destruction and seek security in rocks or in caves and caverns where doves, pigeons, etc., make their nests. It is a picture of piercing persecution soon to descend upon them. Moab overflows with pride, haughtiness and loftiness. They were a package of pride wrapped up and tied with the ribbons of egotism. Were they great? Ask them and they would go promptly into affirmative gear. Heart, head and hand were filled with sinful pride.

v. 30. God knew of the wrath that Moab had exhibited toward Judah. God would not allow Moab to hurt His people. Moabite lies would not effect any type of harm to God's people.

vs. 31,32. Though Moab really deserved no pity yet so severe was to be God's wrath visited upon them that the sensitive seer, Jeremiah, wept for Moab. His cry was inclusive for all Moab. He would mourn for the men of Kirheres, an area especially targeted to feel the deep sting of God's poured-out wrath. Moab was a grape-growing country. The vine of Sibmah is personified with the prophet's weeping linked therewith. The weeping will be as the weeping of Jazer—another Moabite city that felt the deep sting of Jehovah's aroused wrath. Moab was east of the Dead Sea. Her plants are spoken of as going over the sea, i. e., extending into Western Palestine. This means that her power was felt west of the Dead Sea. The sea of Jazer possibly refers to some well known body of water at that time which was near Jazer. The spoiler would be the Chaldean conqueror who would invade and capture the land. The spoiler or plunderer would take as his prey Moab's summer fruits and her vintage (the produce of Moabite vineyards).

v. 33. The despoiling of the land is graphically expressed. (1) Joy and gladness are removed from her fields of plenty. (2) Wine will no longer flow from her winepresses. (3) The treading of grapes and the pressing out of the wine (grape juice) was uniformly a time of rejoicing. The former shouts of joy will turn into "no shouting."

v. 34. Five Moabite cities, Heshbon, Elealeh, Jahaz, Zoar and Horonaim, will all cry in anguish. Moab is likened to a heifer of three years old. The imagery seems to be that as the three-year-old heifer would be unaccustomed to the yoke, so independent Moab would be unfamiliar and unaccustomed to the yoke of captivity soon to descend on them. In her twelve-hundred-year history, Moab had known a foreign yoke imposed on her but few times. Nimrim seems to have been a stream that watered well the area it served. This area shall become desolate or dried up of its former luxuriant plants and foliage.

vs. 35,36. Moab had long been an idolatrous land with Chemosh as chief god. The Lord will cause to cease the idolatrous priest who offered sacrifices in the high places and burned incense to his gods. The pipes mentioned in verse 36 were of the kind played at funerals or other equally sad, solemn occasions. The minstrels and their noise are mentioned in connection with the death of Jairus' daughter in Matthew 9:23. Jesus referred to games children play in Luke 7:32 as they say to their playmates, "We have piped unto you, and ye have not danced; we have mourned to you, and ye have not wept." Deep mourning was appropriate for what was coming on Moab in general and Kirheres in particular. The accumulation of riches they had zealously attained would perish. They would be unable to hang on to them.

vs. 37-39. Ancient exhibitions of grievous anguish and deep dismay were seen in shaved heads, clipped beards, actual mutilations of their bodies and the wearing of coarse sackcloth upon their loins. Lamentations were expressions of deep grief. These would be made upon the flat roofs of their houses; the streets of Moabite cities would be filled with more of the same. God's wrath had broken Moab much like one breaks a vessel in which he no longer has any delight. Beholders of this vast and widespread destruction rained upon malicious Moab would view such with great amazement. Bewilderment will characterize their surveying of the destructive scene. They would see and sense that she was a victim of Jehovah's aroused and extended wrath. Moab would be turned back with the shame of her sins. She was destined to be a derision—an object of great contempt. Moab would be the butt of remarks made by the beholders of her destruction.

vs. 40,41. The antecedant of the **he** is the Babylonian leader— Nebuzaradan—Nebuchadnezzar's field general in the subjugation and discomfiture of Moab. He will be the eagle with his wings spread over Moab. It will not be like Jehovah toward Israel—bearing them upon eagle's wings (Exodus 19:4; Deuteronomy 32:11,12)—but to pounce upon them as coveted prey as the eager eagle does his intended victim. Kerioth, Moabite city, falls; their strongest fortifications will be taken by surprise; their heroes who often shielded them will face the enemy with dread and alarm similar to the mother-to-be in the pangs of coming childbirth.

vs. 42-44. National extinction is at hand for Moab. The reason is that she has magnified herself against God. Danger after danger—fear, pit and snare—will face them. One danger will not much more than be averted until another shall arise with rapidity. God's wrath in full fury will be visited upon them. Twice in this trio of verse we have "saith the Lord." It will come surely and certainly. Moab can be assured of such surety!

v. 45. It is highly unfortunate that on this passage Pulpit Commentary showed its crass modernism by arraying this passage against verse 2 of this chapter and not only accusing Jeremiah of making a slip here but refers to the author of Job as being inconsistent in the other parts of Job with the Prologue. The serious matter is further compound as the writer in PC says, "Nor can we be absolutely certain that our prophecy is exactly as Jeremiah wrote it." The manufacturer of this modernism should have realized that plans for Moabite destruction devised in Heshbon could have been planned (v. 2) without the knowledge of those who thought safety and security would and could be found in that well-fortified city (v. 45). Those who fled there to reach security behind its massive walls and the well-known shadows of its security and safety discovered too late that Heshbon itself was a chosen target for fiery destruction. The force of the enemy drove them to this anticipated site of safety. Allusion to Sihon seemingly had reference to the famed pagan king by that name who once went forth in conquering, destructive action in this very area. Moab is destined for destruction from one end of the land to the other. The crown of the head would either refer to the fall of her men of might or to the fall of her most elevated spots. I prefer the latter view.

v. 46. The weight of woe pronounced on doomed Moab is one of lethal and perilous consequence. Chemosh was their chief god. To him idolatrous Moab looked for protection against any and all enemies. But the lifeless deity was just that—lifeless, helpless, hapless, hopeless! Chemosh could not keep his people from perishing at the cruel and calloused hands of Chaldean conquerors and plunderers. Captivity to a foreign power was now at hand and it would be without any type of segregation—both sons and daughters would be held captives. Even the delicacy of daughters would not make them immune to coming captivity.

MOAB IN THE LATTER DAYS

Paragraph six, very short, consisting of but one verse and concluding this forty-eighth chapter reads, "Yet will I bring again the captivity of Moab in the latter days, saith the Lord. Thus far is the judgment of

Moab'' (v. 47). Moab was at the end of its long existence as a national entity. King and governor would fade the scene. Yet the people of Moab would continue; they would not become extinct as a people. Allusion to the last days seemingly gives this a Messianic application. When Christianity came and sent its clarion call to the ends of the world (Romans 10:18) and when the gospel was proclaimed to every creature on earth (Colossians 1:23), doubtless some of Moabite blood heard, believed and obeyed that soul-saving gospel of God's only begotten Son. ''Thus far'' or to this extent is Moab's judgment. The multitudes of Moabites through the twelve or thirteen centuries that separate them from their father (Lot) were, for the main part, no credit to just Lot or the family of Terah from which he sprang. There are some exceptions and righteous Ruth is one such.

POINTS TO PONDER

(1) Proponents of the no-wrath-of-God teaching should park for a long time with Jeremiah 46, 47 and 48 and learn how utterly foolish their baseless doctrine really is.

(2) Idols were never more impotent to the people who served them than when these same people were under siege and their idols were helpless, hopeless and hapless.

(3) Moab is a graphic exhibition of pride going before destruction and a haughty spirit before a sure fall.

(4) Out of some of the darkest pictures of the Old Testament will sometimes emerge a brilliant, blessed and bright Messianic prophecy of a coming day that will be far, Far, FAR better.

(5) Ruth was a Moabite who rose far above the people and the environment of idolatry that produced her.

DISCUSSION QUESTIONS

1. How is the day of the Lord in the Old Testament usually to be understood?

2. In what sense was Nebuchadnezzar likened to Palestinian mountains such as Tabor and Carmel?

3. How deep and thorough would be the Chaldean bloodshed among the arrogant Philistines?

4. How thorough, humiliating and painful would be the collapse of Moab at Chaldean hands?

5. How do Matthew 9:23 and Luke 7:32 tie in with Jeremiah 48:35,36?

MULTIPLE-CHOICE: Underline correct answer

1. The three powers occupying the thrust of Jeremiah 46, 47 and 48 are: (A) Syria, Assyria and Babylon; (B) Medo-Persia, Elam and Greece; (C) Phoenicia, Lebanon and Arabia; (D) Egypt, Philistia and Moab.
2. (A) Egypt; (B) Ethiopia; (C) Libya; (D) Cyrene—was known as the proverbial "Land of the Nile."
3. Migdol, Noph and Tahpanhes were cities of: (A) Judah; (B) Babylonia; (C) Egypt; (D) Assyria.
4. Gaza, Ashdod, Gath, Ashkelon and Ekron were: (A) Moabite; (B) Judaean; (C) Egyptian; (D) Philistine—cities.
5. Nebo, Misgab, Heshbon and Horonaim were geographical locations associated with: (A) Egypt; (B) Philistia; (C) Phoenicia; (D) Moab.

SCRIPTURAL FILL-IN: Only one word is required in each blank

1. "_____ is like a _____ fair _____ , but _____ cometh; it _____ out of the _____ ."
2. ". . .but _____ will not _____ a _____ end of thee, but _____ thee in _____ ; yet will I not _____ thee _____ unpunished."
3. "O thou _____ of the _____ , how _____ will it be ere thou be _____ ? put up _____ into thy _____ , rest, and be _____ ."
4. "_____ be _____ that _____ the _____ of the Lord _____ , and _____ be _____ that _____ back his _____ from _____ ."
5. "And _____ shall be _____ from _____ a _____ , because _____ hath _____ himself _____ the _____ ."

393

TRUE OR FALSE: Put either a "T" or "F" in the blanks

_____ 1. Jeremiah was a prophet to Judah only and gave no prophetic pronouncements to any other nation.
_____ 2. The Moabites enjoyed a very honorable origin as set forth in Genesis 19.
_____ 3. For the victors to take back home the very gods of the nations they had just conquered was the highest proof possible of how total the victory had been.
_____ 4. Pride was never a besetting sin among the Moabite people.
_____ 5. Jehovah was well pleased with the Moabite people in Jeremiah's era.

THOUGHT QUESTIONS

1. How is every religious falsehood like Pharaoh in the battle with Babylon—endless chatter or all sound and no substance?

2. Why was the answer on Biblical evidence given the Prussian leader, Frederick the Great, a wise and weighty answer?

3. What is so utterly foolish about placing any trust in a lifeless idol?

4. How would a person ever explain the book of Jeremiah if he denied all of Jehovah's wrath?

5. How does Pulpit Commentary show its modernism on Jeremiah 48:45?

CHAPTER TWENTY-THREE

VENGEANCE VISITED ON
NEIGHBORING NATIONS (NO. 2)
Jeremiah 49

Be it kept firmly fixed in mind that Jeremiah was a prophet to the nations as well as to Judah and Jerusalem (Cf. 1:10). In the forty-ninth division of this prophetic work, the prophet to the nations, addresses messages of judgment relative to the Ammonites, the Edomites, the Damascenes, the Kedarenes, the Hazorites and the Elamites. Paragraph headings aid us in the study of this chapter as they have throughout this study in Jeremiah.

PROPHETIC JUDGMENT OF AMMONITES

Paragraph 1 of Jeremiah 49 reads,

> **Concerning the Ammonites, thus saith the Lord; Hath Israel no sons? hath he no heir? why then doth their king inherit Gad, and his people dwell in his cities? Therefore, behold, the days come, saith the Lord, that I will cause an alarm of war to be heard in Rabbah of the Ammonites; and it shall be a desolate heap, and her daughters shall be burned with fire: then shall Israel be heir unto them that were his heirs, saith the Lord. Howl, O Heshbon, for Ai is spoiled: cry, ye daughters of Rabbah, gird you with sackcloth; lament, and run to and fro by the hedges; for their king shall go into captivity, and his priests and his princes together. Wherefore gloriest thou in the valleys, thy flowing valley, O backsliding daughter? that trusted in her treasures, saying, Who shall come unto me?**

Behold, I will bring a fear upon thee, saith the Lord God of hosts, from all those that be about thee; and ye shall be driven out every man right forth; and none shall gather up him that wandereth. And afterward I will bring again the captivity of the children of Ammon, saith the Lord (49:1-6).

vs. 1,2. Ammon was of close kin to Moab. Both nations were descendants of Lot through the drunken oriented unions with his two daughters. The Ammonites were descendants of Lot by his younger daughter (Genesis 19:38). The country of Ammon lay to the north of Moab and to the east of the Jordan. The Arabian desert bounded Ammon on the east and Syria on the north. When Assyria had taken Gad, also east of Jordan, and the other Northern tribes into captivity, Ammon quickly invaded and took for herself Gad's tribal territory. They took it by might—not by right. The prophet lashes out with stinging queries triggered by justice. Gad had closer kin than that of Ammon who should have been the rightful heirs. Israel was not void of heirs. With the Northern tribes taken the next of kin would have been Judah. Ammon ignored this well-known principle of who properly heired an abandoned land. Ammon invaded the forsaken land and settled her people in its abandoned cities. For this and her other sins Ammon must pay and pay dearly. Rabbah was by far the main Ammonite city. War will come to Rabbah without fail. Though fortified and built on a heap, an eminence higher than surrounding territory, the city will become desolate. Her daughters shall be burned with fire. This has reference to the unwalled and unprotected cities and villages near her. The territory that they took from Israel shall again be Israel's. God's people had not permanently left that land; they would return under the Restoration decrees of the Persian Cyrus.

vs. 3,4. Heshbon is charged to howl due to coming miseries by the Chaldean conquerors—God's avenging rod of chastisement upon these people. Ai faces a spoiling. It is highly unlikely that this Ai refers to the Ai in Canaan, west of Jordan and that was near Bethel (Cf. Genesis 12:8; 13:3—ASV). Ai evidently was an Ammonite city though only mentioned here. Daughters of Rabbah would be the people in cities and villages near the capital city and which look to the Ammonite metropolitan power for safety and security. None would be forthcoming.

These unprotected people might as well gird themselves with sackcloth reminiscent of coming anguish. Their lips might as well be turned toward lamentations for such were destined to come for a surety. "Their king" seemingly has reference to their chief god—Milcom. Along with the priests, the princes and the people who served him, he shall be taken captive. Ammon had boasted of her fruitful valleys that made her a land flowing with milk and honey. No longer would there be any glory in such. Ammon was a backslider. She had turned her back on the truth she formerly knew. Trust had been placed in her treasures—not in the truth. Confidence had been placed in her wealth—not in that wisdom that descends from above (Cf. James 3:17,18). So great was her boast in her geographically protected valleys that she doubted seriously that any power could rout her.

vs. 5,6. Where there had been no fear, there will be fear, terror and alarm. The Lord will see surely to the coming of such. Such will come from those who besiege the nation doomed to punishment. Every man will be driven forth and self-preservation will be the number one priority. No one will care for others. There will be none to gather up and preserve the aimless fugitives. Jehovah promises later to bring back these captives. This may partly have been fulfilled under Cyrus who had a rather humane policy relative to captured subjects in allowing them a return to their native land. More fully it likely refers to any of this family who accepts Christ in the Messianic Age of gospel proclamation.

PROPHETIC JUDGMENT OF EDOMITES

Paragraph 2 of Jeremiah 49 reads,

> **Concerning Edom, thus saith the Lord of hosts; is wisdom no more in Teman? is counsel perished from the prudent? is their wisdom vanished? Flee, ye, turn back, dwell deep, O inhabitants of Dedan; for I will bring the calamity of Esau upon him, the time that I will visit him. If grape-gatherers come to thee, would they not leave some gleaning grapes? if thieves by night, they will destroy till they have enough. But I have made Esau bare. I have uncovered his secret places and he shall not be able to hide himself: his seed is spoiled, and his brethren, and his neighbours, and he is not. Leave thy fatherless**

397

children, I will preserve them alive; and let thy widows trust in me. For thus saith the Lord; Behold, they whose judgment was not to drink of the cup have assuredly drunken; and art thou he that shall altogether go unpunished? thou shalt not go unpunished, but thou shall surely drink of it. For I have sworn by myself, saith the Lord, that Bozrah shall become a desolation, a reproach, a waste, and a curse; and all the cities thereof shall be perpetual wastes. I have heard a rumour from the Lord, and an ambassador is sent unto the heathen, saying, Gather ye together, and come against her, and rise up to the battle. For, lo, I will make thee small among the heathen, and despised among men. Thy terribleness hath deceived thee, and the pride of thine heart, O thou that dwellest in the clefts of the rock, that holdest the height of the hill: though thou shouldest make thy nest as high as the eagle, I will bring thee down from thence, saith the Lord. Also Edom shall be a desolation: every one that goeth by it shall be astonished, and shall hiss at all the plagues thereof. As in the overthrow of Sodom and Gomorrah and the neighbour cities thereof, saith the Lord, no man shall abide there, neither shall a son of men dwell in it. Behold, he shall come up like a lion from the swelling of Jordan against the habitation of the strong: but I will suddenly make him run away from her: and who is a chosen man, that I may appoint over her? for who is like me? and who will appoint me the time? and who is that shepherd that will stand before me? Therefore hear the counsel of the Lord, that he hath taken against Edom; and his purposes, that he hath purposed against the inhabitants of Teman: Surely the least of the flock shall draw them out: surely he shall make their habitations desolate with them. The earth is moved at the noise of their fall, at the cry the noise thereof was heard in the Red Sea. Behold, he shall come up and fly as the eagle, and spread his wings over Bozrah: and at that day shall the heart of the mighty men of Edom be as the heart of a woman in her pangs (49:7-22).

vs. 7,8. It would be well for each interested student to read with care the short (one chapter) book of Obadiah along with this section of study. Edom is the thrust of Obadiah's prophecy. The Edomites were descendants of Esau, older twin brother of Jacob—father of the Israelites. Teman was located in Edom and was famed for its wisdom. Eliphaz, one of the three friends of Job, was a Temanite (Job 2:11; 4:1). Wisdom had fled the scene in Teman; counsel forsook the prudent; wisdom was no more. Negative answers are demanded the queries of verse 7. Calamity was coming. Edom is charged to flee, turn back and dwell deep. Though some think the imagery is of the Arabians who, in a time of danger, would strike tents, pack up essentials and head deep into the desert, yet more likely the imagery is to seek out their deep caves, caverns and mountainous retreats with which they were deeply familiar. Coming punishment is styled as Esau's calamity. The allusion seems to be of Esau who could not reverse what had been given by Isaac to Jacob though he sought to do so with tears (See Genesis 25,26,27; Hebrews 12:16,17). God promised to visit Esau. This was to be a visitation of wrath.

vs. 9,10. During vintage and harvest grape gatherers would leave some grapes behind; thieves would take only enough to satisfy and would leave the rest. But Esau is not to fare even this well. Esau, progenitor put for the Edomite people, is to be made bare; the enemy will strip Edom of everything. No longer will Edom be able to hide among rocky caverns and in deep recesses in their mountainous retreats and escape any reprisals from their enemies. God had uncovered his secret places. His seed or descendants will be spoiled (destroyed). Brethren and neighbors will share in the fate. "He is not" refers to their decease.

vs. 11,12. Fatherless children and widows would refer to the widespread deaths that would come to Edomite men leaving their children minus fathers and their wives as widows. Yet God, always the champion of widows and fatherless, will supply their needs. The very God Edomite men despised will preserve their fatherless sons and daughters and their wives left bereft of husbands. What a stinging statement this should have been to the pomp, pride and defiance of Edomite men. The very one they hated would preserve their children, their wives. It would be normally expected that God's people would not have to drink (figuratively) of God's cup of affliction. Yet the cup of God's wrath had been poured upon them and that quite heavily. If God's covenant people did not escape punishment for their sins, surely non-covenant Edom need not think they will escape. Both negatively and positively God assures Edom of coming calamity. Negatively, Edom is told she shall not go unpunished. Positively, they (Edom) would surely drink of that cup.

vs. 13,14. Jehovah could swear by none greater and therefore swore by himself (Cf. Hebrews 6:13,14). Jehovah swore that Bozrah would become a desolation (void of population), a reproach (contemptible), a waste (a destroyed city) and a curse (a hiss and a byword). All its suburbs would lie in perpetual (not a temporary judgment by any means) waste. Word came from God of what was to be. An ambassador (herald) was sent from God to the heathen that they rise up to do battle with these Edomites.

vs. 15,16. Edom was to become of little value among the family of heathen nations of which they were a part. Neighboring nations will feel nothing but disdain and contempt for Edom. Edom has been a ruffian among the nations. Edomites would attack their neighbors to plunder and kill and then dart back quickly to their safeguards in the craggy regions of mountainous safety. Edom had become a deceived people. They were a proud and independent people and felt they were invincible in their impregnable strongholds in mountainous Edom. They trusted totally in the safety of their rock clefts and the height of the hills they controlled. Even if they built their safe retreats as high as the eagle does her nest, yet God had decreed that Edom would be brought down. God had so willed it; it would transpire.

vs. 17,18. Without fail Edom will become desolate. What a slap in the face of her persistent pride. So great will be her downfall that neighboring beholders will stand in utter amazement. Beholders will hiss (belittle and heap scorn) upon plague-ridden Edom. The destruction will be as complete and thorough as that which was visited upon Sodom, Gomorrah, Zeboim and Admah (Genesis 19; Deuteronomy 29:23). It will be as forlorn and desolate as was the doomed quartet of Jordan Plain cities in Abraham's age.

vs. 19,20. The avenging power to humble proud Edom will be the Chaldeans. The "he" would be their leader—Nebuchadnezzar. He is likened to a lion that has to leave its haunt on Jordan's banks when the river floods. He will invade the habitation of the strong. Who does the sudden running? It is not likely that Nebuchadnezzar will do such for he is the fierce, determined invader. Much more likely it refers to the invaded or Edom. Another plausible explanation for this confessedly difficult verse is that the Chaldean conqueror would make very quick order of the Edomite destruction and quickly be called to another sphere of needed action. God would use the choicest of warriors to bring Edom down. He will set the time for its accomplishment. Edom will be unable to appoint any shepherd that will defeat the lion (Chaldea) Jehovah will send among these prideful descendants of Esau. Edom is charged to hear God's counsel. Jehovah has a purpose and it shall be accomplished. No one will circumvent it. God has willed Teman's destruction. Even the weakest of Chaldean hosts will be able to accomplish this. The Chaldean invader will not fail. Teman is destined for desolation.

vs. 21,22. Graphic figures of speech are employed here. So great will be Edom's downfall that the earth will take notice and be moved. The Red Sea was of some measurable distance and yet would hear of Edom's downfall. Widespread would be the news of her fall. Nebuchadnezzar's coming as the Chaldean conqueror of Edom is likened to the high-flying eagle. His wings of destruction will hover over and fall upon Bozrah. Edom's mighty men will know of fear and dread in that day similar to a woman in her pangs. Childbirth pains throughout the Bible are often employed to suggest deep discomfort and great anguish of soul.

PROPHETIC JUDGMENT OF THE DAMASCENES

Paragraph 3 of Jeremiah 49 reads,

> **Concerning Damascus. Hamath is confounded, and Arpad: for they have heard evil tidings: they are faint-hearted; there is sorrow on the sea; it cannot be quiet. Damascus is waxed feeble, and turneth herself to flee, and fear hath seized on her: anguish and sorrows have taken her, as a woman in travail. How is the city of praise not left, the city of my joy! Therefore her young men shall fall in her streets, and all the men of war shall be cut off in that day, saith the Lord of hosts. And I will kindle a fire in the wall of Damascus, and it shall consume the palaces of Benhadad (49:23-27).**

vs. 23,24. This prophetic pronouncement applies to Damascus but not it alone. Damascus was perhaps the most important city of Syria. It lay some one hundred fifty miles northeast of Jerusalem. It is one of the oldest cities in the world with a continuing history and is still frequently in the news today when events occur in the Arabic land of Syria. At that time Syria was divided into the northern part with Hamath on the Orontes River as chief city and the southeastern part with Damascus as chief city. Arpad was another Syrian city. Hamath and Arpad are confounded or ashamed. Evil tidings have been received by these Syrian cities. Babylon is coming; captivity is on their threshold. All courage has left them. No strength remains in their trembling hearts. "Sorrow on the sea" may refer to the fact that the Babylonian scourge will reach all the way to the seacoast but much more likely that just as the sea is troubled and minus rest, so they would be troubled and filled with unease and unrest. "It cannot be quiet" adds traditional strength to the latter explanation as the true meaning. Once powerful Damascus that made neighboring nations fear and quake is reduced to a national weakling herself. She is feeble. There is no strength to **fight** and so she turns to **fleeing** as her final option in the wake of the Chaldean invasion. Fear, dread and alarm permeate her whole person. In anguish and sorrows, she is like the expectant mother in the travail of approaching childbirth.

v. 25. Damascus was once a city highly praised for its beauty, power and stability. Such has vacated her. "The city of my joy" likely refers to the impression the Damascenes felt toward their beloved city. It is highly unlikely Jeremiah would call it the city of HIS joy. Neither would Jehovah for that city had long despised Jehovah and His people to the south. Damascus would not be spared in the capture of cities and nations by Nebuchadnezzar and his Chaldean conquerors.

vs. 26,27. This city was no stronger than the military men who protected her. Yet the prophetic picture is a forlorn and pathetic one indeed. Her young men will fall in the streets; her men of war shall be cut off. Such is sure. Jehovah has so stated. He is Lord of hosts (power) and his will shall be accomplished without fail. Fiery destruction awaits Damascus' wall. When a wall fell in that ancient age the city fell with rapidity. The palaces of Benhadad faced destruction. There were at least three Syrian rulers in Damascus who were called Benhadad. Consumption of the king's palaces was a synonym that the city would be completely overthrown.

PROPHETIC JUDGMENT OF KEDAR AND HAZOR

Paragraphs 4 and 5 of Jeremiah, both of which touch the very same people, reads,

402

Concerning Kedar, and concerning the kingdoms of Hazor, which Nebuchadrezzar king of Babylon shall smite, thus saith the Lord; Arise ye, go up to Kedar, and spoil the men of the east. Their tents and their flocks shall they take away: they shall take to themselves their curtains, and all their vessels, and their camels; and they shall cry unto them, Fear is on every side. Flee, get you far off, dwell deep, O ye inhabitants of Hazor, saith the Lord; for Nebuchadrezzar king of Babylon hath taken counsel against you, and hath conceived a purpose against you. Arise, get you up unto the wealthy nation, that dwelleth without care, saith the Lord, which have neither gates nor bars, which dwell alone. And their camels shall be a booty, and the multitude of their cattle a spoil: and I will scatter into all winds them that are in the utmost corners; and I will bring their calamity for all sides thereof, saith the Lord. And Hazor shall be a dwelling for dragons, and a desolation for ever: there shall no man abide there, nor any son of man dwell in it (49:28-33).

Verses 28 and 29 form a paragraph and verses 30-33 form another paragraph. The same people are prophetically addressed in both paragraphs.

vs. 28,29. Kedar and Hazor (not to be confused with the four or more Palestinian towns having this same appellation) were territories east of Palestine and belonging to the Arabian people. According to Genesis 25:13, Kedar was a son of Ishmael and grandson of Abraham through Hagar. People of this area, long known for their rejection of Jehovah, were destined to taste of Nebuchadrezzar's unleashed fury. The Babylonian monarch had been given a charge from Jehovah to smite and spoil. They are referred to as men of the east, i. e., east of Palestine. These Arabians were nomads. The spoils to be taken by Nebuchadrezzar would be their tents, flocks, their curtains (connected with their tents), their vessels and their camels. Arabians had but little of anything else that a conqueror would consider as worthy of spoils. The invaded Arabians will face fear on every side. Refuge in Kedar and Hazor will fail them.

vs. 30,31. Their only chance of survival was to flee deep into the forbidding Arabian desert. This is especially addressed to Hazor and its inhabitants. The reason behind the fleeing decree is crystal clear. Nebuchadnezzar has already laid plans for your death and destruction. His purpose or strategy is already formulated. Its fierce execution but remains and that will soon be forthcoming and perhaps not later than 580 B. C. Verse 31 is what the Babylonian monarch would do. He would invade the wealthy land (land at ease—ASV), that has ever had little to fear from opposing nations and who felt secure enough that they lived minus walled cities with gates and bars and were independent enough that they formed no ties of strength with nearby neighboring nations or more remote powers. One commentator has said that the Chaldean invasion of these people would be but a holiday march. That is how free of resistence the Chaldeans would face.

vs. 32,33. The Babylonian victors will take Arabian camels as their booty and Arabian cattle as their spoil. God will see to it that the invaded Arabians will be scattered far and wide; calamity will hit them on all sides and with full fury unleashed. Hazor of the Arabians will be desolate save for the dragons (jackals) dwelling there. Human habitation of a permanent nature there will be none! Thorough and complete would be its discomfiture and its destruction. Babylon would put them to rout with rapidity.

PROPHETIC JUDGMENT AGAINST THE ELAMITES

Paragraph 6 of Jeremiah 49 reads,

The word of the Lord that came to Jeremiah the prophet against Elam in the beginning of the reign of Zedekiah king of Judah, saying, Thus saith the Lord of hosts; Behold, I will break the bow of Elam, the chief of their might. And upon Elam will I bring the four winds from the four quarters of heaven, and will scatter them toward all those winds; and there shall be no nation whither the outcasts of Elam shall not come. For I will cause Elam to be dismayed before their enemies, and before them that seek their life: and I will bring evil upon them, even my fierce anger, saith the Lord; and I will send the sword after them, till I have consumed them: And I will set my throne in Elam, and will destroy from thence the king and the princes, saith the Lord (49:34-38).

vs. 34-36. Again Jeremiah's inspiration is vouchsafed as it is throughout this book and in the aggregate nearly five hundred times in Jeremiah's writings. The prophecy was given near the time Zedekiah began to reign which would make it around 597 B. C. The prophecy is against Elam. Elam was a son of Shem as per Genesis 10:22. The country was located east of Chaldea, north of the Persian Gulf and in the general area of Persia. The country lay northeast of Palestine. Jehovah, the God of power, speaks with authority permeating each syllable. Elam's bow would be broken. This was their chief weapon and they were powerfully proficient in its lethal employment. But as chief of their might, it would be an impotent weapon. The enemy, probably Nebuchadnezzar, would descend upon them from the four winds. His warriors would come from every direction. Elam would be scattered toward all the winds. As outcasts from their own nation, they would seek refuge among all the nations.

vs. 37,38. Elam would be dismayed before her enemies. She will become the prey for those who seek her life. She rests under Jehovah's strong displeasure and evil (appropriate punishment) awaits her for sure. The sword (lethal weapon) will pursue them till they are consumed. God's throne would be set in Elam. This may refer to the throne of the power God would use in chastising Elam. Governmental leaders face destruction.

PROPHETIC HOPE FOR ELAM AT LAST

Paragraph 7 of Jeremiah 49 consisting of but one verse, reads, "But it shall come to pass in the latter days, that I will bring again the captivity of Elam, saith the Lord" (v. 39). Elam did not fare well at all under the Chaldeans but fared much, much better under the far more humane Cyrus of Persia when they were restored to their land and became a powerful people again. There were Elamites present for Pentecost as per Acts 2:9 and this passage here in Jeremiah 49:39 likely finds it richer and fuller fulfillment in Messianic times when Elamites, and all other nations of men, had access to freedom from the worst type of captivity of all—captivity to Satan and sin!

POINTS TO PONDER

(1) Self-preservation in times of crises leads quickly to selfishness and not selflessness.

(2) All the earthly wisdom for which Teman was so noted could not save this Edomite city from coming calamity.

(3) Edom shows strikingly what happens when a person or people are too full of sinful pride.

(4) Jeremiah 49 exhibits clearly that God is ruler over all nations—not just the people of Palestine.

(5) Those who claim there is NO wrath in Jehovah's character would do well to park at Jeremiah 49, do indepth study therein and for as long as it takes to be convinced.

DISCUSSION QUESTIONS

1. What is the prophetic thrust of Jeremiah 49?

2. Discuss the infamous origin of the Ammonites as portrayed so sadly in Genesis 19.

3. What is meant by Esau's calamity and give its apparent background?

4. Discuss in some detail the coming calamity to Damascus from the Chaldean invaders.

5. Discuss in some detail the coming calamity upon Elam.

MULTIPLE-CHOICE: Underline correct answer

1. Lying north of Moab, east of Jordan, west of the Arabian desert and south of Syria was: (A) Damascus; (B) Edom; (C) Elam; (D) Ammon.
2. Rabbah, Heshbon and Ai were cities belonging to: (A) Ammon; (B) Damascus; (C) Elam; (D) Edom.
3. Obadiah, shortest book of the Old Testament, is a prophetic discourse about the destruction of: (A) Nineveh; (B) Damascus; (C) Jerusalem; (D) Edom.
4. In the book of Job: (A) Eliphaz; (B) Bildad; (C) Zophar; (D) Elihu—was a Temanite, i.e., one from the Edomite country.
5. Sodom, Gomorrah, Zeboim and Admah were: (A) Edomite cities of great wickedness; (B) cities noted especially for their

righteousness; (C) Ammonite cities destined for destruction by the cruel Chaldeans; (D) cities of the Jordan Valley in Abraham's era who were destroyed due to their great wickedness.

SCRIPTURAL FILL-IN: Only one word required in each blank

1. ". . . O _____ daughter? that _____ in her _____ , saying, _____ shall _____ unto _____ ?"

2. ". . . for _____ will _____ the _____ of _____ upon him, the _____ that _____ will _____ him."

3. "_____ , lo, _____ will _____ thee _____ among the _____ , and _____ among _____ ."

4. "_____ is the _____ of _____ not _____ , the _____ of _____ joy!"

5. "_____ , I will _____ the _____ of _____ , the _____ of their _____ ."

TRUE OR FALSE: Put either a "T" or "F" in the blanks

_____ 1. Relative to land she took over Ammon always followed principles of integrity and honor.
_____ 2. The Edomites were descendants of Jacob (later called Israel).
_____ 3. There is no instance in all the Bible of where God ever swore by Himself.
_____ 4. Damascus is one of the oldest, if not oldest, continuing cities on earth.
_____ 5. Nebuchadnezzar was the Lord's appointed smiter and spoiler of the wicked nations of that evil area.

THOUGHT QUESTIONS

1. Discuss how people today for the most part trust in their earthly treasures and not in heavenly truth.

2. Edomite trust in her mountainous retreats should be what kind of lesson to materialistic America who largely has forgotten God?

3. What kind of needed lesson can we learn from the way Edom treated its neighbors and the reaped punishment they later received for the same?

4. How does this chapter reflect fully the authority that resides in the great and glorious God of heaven?

5. What tremendous tie exists between Jeremiah 49:39 and Acts 2:9?

CHAPTER TWENTY-FOUR

VENGEANCE ON BABYLON (NO. 1)
Jeremiah 50

Throughout this prophetic product by the weeping prophet from Anathoth, Babylon has been the avenging agent of Jehovah in chastising Jerusalem, Judah and surrounding nations for their enormous crimes against God and man. In this chapter and the subsequent one, Jeremiah 51, longest one of the whole book, Babylon itself becomes the victim of God's aroused indignation. Babylon's payday for her own crimes and transgressions will surely come. Habakkuk faced a problem in this prophetic era how God could use a sinful people like the Chaldeans to punish His own sinful people of Judah. Habakkuk was led to see that Chaldea's day of punishment for her sins would also occur. If Habakkuk had had access to all of Jeremiah's book in general and these two chapters in particular, he would have seen even more clearly the solution to the problem that plagued him. Intermixed with the judgments soon to afflict Babylon, there is redemption promised to Israel. In fact, my Bible has as the one line summary of this entire chapter, "Judgment of Babylon, and redemption of Israel."

BABYLON'S FALL PREDICTED

Paragraph 1 of Jeremiah 50 reads,

The word that the Lord spake against Babylon and against the land of the Chaldeans by Jeremiah the prophet. Declare ye among the nations, and publish, and set up a standard; publish, and conceal not: say, Babylon is taken, Bel is confounded, Merodach is broken in pieces; her idols are confounded, her images are broken in pieces.

409

For out of the north there cometh up a nation against her, which shall make her land desolate, and none shall dwell therein: they shall remove, they shall depart, both man and beast (50:1-3).

vs. 1,2. The message is Jehovah's; the prophetic penman of the message is Jeremiah; the prophecy of doom and destruction concerns Babylon (the Chaldeans); the time of the prophecy, according to Jeremiah 51:59, was in Zedekiah's fourth year (about 593 B. C.). It was a message to be made known among the nations for Babylon had plagued and plundered all nations in her heyday of empire greatness. The nations would rejoice to hear of Babylon's demise. A standard was to be set, i. e., the place established where the nations would meet to hear of Babylon's fall. The message was to be published (the positive); it was not to be concealed (the negative). The message is plain and pointed. (1) Babylon is taken. Babylon's demise was so certain that the prophet spoke of it as already taking place though it was more than a half century yet in the future. (2) Bel is confounded. Bel was chief Babylonian deity and corresponded to the Baal deity of the Middle East countries. Baal was viewed as the sun god. Bel also corresponded to the Jupiter of other pagan people. (3) Merodach is broken in pieces. This was another Babylonian idol though some commentators think they—Bel and Merodach—were one and the same. Nebuchadnezzar must have fondly favored Merodach since he named his son Evil-Merodach. In the aggregate all Chaldean idols are confounded ("put to shame"—ASV) and broken to pieces. They were not able even to preserve themselves to say nothing of aiding the empire that adored them.

v. 3. Babylon's conqueror will come from the north. The Medes and Persians would write finis to the saga of Chaldean might and glory. Cyrus and the Persians did it; Darius and the Medes did it. Mighty Babylon which was once densely populated would know a desolation almost minus parallel; it would be a place minus population. Both man and beast will vacate the desolate land and that in mass form. In any listing of great cities of today, one would seek in vain to find Babylon. It is city strictly of the past—not of present—not of future.

HOPEFUL ASSURANCE FOR ISRAEL

Paragraph 2 of Jeremiah 50 reads,

In those days, and in that time, saith the Lord, the children of Israel shall come, they and the children of Judah together, going and weeping: they shall go, and seek the Lord their God. They shall ask the way to Zion with their faces thitherward, saying, Come, and let us join ourselves to the Lord in a perpetual covenant that shall not be forgotten. My people hath been lost sheep: their shepherds have caused them to go astray, they have turned them away on the mountains: they have gone from mountain to hill, they have forgotten their restingplace. All that found them have devoured them: and their adversaries said, We offend not, because they have sinned against the Lord, the habitation of justice, even the Lord, the hope of their fathers. Remove out of the midst of Babylon, and go forth out of the land of the Chaldeans, and be as the he goats before the flocks (50:4-8).

vs. 4,5. The time for Israelite release from their Babylonian captors is when Babylon falls to the invading power from the north—the Medes and Persians. Cyrus promptly gave any and every willing Jew permission to return to Palestine as per 2 Chronicles 36:22,23 and Ezra 1:1-3, verses of repetition. Children of Israel and children of Judah are both included. Israel had been taken to Assyria in 722 B. C.; Judah had been taken to Babylon in 586 B. C. Cyrus now controlled all these land areas and the people contained therein. Those ready will return. Tears of penitence will flood their eyes and soil their changed faces. In their return, one thing will be dominant—the reverent seeking of the Lord. Inquiry will be made for the way to Zion. The old paths will not be rejected as an earlier generation of rebels had done in Jeremiah 6:16,17. Their faces will be toward Jerusalem. Their feet will be traveling in that direction. To one another they shall extend a warm and gracious COME to form a perpetual covenant (agreement) with God—a covenant neither to be forgotten nor forsaken. Their whole history up to that time had been filled to overflowing with covenant abandonment and law violations of the deepest dye.

vs. 6,7. Jehovah viewed them as lost sheep. Their shepherds—kings, prophets and priests—have led them astray. These pseudo kings, prophets and priests had encouraged them to come to the mountains and high

411

hills and when they had seduced them into idolatrous orgies without end. Their restingplace was God. Him they had ignored and forgotten. Their enemies, in essence, said that they incurred no blame in what they inflicted on idolatrous Israel for Israel had sinned against their holy God even though He was their Lord, their habitation of justice and the only hope of their fathers.

v. 8. With rapidity and promptness, Israel is charged to move out of the doomed city—Babylon—and to depart the about-to-be-destroyed land—Chaldea. They were charged to be as the he goats which charge ahead of the more timid in the flocks and serve as inspirational leaders to those in the rear. This prompt exit would be essential if they hoped to avoid the catastrophe coming to Chaldea.

DESTRUCTION TO BABYLON WILL BE WIDE, DEEP AND THOROUGH

Paragraph 3 of Jeremiah 50 reads,

> **For, lo, I will raise and cause to come up against Babylon as assembly of great nations from the north country: and they shall set themselves in array against her; from thence she shall be taken: their arrows shall be as of a mighty expert man; none shall return in vain. And Chaldea shall be a spoil: all that spoil her shall be satisfied, saith the Lord. Because ye were glad, because ye rejoiced O ye destroyers of mine heritage, because ye are grown fat as the heifer at grass, and bellow as bulls; Your mother shall be sore confounded; she that bare you shall be ashamed: behold, the hindermost of the nations shall be a wilderness, a dry land, and a desert. Because of the wrath of the Lord it shall not be inhabited, but it shall be wholly desolate: every one that goeth by Babylon shall be astonished, and hiss at all her plagues. Put yourselves in array against Babylon round about: all ye that bend the bow, shoot at her, spare no arrows: for she hath sinned against the Lord. Shout against her round about: she hath given her hand: her foundations are fallen, her walls are thrown down: for it is the vengeance of the Lord: take vengeance upon her; as she hath done, do unto her. Cut**

412

**off the sower from Babylon, and him that handleth the
sickle in the time of harvest: for fear of the oppressing
sword they shall turn every one to his people, and they
shall flee every one to his own land (50:9-16).**

vs. 9,10. The assigned destroyer of Babylon has already been
determined by omniscient and omnipotent Jehovah. Jehovah will stir
them up, awake them to their God-appointed task of chastising a now
arrogant, sinful people. Babylon will be the target of the avenging power
that will come from the north. Though it will be the Medes and Persians,
yet they will have in the aggregate of their armies men from several
nations. These are from great nations. They will be powerful enough
to do Jehovah's bidding. Babylon will be totally impotent in averting
such. They will make their approach from the north country, i. e., north
of Babylon though not all in the Medo-Persian army would be from
the north. They have one design—the conquering of the Chaldeans; this
is their driving purpose. Their arrows will be so expertly aimed that
none shall miss the target—Babylon. The Chaldeans who had spoiled
so many others now will become the spoiled; she who had conquered
so many others will now become the conquered, the vanquished herself.
Those who conquer physical Babylon shall be satisfied in the spoils they
take.

vs. 11,12. Though Babylon had been Jehovah's accepted and assigned
rod to chastise sinful Judah, yet Babylon exulted or found fiendish delight
in what they inflicted on besieged Judah and Jerusalem as they attacked
and conquered God's heritage, viz., Judah. Babylon had become as a
well-fed heifer or a bellowing bull. Her arrogance and wantonness must
be punished and this the Medes and Persians would do. Babylon is spoken
of as mother. For many years before her demise as the great world power
of her day, she had considered herself as the mother-city, the Queen
of the whole world. Spiritual Babylon does the same in Revelation 18.
Yet mighty Babylon is to be brought low—very low. Her own people
will become ashamed of her. She who once ruled the world will become
weak and impotent. In Daniel's early days, Babylon and its king
constituted the head of gold (Daniel 2:31ff). Now she is destined to be
the lowest of nations. She will be depopulated; she will become a dry,
arid and deserted land. What once was a flourishing city will become
a famished, forsaken land. Babylon indeed is to be brought low—very low.

vs. 13,14. Jehovah's aroused wrath calls for flourishing Babylon to be void of people. Desolation of the deepest dye awaits it. Passers-by will stand in astonishment, in amazement, in bewilderment and shall show utter contempt for the plagued city. Merciful sympathy will be absent as they view a city brought to utter desolation. The charge to the avenging army calls for total destruction. No effort is to be spared in her total demolition. Archers are charged to bend their bows, shoot their arrows and let none miss the target. The why is summed up concisely, "for she hath sinned against the Lord." This proves conclusively that non-Israelites prior to Calvary were under a law to God. It was not Mosaic law since that was to Isrrael only (Deuteronomy 5:3-5) and so it must have been patriarchal law that continued for all non-Israelites. Had Babylon been under no law they could have sinned against the Lord of heaven (Cf. Romans 4:15; 5:13). Babylon had not violated its own laws but had sinned against higher law—Jehovah's law.

vs. 15,16. Those attacking Babylon are urged to sound the necessary war cries to inspire all their fighting comrades to take the city. She has yielded her hand; her foundations or security systems are destroyed; her walls are no more an obstacle to keep out the attackers. Jehovah determines that vengeance is now required. He demands it to be done. As she has done to others, now do to her. This is the well-known law of retribution. Strikingly similar is what is said of Spiritual Babylon in the final book of Holy Writ,

> **For her sins have reached unto heaven, and God hath remembered her iniquities. Reward her even as she rewarded you, and double unto her double according to her works: in the cup which she hath filled fill to her double. How much she hath glorified herself, and lived deliciously, so much torment and sorrow give her: for she saith in her heart, I sit a queen, and am no widow, and shall see no sorrow (Revelation 18:5-7).**

Babylon had sown the wind; now she must reap the whirlwind (Cf. Hosea 8:7). The charge goes forth relative to sowers of seed and handlers of harvest sickles. Both were to be cut off. Hence, there were to be no planting seasons, no harvest seasons. Gardens and fields of grain were to be no more. Conquerors usually spare agriculturalists but not in this instance. Inhabitants in Babylon, for fear of the oppressing sword, shall flee the doomed city. Those brought to Babylon as captives will flee to their own lands.

ISRAEL'S RESTORATION

Paragraph 4 of Jeremiah 50 reads,

Israel is a scattered sheep; the lions have driven him away: first the king of Assyria hath devoured him; and last this Nebuchadrezzar king of Babylon hath broken his bones. Therefore thus saith the Lord of hosts, the God of Israel; Behold, I will punish the king of Babylon and his land, as I have punished the king of Assyria. And I will bring Israel again to his habitation, and he shall feed on Carmel and Bashan, and his soul shall be satisfied upon Mount Ephraim and Gilead. In those days, and in that time, saith the Lord, the iniquity of Israel shall be sought for, and there shall be none; and the sins of Judah, and they shall not be found: for I will pardon them whom I reserve (50:17-20).

vs. 17,18. God's people had been scattered like scared sheep; lions (first the Assyrians with Israel and second the Babylonians with Judah) have devoured and broken bones. There seems to be a progression here with being scattered, devoured and the breaking of bones. Assyria had already been destroyed by the Medes and Chaldeans; now it is Babylon's turn to be punished. The Medo-Persians will be the assigned avengers on proud, defiant and bloodthirsty Babylon.

vs. 19,20. Restoration, prosperity and pardon are key thoughts in this duet of verses. Israel will be restored to the land of her nativity. Prosperity is set forth in the feeding on Carmel and Bashan and Israel's satisfaction upon Mount Ephraim and Gilead. These were four fertile areas in Palestine. Both Israel and Judah are mentioned in verse 20. Pardon will be their rich possession because no iniquity will be found in Israel and no sin in Judah. This pictures a penitent people who have become a pardoned people. The captivity cured Israel and Judah of their long, besetting sins of idolatry.

JEHOVAH ORDERS TOTAL DEMOLITION
FOR WICKED BABYLON

Paragraph 5 of Jeremiah 50 reads,

Go up against the land of Merathaim, even against it, and against the inhabitants of Pekod: waste and utterly destroy after them, saith the Lord, and do according to all that I have commanded thee. A sound of battle is in the land, and of great destruction. How is the hammer of the whole earth cut asunder and broken! how is Babylon become a desolation among the nations! I have laid a snare for thee, and thou art also taken, O Babylon, and thou wast not aware: thou art found, and also caught, because thou hast striven against the Lord. The Lord hath opened his armoury, and hath brought forth the weapons of his indignation: for this is the work of the Lord God of hosts in the land of the Chaldeans. Come against her from the utmost border, open her storehouses: cast her up as heaps, and destroy her utterly: let nothing of her be left. Slay all her bullocks; let them go down to the slaughter: woe unto them! for their day is come, the time of their visitation. The voice of them that flee and escape out of the land of Babylon, to declare in Zion the vengeance of the Lord our God, the vengeance of his temple. Call together the archers against Babylon: all ye that bend the bow, camp against it round about; let none thereof escape: recompense her according to her work; according to all that she hath done, do unto her: for she hath been proud against the Lord, against the Holy One of Israel. Therefore shall her young men fall in the streets, and all her men of war shall be cut off in that day, saith the Lord. Behold, I am against thee, O thou most proud, saith the Lord God of hosts: for thy day is come, the time that I will visit thee. And the most proud shall stumble and fall, and none shall raise him up: and I will kindle a fire in his cities, and it shall devour all round about him (50:21-32).

416

v. 21. The charge is given the Medes and Persians since they were to be God's avenging rod to chastise and destroy Babylon. Merathaim seemingly was a symbolical term for the land to be taken. Its meaning is "double rebellion." Babylon was rebellious against God by both her idolatry and her almost unparalleled pride. Look at what God did in bringing prideful Nebuchadnezzar down in Daniel 4. Babylon had striven against the Lord and had been proud against Him (vs. 24,29). Pekod may have been a Babylonian town or again we may have a symbolic term employed to set forth coming punishment on arrogant, idolatrous Babylon. Medo-Persia receives a charge from God to waste and destroy Babylon. Medes and Persians were to do all Jehovah commanded.

vs. 22,23. War cries of coming battles fill the doomed land. Great destruction hovers over Babylon. According to Daniel 5 the city was more interested in PARTYING than in PREPARING to meet the coming enemy. Babylon had been the hammer of the whole earth; it had been the Lord's scourge to punish rebellious nations; it had beaten to pieces other nations; now it is Babylon's time to be brought low by the powerful twin arms of the mighty Medes and the powerful Persians. She who once thrived and flourished as mistress of the world is destined toward desolation. Her fall would be as meteoric as had been her rise under powerful Nebuchadnezzar.

v. 24. God laid a snare for Babylon; she was taken almost before she knew what was happening. If Herodotus, father of history, is correct, Cyrus diverted the waters of Euphrates, which flowed through Babylon, into another channel and entered the city by the channel now empty of flowing waters. Another view accepted by some is that a traitor from within opened the gates to the invaders while the city leaders were in drunkenness and debauchery. Either view would fit this verse which speaks of Babylon's being taken without awareness of what was occurring. Babylon's sin of striving against the Lord has caught up with her.

vs. 25-27. Jehovah is portrayed here as opening up His armory of weapons for the Medes and Persians to use against doomed Babylon. Weapons used against Babylon are considered here as the weapons of God's own indignation. This is HIS work; the Medes and Persians are HIS agents in destroying prideful, rebellious and idolatrous Babylon. He is styled here Lord of hosts which exhibits His power at work throughout all this. Medo-Persia is charged to come against her from the utmost border. The order calls for total destruction to be visited on the proud Chaldean capital. Jehovah charged Medes and Persians to open her storehouses. It is said that when Babylon was conquered, she had sufficient provisions to last for many years. She was not starved into subjection as Jerusalem had been. The ordered destruction is graphically portrayed. (1) She is to be cast up as heaps; (2) she is to be destroyed utterly; (3) nothing is to be left her; (4) her bullocks, warriors and choice young men are to be slain; (5) they are to go down to slaughter (imagery of where animals were slain in the lower part of the city); (6) a woe of weight is pronounced against them; (7) the day of their punishment has come; (8) God's visitation of His aroused wrath is upon them.

v. 28. Jewish fleers from the doomed city will escape and bring news of Babylon's demise to Zion. The thrust of their heralded message will be that God's vengeance has been taken out on Babylon for what Babylon had done to His temple. With a powerful play on words, Adam Clarke has this to say on verse 28, "Zion was desolated by Babylon; tell Zion that God hath desolated the desolator."

vs. 29,30. Bow and arrow formed a prominent part of ancient military weapons. Medes and Persians were proficient in the skilled usage of such. Medo-Persian archers are charged to assemble and discharge their work with bow and arrow proficiently. No Chaldean is to escape. Babylon is to be done as she has done to countless others. The imagery here is strikingly similar to that set forth against spiritual Babylon in Revelation 18:5-7. The well-known law of sowing and reaping applies to nations as well as to individuals (Cf. Galatians 6:7,8). Why? A reason is given— her pride against God. According to Proverbs 6:16-19, there are seven things God deems to be abominations, things He hates. The proud look (haughty eyes—ASV) heads the loveless list. Babylon and pride were almost synonyms in that ancient era. What a price she must now pay. (1) Her choice young men will be slain inside the very city, on its very streets. (2) Her stalwart, powerful men of war will be cut off. How sure is all this? The Lord said it; that settled its surety.

vs. 31,32. Babylon will be impotent in standing or in resisting the Medo-Persian invaders because God was opposed to Babylon and was giving power, impetus and direction to the invaders from the north. Again the intolerable pride of arrogant Babylon is delineated and with God's signal disfavor and disapproval. Demise is at hand; divine visitation of wrath hovers over the now doomed city. Babylon men of insufferable pride are going to stumble and fall; no one will be there to lift them up again. Fiery destruction with total devastation awaits these proud, disdainful sinners. Payday for sin in this life is now theirs. Hell is God's eternal payday for all who strive against God and are proud against Him. Note how often pride is mentioned as one of Babylon's primary sins. The lesson Jehovah taught Nebuchadnezzar relative to pride and its lethal dangers in Daniel 4 did not make a measurable dent with the generation that came next. Babylon totally failed to realize that "Pride goeth before destruction, and a haughty spirit before a fall" (Proverbs 16:18). Let each of us not forget that pride is one of the three prongs of worldliness (1 John 2:15-17) and that God resists (military term where God marshals Himself against) the proud but gives grace to the humble (James 4:6; 1 Peter 5:5).

JEHOVAH: NOT FORGETFUL OF HIS PEOPLE

Paragraph 6 of Jeremiah 50 reads,

> **Thus saith the Lord of hosts; The children of Israel and the children of Judah were oppressed together: and all that took them captives held them fast; they refused to let them go. Their Redeemer is strong: the Lord of hosts is his name: he shall throughly plead their cause, that he may give rest to the land, and disquiet the inhabitants of Babylon (50:33,34).**

v. 33. Jehovah speaks as the authoritative one, the all-powerful one. Israel and Judah are spoken of together because both had been and still are oppressed and in virtually the same general area—the former in Assyria and the latter in Babylon. Any good map of Bible Lands will show the close proximity of these two aggressive powers. When Babylon came to world power, she superseded Assyria and assimilated the area Assyria once ruled with might and maliciousness. Both Assyria and Babylon had held Israel and Judah in a strictly captive condition; they refused to let them go. Medo-Persia would grant them freedom to return to Palestine and would partly finance building their nation and their temple again.

v. 34. Jehovah is portrayed here as Israel's and Judah's Redeemer. The imagery is very striking. He is their GOEL which means he acts as Israel's and Judah's nearest kinsman who was the assigned and accepted avenger for wrongs afflicted. This concept permeates the entire Old

419

Testament, i. e., the nearest of kin came to the avenging rescue of a kinsman done wrong. Jehovah is strong. The Chaldeans had been strong but now were weak. Jehovah promises to plead the cause of His people. How throughly would He do this? In the Hebrew text we have "the triple repetition of the same word; lit. in pleading He will plead their plea" (Cook and Fuller, THE BIBLE COMMENTARY ON PROVERBS— EZEKIEL, p. 270). Jehovah promises rest to the land that has been torn by war. Babylonian warriors will no more make the world weary with their battle cries and destructive tactics. Jehovah has disquieted permanently Babylonian warfare on surrounding nations.

BABYLON WILL NOT BE SHOWN MERCY

Paragraph 7 of Jeremiah 50 reads,

> A sword is upon the Chaldeans, saith the Lord, and upon the inhabitants of Babylon, and upon her princes, and upon her wise men. A sword is upon the liars; and they shall dote: a sword is upon her mighty men; and they shall be dismayed. A sword is upon their horses, and upon their chariots, and upon all the mingled people that are in the midst of her; and they shall become as women: a sword is upon her treasures; and they shall be robbed. A drought is upon her waters; and they shall be dried up: for it is the land of graven images, and they are mad upon their idols. Therefore the wild beasts of the desert with the wild beasts of the islands shall dwell there, and the owls shall dwell therein: and it shall be no more inhabited for ever; neither shall it be dwelt in from generation to generation. As God overthrew Sodom and Gomorrah and the neighbour cities thereof, saith the Lord; so shall no man abide there, neither shall any son of man dwell therein. Behold, a people shall come from the north, and a great nation, and many kings shall be raised up from the coasts of the earth. They shall hold the bow and the lance: they are cruel, and will not shew mercy: their voice shall roar like the sea, and they shall ride upon horses, every one put in array, like a man to the battle, against thee, O daughter of Babylon. The king

420

of Babylon hath heard the report of them, and his hands waxed feeble: anguish took hold of him, and pangs as of a woman in travail. Behold, he shall come up like a lion from the swelling of Jordan unto the habitation of the strong: but I will make them suddenly run away from her: and who is a chosen man, that I may appoint over her? for who is like me? and who will appoint me the time? and who is that shepherd that will stand before me? Therefore hear ye the counsel of the Lord, that he hath taken against Babylon; and his purposes, that he hath purposed against the land of the Chaldeans: Surely the least of the flock shall draw them out: surely he shall make their habitation desolate with them. At the noise of the taking of Babylon the earth is moved, and the cry is heard among the nations (50:35-46).

vs. 35,36. Sword is a lethal weapon. It is a weapon of war. Babylon had long used the sword upon its enemies. Now the sword hangs upon Chaldea. This warfare will affect Babylonian inhabitants; princes will not be spared; wise men will not escape its lethal effects. A sword is upon the liars. This probably includes the Babylonian astrolgers, soothsayers, fortune-tellers, boasters, etc. These men had great influence upon an age filled with ignorance and superstition. They shall dote means that their foolishness would humiliate them, throw them into a state of confusion and their folly would be evident to all their former devotees. Babylon had long depended on her men of military might to protect her and conquer nations under her banner. Now those same mighty men face this lethal sword. Their power would be gone. They will feel terror, know alarm and experience utter confusion.

vs. 37,38. Their horses and chariots will experience the lethal effects of the sword (the warfare brought on by the invading Medes and Persians). The mingled people would be the foreigners brought into Babylon and which probably served as mercenaries to aid Chaldean interests. Their men of might will lose their manly strength and prowess. They are likened to women. As a general rule, women, though superior to men in a number of ways, are not as strong physically as men. This is why wars have usually been fought, at least on the front lines, by men. The sword (warfare) will devour Babylon of her vast treasures many of which had

421

been gathered as spoils of Babylonian victories in the past. Babylon's prized waters are dried up. This always spells doom for a nation due to water's essentiality. This may refer to the drying up of the Euphrates' channel, diverting the water elsewhere, and the means of Medo-Persian entrance into the opulent city. One of Babylon's grave crimes was its utter fascination and total enamoring of idols. Their idols were more designed to terrorize them than to attract them. Babylon was mad upon idolatry.

vs. 39,40. Babylon shall be so thoroughly destroyed and made desolate as to be a place where only doleful and wild creatures (wild beasts, wolves, owls, ostriches, etc.,) shall have a dwelling there. Human habitation will not be found there from generation to generation. Isaiah 13:19-22 should be read in connection with what Jeremiah portrays. Sodom and Gomorrah are mentioned by both Jeremiah and by Isaiah (Jeremiah 50:40; Isaiah 13:19-22). These Jordan Plain cities, plus Admah and Zeboim, experienced a total overthrow. In all probability, the Dead Sea now covers these destroyed cities. Just that complete will be Babylon's overthrow. This once flourishing and properous area will be as free of human population as the cities of Sodom, Gomorrah and their neighboring cities. What a picture of utter destruction is penned here by God's prophet.

vs. 41-43. The language here is strikingly similar to what we have in 6:22-24. There it describes Babylon's attack on Zion; here it describes Medo-Persia's invasion of Babylon. The invader in chapter six becomes the invaded in chapter fifty. How quickly military roles can be reversed. Medo-Persia lay north and east of Babylon. The invasion came from the north. The Medes and Persians were the great world power from about 539 B. C. to the days of Alexander the Great a full two centuries later. A number of kings ruled from the Medo-Persian throne and some of them were very powerful as the books of Ezra, Nehemiah and Esther fully reveal. Bow and lance were weapons in the Medo-Persian armory. They were cruel and merciless. War can hardly be waged minus both of these ingredients. Look at Haman's cruelty and the rapidity that Ahasuerus, king of Persia in that era, granted Haman's request to destroy an entire people—the Jews—in the Empire (Cf. Esther 3). A voice roaring like the sea would be one of authority and that would strike terror in the hearts of the invaded. Medes and Persians would be horsemen. The Medo-Persian warriors would be so ordered in uniform military action that it would seem as though the army was composed of just one man. Daughter of Babylon refers to the whole people—target of the Medo-Persian invasion. The king of Babylon here apparently refers to Belshazzar. He feels feeble; fear and anguish tug at his uneasy heartstrings; he is likened to a woman in the throes of painful childbirth. Daniel 5 is an excellent commentary on verse 43 and should be read by every interested student.

vs. 44-46. These verses are strikingly similar to 49:19,20. There Edom is the invaded target; here Babylon is the invaded target. The lion is Medo-Persia that comes to tear, devour, destroy. The imagery is of the lion that is forced to leave the underbrush along Jordan due to its flooded condition. The habitation of the strong here is Babylon. With relative ease, Medo-Persia will take Babylon—long considered an invincible city. God has willed her collapse and Babylon can post no leader that can resist the heavenly decree that it shall fall and fall permanently. God speaks His counsel to Babylon. Reference to the least of the flock refers to the ease and success of Medo-Persia's conquering of the Chaldean capital. Almost overnight Babylon will go from a FLOURISHING power to a FAMISHED people. Their once prosperous city is destined for forlorn misery and desolate destruction. Babylon's fall will enlist the world's wonder and amazement. Adam Clarke well comments, "The taking of Babylon was a wonder to all the surrounding nations. It was thought to be impregnable."

POINTS TO PONDER

(1) Predictive prophecy punctuates all this chapter.

(2) Arrogance helped to pave the way for Babylon's demise as world power.

(3) It is folly to the nth degree for proud, defiant and rebellious man to think he can strive successfully against the Sovereign Ruler of the whole universe.

(4) All Babylonian idols in the aggregate proved to be absolutely worthless when the Medes and Persians attacked the great city on the Euphrates.

(5) What Jeremiah predicted in this chapter was fulfilled minutely and precisely just a very few decades later.

DISCUSSION QUESTIONS

1. Summarize introduction.

2. Discuss the changes to be found in the returning captives to their homeland again.

3. Discuss the two views of how the Persian Cyrus conquered with relative ease the almost impregnable Babylon.

4. How is the ordered destruction of Babylon portrayed so graphically in some eight descriptions?

5. Why are Sodom and Gomorrah brought into the picture in depicting Babylon's total demise as a nation?

MULTIPLE-CHOICE: Underline correct answer

1. (A) Habakkuk; (B) Joel; (C) Judah; (D) Micah—had a problem over a sinful nation like Babylon being God's avenging rod of correcting sinful Judah.
2. The new world power who would conquer Babylon and bring her prostrate was to be: (A) Assyria; (B) Medo-Persia; (C) Greece; (D) Rome.
3. Cyrus the Persian: (A) refused to allow any Jew to return to Palestine; (B) allowed all Jews so dispositioned to return to their homeland; (C) slew all Jews in his realm; (D) was far more inhumane than Nebuchadnezzar and the Chaldeans ever dared be.
4. (A) Jerusalem; (B) Babylon; (C) Damascus; (D) Tyre—considered herself the mother-city, the Queen of the whole world.
5. (A) Nebuchadnezzar; (B) Belshazzar; (C) Evil-Merodach; (D) Darius the Mede—in Daniel 4 was taught a great lesson on the folly of human pride and the worth of humility.

SCRIPTURAL FILL-IN: Only one word required in each blank

1. "They shall _____ the _____ to _____ with their _____ thitherward, saying, _____, and

424

let us _____ ourselves to the _____ in a _____ covenant that _____ not be _____ ."

2. "_____ , I will _____ the _____ of _____ and his _____ , as _____ have _____ the _____ of _____ ."

3. "Their _____ is _____ ; the _____ of _____ is his _____ : he shall throughly _____ their _____ , that he may _____ rest to the _____ , and _____ the _____ of Babylon."

4. "A _____ is _____ her _____ ; and they _____ be _____ up: for it is the _____ of graven _____ , and they are _____ upon their _____ ."

5. "At the _____ of the _____ of _____ the _____ is _____ , and the _____ is _____ among the _____ ."

TRUE OR FALSE: Put either a "T" or "F" in the blanks

_____ 1. Cyrus and Darius were the two final kings who ruled Babylon in her declining days.

_____ 2. Babylon would be dealt only a slight blow by invading Medes and Persians.

_____ 3. Hosea 8:7 totally negates the law of sowing and reaping.

_____ 4. Throughout the Bible penitence always precedes pardon.

_____ 5. Arrogance among the human family has never been of any particular concern to God.

THOUGHT QUESTIONS

1. How does the predicted fall of Babylon exhibit clearly the law of sowing and reaping? Tie in also what is said of Spiritual Babylon in Revelation 18:5-7.

2. Discuss the enormity of our sinning "against the Lord."

3. Discuss Babylon as being under law to God, what law it could not have been and what law it had to be.

4. What great lesson should our generation learn from Daniel 5 relative to a love for PARTYING and an adamant refusal toward PREPARING to meet God in final judgment.

5. List some dangers we face from pride today and what are some of its current exhibitions?

CHAPTER TWENTY-FIVE

VENGEANCE ON BABYLON (NO. 2)
Jeremiah 51

During the last half of Jeremiah's era, Babylon had been the dominant power of the world. This was especially true since Nineveh's fall and Assyria's collapse around 612 B. C. Babylon had been the mistress of the world; she had been the scourge of the world; she had been Jehovah's chastening rod not only for His people but for numerous neighboring nations as well. She was arrogant, ruthless, selfish and idolatrous to the core. Now her payday for sin is predicted by Jeremiah in chapters 50 and 51. Jeremiah wrote of her destruction some five decades before it materialized. Fulfillment occurred in precise, severe fashion under the cruel Medes and Persians—God's chastenings rod for proud and mighty Babylon.

The KJV gives only two paragraph headings to this chapter (recall that paragraph divisions are the works of men). The ASV gives many more and I shall use its paragraph divisions though the scriptural quotations will be from the beloved and revered KJV. This will enable our study to be uniform by heading sections along shorter paragraph divisions. This is by far the longest chapter in the entire book.

BABYLON TO BE SEVERELY RECOMPENSED FOR HER SINS

Paragraph 1 of Jeremiah 51 reads,

Thus saith the Lord; Behold, I will raise up against Babylon, and against them that dwell in the midst of them that rise up against me, a destroying wind; And will send unto Babylon fanners, that shall fan her, and shall empty her land: for in the day of trouble they shall be against

427

her round about. **Against him that bendeth let the archer bend his bow, and against him that lifteth himself up in his brigandine: and spare ye not her young men; destroy ye utterly all her host. Thus the slain shall fall in the land of the Chaldeans, and they that are thrust through in her streets. For Israel hath not been forsaken, nor Judah of his God, of the Lord of hosts; though their land was filled with sin against the Holy One of Israel. Flee out of the midst of Babylon, and deliver every man his soul: be not cut off in her iniquity; for this is the time of the Lord's vengeance; he will render unto her a recompence. Babylon hath been a golden cup in the Lord's hand, that made all the earth drunken: the nations have drunken of her wine; therefore the nations are mad. Babylon is suddenly fallen and destroyed: howl for her; take balm for her pain, if so be she may be healed. We would have healed Babylon, but she is not healed: forsake her, and let us go every one into his own country: for her judgment reacheth unto heaven, and is lifted up even to the skies. The Lord hath brought forth our righteousness: come, and let us declare in Zion the work of the Lord our God (51:1-10).**

vs. 1-4. Jeremiah speaks God's word. This is just one of nearly five hundred allusions he makes to his inspiration. Babylon's enemy will be raised up by Jehovah; this is to be His doing. The enemy is Medo-Persia. The invaders are likened to a destroying wind. People in the Middle East were well acquainted with the parching, drying and destructive winds that blew. The enemies, the Medes and Persians, were likened to fanners. Babylon is destined to be fanned and emptied. The imagery is of grain that has been trodden and then pitched into the air. The wind would drive away the worthless chaff. Babylon has now become chaff that must be destroyed. The enemies will surround the doomed Chaldean capital. The Babylonian archer will be defenseless against the Persian archer who comes against him. The Babylonian is defenseless, even in his brigandine (coat of armor) against the invader. Medo-Persia is charged to destroy her young men (warriors) and all her host (all the Chaldean defenders). Widespread destruction is herein depicted as the slain, by the masses, will fall on Chaldean territory and the Babylonian land will be strewn full of corpses.

vs. 5,6. Israel and Judah, though violators of God's law and now in captive punishment, have not been abandoned of Jehovah God. God's people are charged to flee with rapidity from doomed Babylon. This they must do if they hoped to escape the severe punishment soon to be meted out to wicked Babylon. Babylon is now ripe to receive God's vengeance; the time of her punishment draws near.

vs. 7, 8. In this duet of verses, Babylon is set in marked contrast. She had been the golden cup in Jehovah's hand. In Daniel's early days, Nebuchadnezzar was the head of gold observed in the great metallic image (Daniel 2). In Isaiah 14:4, she is called the golden city. By her power and might she had made all nations drunken due to drinking the wine in her cup whether they drank voluntarily or by compulsion. Babylon falls with a sudden impact. Her destruction will come quickly. Those long interested in her are told to howl for her and seek balm for her healing in case she might be healed. But healing, as the next verse indicates, will be out of the question.

vs. 9,10. Her former devotees and aides from other nations would have healed her but her wound was incurable. Prudent policy called for their abandoning her to her God-allotted destruction. Survival called for them to leave her and get to their own country. They say in her destruction that this was God's vengeance visited on the doomed metropolis. Graphically, her demise is pictured as a judgment heaven high, sky high. Verse 10 gives the Jewish response. Jehovah has vindicated His own righteous cause. This He does for the sake of His cause and not for any merits Israel and Judah might have. Declaration was to be made in Zion (Jerusalem) of the work God would accomplish.

THE MEDES ARE RAISED UP TO DO GOD'S BIDDING

Paragraph 2 of Jeremiah 51 reads,

> **Make bright the arrows; gather the shields: the Lord hath raised up the spirit of the kings of the Medes: for his device is against Babylon, to destroy it; because it is the vengeance of the Lord, the vengeance of his temple. Set up the standard upon the walls of Babylon, make the watch strong, set up the watchmen, prepare the**

ambushes: for the Lord hath both devised and done that he spake against the inhabitants of Babylon. O thou that dwellest upon many waters, abundant in treasures, thine end is come and the measure of thy covetousness. The Lord of hosts hath sworn by himself, saying, Surely I will fill thee with men, as with caterpillars; and they shall lift up a shout against thee (51:11-14).

vs. 11,12. Making bright the arrows means polishing and sharpening them for the ensuing battle. Gather the shields means to man them. Only the Medes are specifically mentioned. This may be due to their greater prominence. Darius was the Mede; Cyrus was the Persian. The former was uncle to the latter. It is said that Cambyses, father of Cyrus, sent his son with 30,000 men to aid Darius in the Chaldean conflict. The Lord has put into the heart of Darius and Cyrus the spirit to destroy Babylon. God has decreed it; no power can avert its occurring. This is His vengeance; it is the vengeance of His temple which Babylon destroyed in 586 B. C. and had profaned its holy vessels which had been taken (Cf. Daniel 5:1-4). Babylonian lords were so engaged in this profanation the very night Babylon fell to Medes and Persians. The standard to be set up on Babylon's walls was the flag or ensignia representative of the nation. Recall the raising of "Old Glory" on Iwo Jima during the US-Japanese conflict in World War II. Making the watch strong calls for the pressing of the siege. There would be no retreat for the invading army. Watchmen are given this charge. The ambushes are to be in a state of readiness as the city is taken. The Lord has willed the city's fall. Babylon is now the object of His aroused wrath.

vs. 13,14. Babylon was a city well-favored by many waters. The Euphrates ran through the city. The canals, dykes, tributaries, a large nearby lake, etc., would be included in the comprehensive term. Babylon looked to its waters not only for irrigating the entire area, which they did, but for protection as well. Babylon was a rich, opulent city. She was richly endowed by her geographical location but spoils of war had greatly enriched the aggressive city on the Euphrates. Yet her end has come. No longer will it be the greedy, covetous and grasping city. Jehovah is so serious relative to her collapse that He even took an oath with Himself as the standard of the swearing (not cursing but a solemn assurance of what He intended to do). Jehovah said He will fill the doomed Chaldean capital with men. Though some see in this an allusion to the myriads of Chaldeans who lived there, it seems better to see it as reference to the vast Medo-Persian army. The Chaldeans already filled the city. There would be no point to an allusion like that. The invaders are likened to an army of caterpillars (cankerworms or locusts) who destroy everything in their targeted path. This army of devouring locusts (Medes and Persians) will lift up the shout (the battle cry) against the now besieged metropolis.

POWERFUL JEHOVAH IS INVINCIBLE

Paragraph 3 of Jeremiah 51 reads,

He hath made the earth by his power, he hath established the world by his wisdom, and hath stretched out the heaven by his understanding. When he uttered his voice, there is a multitude of waters in the heavens; and he causeth the vapours to ascend from the ends of the earth: he maketh lightnings with rain, and bringeth forth the wind out of his treasures. Every man is brutish by his knowledge; every founder is confounded by the graven image: for his molten image is falsehood, and there is no breath in them. They are vanity, the work of errors: in the time of their visitation they shall perish. The portion of Jacob is not like them; for he is the former of all things: and Israel is the rod of his inheritance: the Lord of hosts is his name (51:15-19).

These verses are a repeat from 10:12-16. There God is showing with what ease He can defeat lifeless gods; here He shows with what ease He can put down an earthly monarchy—the Babylonian government. There is nothing wrong in repetition; in fact there is much to commend its great, long-term value.

vs. 15,16. Reflected here are God's omnipotence and omniscience respectively. By His power He made earth. By His wisdom and understanding He established the world and stretched out the heaven. Genesis 1 is an inspired commentary on this concise statement in verse 15. He utters His voice and thunders bellow forth; He gives charge and waters evaporate to form clouds later to fall back to earth as refreshing rains. He is the author of lightnings; the winds are ever under His control.

431

vs. 17,18. Foolish and senseless is any man who has idolatrous tendencies. Such behavior sinks him to the low level of a dumb brute. Idolatry is a system of total falsehood; it has no truth linked therewith. The idols are minus breath, actuality or ability to bless and protect. This is why they are vanity or filled with emptiness. Error and falsehood have formed and fashioned them. When God's visitation comes on Babylon, they will have neither power to protect themselves nor those who made and worshipped them.

v. 19. Jacob's portion is vastly different than the lot of the heathen. Jacob's portion is Jehovah and what He has done for His well-favored people even though they frequently were unworthy. Jehovah, not pagan idols, is the true source from whom all blessings flow and flow abundantly. From Him Israel receives its inheritance. As Lord of hosts He is powerful and proficient in blessing Israel.

BABYLON TO BE POWERLESS AGAINST ALL POWERFUL JEHOVAH

Paragraph 4 of Jeremiah 51 reads,

> **Thou art my battle axe and weapons of war: for with thee will I break in pieces the nations, and with thee will I destroy kingdoms; And with thee will I break in pieces the horse and his rider; and with thee will I break in pieces the chariot and his rider; With thee also will I break in pieces man and woman; and with thee will I break in pieces old and young; and with thee will I break in pieces the young man and the maid; I will also break in pieces with thee the shepherd and his flock; and with thee will I break in pieces the husbandman and his yoke of oxen; and with thee will I break in pieces captains and rulers. And I will render unto Babylon and to all the inhabitants of Chaldea all their evil that they have done in Zion in your sight, saith the Lord (51:20-24).**

vs. 20-24. Babylon had been God's hammer, battle axe and weapon against sinful nations. Now Babylon will be on the receiving end of reaped punishment. God had used Babylon to break nations into pieces and in the destruction of kingdoms. Now Babylon is to be broken and destroyed. Babylon has broken horse, rider and chariot. Now her horses,

432

riders and chariots must be broken. Babylon had been indiscriminate in slaying their captured subjects—men, women, old, young man and maiden. Now her invaders—Medes and Persians—will be indiscriminate in slaying myriads of the Babylonians with no regard to age, sex or station in life. Babylon had destroyed shepherd, flock, disrupted agricultural pursuits and broken governmental rulers. God will now return upon Babylon just punishment for the Babylonian wrongs inflicted upon Zion—God's people. Babylon is now to receive what she formerly gave others. Payday has come for Babylon and her iniquities.

THE DESTROYING MOUNTAIN—BABYLON— NOW TO BE DESTROYED

Paragraph 5 of Jeremiah 51 states,

Behold, I am against thee, O destroying mountain, saith the Lord, which destroyest all the earth: and I will stretch out mine hand upon thee, and roll thee down from the rocks, and will make thee a burnt mountain. And they shall not take of thee a stone for a corner, nor a stone for foundations; but thou shalt be desolate for ever, saith the Lord (51:25,26).

v. 25. Jehovah addresses Babylon. The Chaldean capital is called "destroying mountain." The destructive part of the term derives from the havoc she had made of all her neighbors—those nearby and those more distant. The mountain part is from her eminence—not geographical position for she was in a low-lying area. She had been a destroyer of the whole earth. Now God proposed to bring her down. In her days of conquering glory, she had been like a burning volcano spreading the lava of her destruction everywhere. Now she was a burned out mountain ready to be flattened out permanently.

v. 26. Medo-Persia will not take the city because she needs Babylon's property for herself. She will have another purpose in its devastation. Being the new mistress of the world superceded her desire for Babylonian spoils though there would be an abundance of that also. Medo-Persia will reduce the prosperous, powerful and prominent Babylon to a permanent area of forlorn desolation. How sure will it be? The Lord said it; that settled the matter once and for all.

433

MEDO-PERSIA AND HER ALLIES AGAINST BABYLON

Paragraph 6 of Jeremiah 51 reads,

> **Set ye up a standard in the land, blow the trumpet among the nations, prepare the nations against her, call together against her the kingdoms of Ararat, Minni, and Ashchenaz; appoint a captain against her; cause the horses to come up as the rough caterpillers. Prepare against her the nations with the kings of the Medes, the captains thereof, and all the rulers thereof, and all the land of his dominion. And the land shall tremble and sorrow: for every purpose of the Lord shall be performed against Babylon, to make the land of Babylon a desolation without an inhabitant. The mighty men of Babylon have forborn to fight, they have remained in their holds: their might hath failed; they became as women: they have burned her dwellingplaces; her bars are broken. One post shall run to meet another, and one messenger to meet another, to shew the king of Babylon that his city is taken at one end, And that the passages are stopped, and the reeds they have burned with fire, and the men of war are affrighted (51:27-32).**

vs. 27,28. God gives this clear military charge that Medo-Persia be in a state of readiness for Babylon's invasion. The standard or flag is to be hoisted; the trumpet calling men together for war is to be sounded. Medo-Persia had already conquered other areas and these, as her military aides, are called to do their part. The leader is to be appointed; the military stallions are to come as though they were locusts. Medo-Persia was to come with thorough preparation on her part. In power and might, she is directed to come.

vs. 29,30. Babylon, long the invincible and impregnable power of all earth, will now know fear and quaking. Nothing shall fall to the ground void of fulfillment which God planned in Babylon's demise as world power. God had decreed for her bleak, dreary desolation and that surely would be her lot subsequent to the Medo-Persian victory. Babylonian warriors realize the futility of putting forth any military effort. They refuse to leave their holes of protection to come forth with a fight. Their

434

might has evaporated. In physical prowess, they have become weak like women would be in military combat. All in which they trusted is now gone; there is no more a shield to protect them. Even their houses were in flames; the bars of her city gates were broken.

vs. 31,32. Posts and messengers were men of great speed who took messages from one place to another. In conveying messages of what was happening at the end of the city, where Medes and Persians had entered, to the city-center where the king resided, they would run into each other. Nabonidas, last king of Babylon, was not present when the city fell. His son, Belshazzer who co-ruled with him, was in the city as Daniel 5 portrays. Medo-Persia now controlled the passages or the fords of the river that divided the city. Reeds that grew on the banks of the great river were set aflame. This would greatly startle the city that was at ease that night. Men of war lost their courage and knew only fright and fear.

JEHOVAH TO EXTRACT A HIGH PRICE OF BABYLON

Paragraph 7 of Jeremiah 51 reads,

For thus saith the Lord of hosts, the God of Israel; The daughter of Babylon is like a threshingfloor, it is time to thresh her: yet a little while, and the time of her harvest shall come. Nebuchadrezzar the king of Babylon hath devoured me, he hath crushed me, he hath made me an empty vessel, he hath swallowed me up like a dragon, he hath filled his belly with my delicates, he hath cast me out. The violence done to me and to my flesh be upon Babylon, shall the inhabitant of Zion say; and my blood upon the inhabitants of Chaldea, shall Jerusalem say. Therefore thus saith the Lord; Behold, I will plead thy cause, and take vengeance for thee; and I will dry up her sea, and make her springs dry. And Babylon shall become heaps, a dwellingplace for dragons, an astonishment, and an hissing, without an inhabitant. They shall roar together like lions: they shall yell as lions' whelps. In their heat I will make their feasts and I will make them drunken, that they may rejoice, and sleep a perpetual sleep, and not wake, saith the Lord. I will bring them

down like lambs to the slaughter, like rams with he goats (51:33-40).

v. 33. All-powerful Jehovah, Israel's God, speaks. "The daughter of Babylon" refers to the entire nation. Feminine references to nations and cities are common in both ancient history as well as in modern parlance. Babylon is likened to a threshingfloor where grain is taken to be threshed out by human feet or more likely by a sledge pulled by oxen. When threshed the mixture of both grain and chaff was thrown into the wind that the chaff might be blown away and the treasured grain fall back to the earth. Then it was gathered up and placed in granaries for future human consumption. Babylon's threshing time is come; her full harvest is on the threshold of events soon to materialize. Harvest time for Babylon is her end punishment, her demise as a powerful nation and even as a continuing kingdom.

vs. 34,35. Zion is the speaker here. Nebuchadrezzar is mentioned here not because he will be king when end-time occurs for he was not. His son and grandson were king and co-king when Medo-Persia took the Chaldean monarchy and its nation. He is mentioned because he was king when the three sets of captives were taken in 605 B. C., 597 B. C., and 586 B. C. Note how this destruction of Zion is depicted so graphically. (1) He hath DEVOURED me; (2) he hath CRUSHED me; (3) he hath EMPTIED me as one would a vessel; (4) he hath SWALLOWED me as a dragon (sea monster) does its prey; (5) he hath FILLED his belly with my delicates (delights or delicacies); (6) He hath CAST me out—led me into distant, disagreeable captivity. Violence meted out to Zion by ruthless Chaldea must now recoil upon the head of Babylon. Blood shed by Babylon in Zion now calls for blood to be shed in the Chaldean capital and shed it would be! Zion and Jerusalem have now had their say. Jehovah has His say in the next subsequent verses.

vs. 36,37. Jehovah promises to be pleader for Zion's cause; He will be the active agent for the vengeance that must be taken on cruel, calloused Chaldea. All-powerful Jehovah says He will dry up her seas and make dry her springs. Babylon was well watered by the Euphrates and the canal, tributary system connected therewith. Babylon had a reservoir system second to none in that era. It was the nation's lifeblood. When dried up this meant the demise of the nation. Babylonian destruction is graphically delineated. (1) She will become heaps, i. e., piles of rubbish. (2) She will become a dwellingplace for dragons (jackals—ASV), the former mistress of the nations will soon be just a haunt for animals. (3) She will be an astonishment. Beholders will observe her total demise in almost unbelievable bewilderment. (4) She will be a hissing. Contempt and ridicule will be her lot. What a plunge for the city that once was the talk of the then known world. (5) She will be minus human habitation. The former masses now become zero population.

vs. 38-40. Daniel 5 should be read along with these verses. Darius the Mede and Cyrus the Persian combined in taking the city when the co-regent and his drunken lords and ladies were yelling or growling like lions. The yells were of revellings, drunkenness, etc. Liquor has always made its native patrons loud and boisterous. The Babylonian leaders were in the heat of drunkenness and their revellings—totally oblivious to the impending doom hanging over their impious heads and perverted hearts. Their city fell when they were living it up, rejoicing in the wine they drank from the vessels once holy and used in Jehovah's temple in Jerusalem. Since the city fell at night many of the revelling Chaldeans and even the sober part of the city retired for the night's rest were slain before the sun arose the next day. Some died in their sleep. They would know that very night a perpetual sleep—one without waking. Babylon is likened to lambs, rams and he goats—ready for slaughter and yet most oblivious to it. Babylon fell with as little resistance given as any city ever has in warfare. There is scarcely a parallel to it either in sacred or profane history. If so, where is the parallel? Perhaps Jericho in Joshua's age would be as close a parallel as could be given.

JEHOVAH'S SEVERE JUDGMENT
ON BABYLON FURTHER DELINEATED

Paragraph 8 of Jeremiah 51 reads,

> **How is Sheshach taken! and how is the praise of the whole earth surprised! how is Babylon become an astonishment among the nations! The sea is come up upon Babylon: she is covered with the multitude of the waves thereof. Her cities are a desolation, a dry land, and a wilderness, a land wherein no man dwelleth, neither doth any son of man pass thereby. And I will punish Bel in Babylon,**

and I will bring forth out of his mouth that which he hath swallowed up: and the nations shall not flow together any more unto him: yea, the wall of Babylon shall fall (51:41-44).

vs. 41-43. Sheshach was the name of a well-known Babylonian idol. It also was a symbolic name for Babylon. There was a feast of some five days held to this idol each year. It was a time of unbridled lusts and dissipation. Babylon's fall may well have occurred during such a drunken and licentious feast. Daniel 5 surely fits such in its depiction of the events of that fatal night in Babylon. Babylon was taken so quickly and completely by Darius and Cyrus that it came as amazement to a beholding world of neighboring nations—both near and remote. Babylon had been the praise of the whole world. With her massive walls, Hanging Gardens and the temple of Belus she was one of the wonders of the ancient world. The coming of the sea upon her and her inundation by the waves should not be taken literally. This is metaphorical language. Just as one upon the sea observes water everywhere so the Medes and Persians would come in such overwhelming numbers that it would seem that the invaders were everywhere. Babylon's fall astonished and bewildered the whole world. Her cities were deserted; her land, long known for its irrigation and fertility, became a dried, famished land; this once populous land now would become a wilderness. No longer would it be a fit or desirable habitat for human beings. No man would live there; none would even wish to visit there.

v. 44. Bel (form of Baal) or Belus was the primary idol of Babylon. Bel would be punished. Numerous had been the offerings that idolatrous Babylonians brought Bel and supposed he had swallowed those sacrifices. This is the supplied imagery. Babylon had swallowed up peoples. She had swallowed up or taken the holy vessels from Jehovah's temple on Mt. Moriah in 586 B. C. These were the very vessels from which the Babylonian revelers were drinking the night the city fell (Daniel 5:1ff). Bel would be totally impotent in even defending himself to say nothing of defending the invaded city. Both treasures and people who had been swallowed up (brought into captivity) would now know a release. Babylon's wall, long its chief shield and means of impregnable security, will fall. It will collapse due to disuse and abandonment.

438

BABYLON TO REAP WHAT IT HAD SOWN

Paragraph 9 of Jeremiah 51 reads,

> **My people, go ye out of the midst of her, and deliver ye every man his soul from the fierce anger of the Lord. And lest your heart faint, and ye fear for the rumour that shall be heard in the land; a rumour shall both come one year, and after that in another year shall come a rumour, and violence in the land, ruler against ruler. Therefore, behold, the days come, that I will do judgment upon the graven images of Babylon: and her whole land shall be confounded, and all her slain shall fall in the midst of her. Then the heaven and the earth, and all that is therein, shall sing for Babylon: for the spoilers shall come unto her from the north, saith the Lord. As Babylon hath caused the slain of Israel to fall, so at Babylon shall fall the slain of all the earth (51:45-49).**

vs. 45,46. Jehovah gives charge to His people who for many decades had been detained in Chaldean captivity to be in a state of readiness relative to leaving the doomed Chaldean capital. By a quick exit, they could save their lives, they could deliver their souls. Babylon was targeted to receive God's wrath. Jewish safety would not be found in the city. Jehovah relays this message to His people in Babylon lest they be discouraged, lest they faint. Rumors of the coming destruction by Medes and Persians will precede the city's invasion and collapse. Two years are mentioned relative to the build-up of Medo-Persian power and their threat against Babylon—long the mistress of the then known world. Violence was hovering over the doomed city and its dominion. Ruler would be against ruler or perhaps the thought is ruler upon ruler. In a short period of time, Nabonidus and Belshazzar, co-rulers of Babylon, were deposed. Darius the Mede (also called Cyaxares) held sway for awhile and then was succeeded by Cyrus the Persian, his nephew.

vs. 47,48. The coming of the days refers to the judgment period soon to descend to the corrupt Chaldean capital. Babylon, like all pagan nations of that day, was seeped in sinful, idolatrous worship. God's coming judgment would be aimed squarely at such just as the ten plagues in Egypt in Exodus were aimed at Egyptian idolatry as well as against stubborn Pharaoh and obstinate Egypt. God will show how very impotent Babylon idols are. They will not even possess power to protect themselves let alone their duped patrons, their superstitious subjects. Medo-Persia was also idolatrous but they destroyed Babylonian idols in the wake of the destruction they wrought. There was no problem in this for idolatrous people thought gods and goddesses were localized and the gods and goddesses of other lands had neither power nor influence over them. Babylon will be confounded or put to shame in seeing just how weak and helpless her treasured Bel and all other gods are. Masses of Babylonian people will be slain in the city's fall. Heaven and earth rejoicing in song refers to the universal delight that will attend Babylon's fall. Babylon had long been the scourge of the nations and her fall brings joy to those long despoiled by her. Her spoilers will come in military conquest of Babylon. They shall take what they want in the city's defeat. "To the victor belongs the spoils" expresses it quite accurately. How sure will it be? The Lord said it; that settled it once and for all.

v. 49. Just retribution must now come to Babylon. She had slain the masses in Israel. Now the masses will be slain in her and because of her sins. One commentator well writes, "Babylon has to answer for the general carnage caused by its wars."

"LET JERUSALEM COME INTO YOUR MIND"

Paragraph 10 of Jeremiah 51 reads,

> **Ye that have escaped the sword, go away, stand not still: remember the Lord afar off, and let Jerusalem come into your mind. We are confounded, because we have heard reproach: shame hath covered our faces: for strangers are come into the sanctuaries of the Lord's house. Wherefore, behold, the days come, saith the Lord, that I will do judgment upon her graven images: and through all her land the wounded shall groan. Though Babylon should mount up to heaven, and though she should fortify the height of her strength, yet from me shall spoilers come unto her, saith the Lord (51:50-53).**

vs. 50,51. In the first of these two verses a charge is given God's people who have escaped the sword. They constitute the remnant. They are told to leave the city and not linger. Death and destruction awaited

440

the city. Though they were far from Canaan, the land God had given them, they were to remember God from distant Babylon. "Let Jerusalem come into your mind." It was their holy city, the place where Solomon's temple once stood, the city they soon would be restoring and rebuilding and the temple that would be rebuilt gracing again Moriah's mount. Do not forget your religious roots which lay in Judah and Jerusalem. The second of these verses seems to be the response from Israel. They confess to being confounded or ashamed. They had heard of what had been done to Jerusalem and their holy temple. Shame covered their faces as they contemplated strangers treading and profaning their sacred sanctuaries. They were a downgraded and despondent people relative to memories of what had happened to Jerusalem.

vs. 52,53. The Lord again becomes speaker. Babylon's punishment is yet future, Jehovah avers. Yet a period of punishment will surely come. Babylonian idols will be destroyed. Widespread will be the wounded who will groan due to their pains and afflictions. There is NO way Babylon will escape such. Even if her fortifications were skyhigh and her strength were of the same height, yet I will surely send her spoilers, her destroyers. How sure will this be? The Lord said it; that settled it!

DOWN, DOWN WILL COME BABYLON'S FAMOUS WALLS

Paragraph 11 of Jeremiah 51 reads,

> **A sound of a cry cometh from Babylon, and great destruction from the land of the Chaldeans: Because the Lord hath spoiled Babylon, and destroyed out of her the great voice; when her waves do roar like great waters, a noise of their voice is uttered: Because the spoiler is come upon her, even upon Babylon, and her mighty men are taken, every one of their bows is broken: for the Lord God of recompenses shall surely requite. And I will make drunk her princes, and her wise men, her captains, and her rulers, and her mighty men: and they shall sleep a perpetual sleep, and not wake, saith the King, whose name is the Lord of hosts. Thus saith the Lord of hosts; the broad walls of Babylon shall be utterly broken, and her high gates shall be burned with fire; and the people shall labour in vain, and the folk in the fire, and they shall be weary (51:54-58).**

vs. 54,55. The cry that ascends is from a city and a land facing grave, grievous destruction. It is a cry of wailing, anguish and affliction. Jehovah is spoiler (destroyer) of Babylon. Medo-Persia will be his agent but the Lord's definite design is back of it all. Babylon's great voice is no more. This may refer to her voice of boasting. The chapters of Daniel 1-4 contain much of the vain boasting for which Babylon was notoriously noted. It may refer to the voice of her revelers. These would have been loud and boistrous the night she fell as per Daniel 5. Whatever the precise nature of the voice, it was to become deafeningly silent. The roaring of her waves and the uttering of the noises of their voice may refer to the vast myriads of Medo-Persian soldiers who would take the city with a storm and with little or no show of Chaldean resistance.

vs. 56,57. Jehovah decreed that Medo-Persia be the spoiler or destroyer of Babylon. When arrogant, reveling Babyon felt secure and was living it up, the Medes and Persians came. The spoiler or destroyer came when Babylon least expected her. The defeat to her men of might and the breaking of her bows sharply delineate the spoiling (destroying) of a once proud people. Jehovah, in strict justice, decreed that Babylon be requited for her mounting sins. Those who think God has no wrath linked with His character have failed totally to view Him as "the Lord God of recompenses." Belshazzar, co-regent, his princes, wise men, captains, rulers and mighty men were engaged in drinking and debauchery the very night the Medes and Persians stormed the well-fortified city. Many of them were put to death that night and began what the prophet called a perpetual sleep. Killed in their drunken stupor, they did not know what took them from this world to the next. How sure would this be? The King of the Universe, the Lord of hosts, said it.

v. 58. Allusion is made to Babylon's broad walls and high gates in this verse. We are told that her walls were one of the wonders of that ancient age. It is said her walls were eighty-seven feet broad and that two chariots each drawn by four horses could meet each other minus collision. The walls were some three hundred feet high. The length of the walls was some sixty miles. Being a square, this meant fifteen miles on each side. There were twenty-five gates for each wall or a total of one hundred. Atop the walls were two hundred and fifty towers. One writer has said that "triple walls encompassed the outer, and the same number the inner city." No wonder the city felt smugly secure behind such a shield of safety. Yet Darius the Mede and Cyrus the Persian took the city with subtle stratagem. These great walls and high gates faced destruction. In vain the people had erected such for they did not thwart Medo-Persia's entrance at all. The builders of these walls and gates had labored to erect something that fire would later destroy. What a weariness it must have been to the proud Babylonian to see his city entered so successfully by a determined enemy.

JEREMIAH'S MESSAGE TO SERAIAH

Paragraph 12 of Jeremiah 51 reads,

The word which Jeremiah the prophet commanded Seraiah the son of Neriah, the son of Maaseiah, when he went with Zedekiah the king of Judah into Babylon in the fourth year of his reign. And this Seraiah was a quiet prince. So Jeremiah wrote in a book all the evil that should come upon Babylon, even all these words that are written against Babylon. And Jeremiah said to Seraiah, When thou comest to Babylon, and shalt see, and shalt read all these words; Then shalt thou say, O Lord, thou hast spoken against this place, to cut it off, that none shall remain in it, neither man nor beast, but that it shall be desolate for ever. And it shall be, when thou hast made an end of reading this book, that thou shalt bind a stone to it, and cast it into the midst of Euphrates: And thou shalt say, Thus shall Babylon sink, and shall not rise from the evil that I will bring upon her: and they shall be weary. Thus far are the words of Jeremiah (51:59-64).

vs. 59,60. Jehovah's spokesman somehow learned that Seraiah, perhaps a brother to Baruch for Neriah is spoken of as being father of both, would be making a trip with Zedekiah to Babylon. It was during Zedekiah's fourth year or around 593 or 594 B. C. Seraiah was a quiet prince. It may have been his task to travel ahead and find a good resting-place for the king when time came to camp for the night. He was a dependable man—one Jeremiah could trust. Jeremiah wrote in a book what was to befall Babylon. The Hebrew word for book here refers to a writing whether long or short.

443

vs. 61,62. Seraiah, upon his arrival in Babylon and surveying the great Chaldean capital, was directed to read the words of this book. Seraiah's response touched the total destruction and desolation soon to overtake Babylon.

vs. 63,64. Old Testament prophets often acted in some remarkable way to give graphic emphasis to their messages. Jeremiah instructs Seraiah to engage in such relative to this book. Upon finishing its perusal he is to attach a stone to it and cast it into the Euphrates. Obviously, the stone would cause the book to sink. Symbolically, this was to show Babylon's demise, one that would be permanent in nature. God would surely bring this upon the Chaldean capital. The allusion to the weariness probably refers to the Chaldeans who would grow weary in defending themselves and succumb to the enemy. "Thus far are the words of Jeremiah." It seems he ended his prophetic work and chapter 52 is the work of another inspired man who provided a historical epilogue or appendage to this great work.

POINTS TO PONDER

(1) In Jeremiah 50, 51, Babylon receives a great and grievous reversal of roles between what is to be and what once was in her case.

(2) The no-wrath-of-God advocates would have a difficult time indeed interpreting Jeremiah 51.

(3) No nation is safe when its leaders are engaged in drunken, licentious orgies, etc.

(4) Idols are totally impotent in helping people whether times be prosperous or adverse.

(5) There are no shields of safety to any city or nation when God wills its demise.

DISCUSSION QUESTIONS

1. Summarize introduction.

2. Discuss the significance of winds in Bible Lands and in Bible times.

3. Describe Babylon prior to her demise.

4. Just how destructive had Babylon once been to Zion as set forth in Jeremiah 51:34,35?

5. Discuss the expression—"Let Jerusalem come into your mind."

MULTIPLE-CHOICE: Underline correct answer

1. Darius and Cyrus are: (A) totally unknown to each other; **(B)** inveterate enemies; (C) uncle and nephew respectively; (D) both opposed to the capture of Babylon.
2. Medo-Persia will be: (A) weak; (B) powerful; (C) a failure; (D) just barely successful in Babylon's capture.
3. Nabonidus and Belshazzar were: (A) a father-son team who last ruled Babylon; (B) spies of Medo-Persia sent into Babylon; (C) conquering generals of the Medo-Persian army; (D) the first and second king respectively of Medo-Persia.
4. Jericho and Babylon both have in common: (A) their never having fallen in a battle; (B) the ease with which each fell in respective battles with the Israelites and Medo-Persia; (C) their never having to face an enemy; (D) their perpetual blessing received from God.
5. The Hanging Gardens are associated with: (A) Shushan; (B) Jerusalem; (C) Babylon; (D) Damascus.

SCRIPTURAL FILL-IN: Only one word required in each blank

1. "The _____ hath _____ forth our _____ : come, and let us _____ in _____ the _____ of the _____ our _____ ."
2. "_____ thou that _____ upon many _____ , abundant in _____ , thine _____ is _____ , and the _____ of thy _____ ."
3. "And _____ shall become _____ , a _____ for _____ , an _____ , and an _____ , without an _____ ."
4. "So _____ wrote in a _____ all the _____ that shall _____ upon _____ , even

all these _____ that are _____ against
_____ ."

5. "And _____ shalt _____ , Thus shall
_____ sink and shall not _____ from the
_____ that I will _____ upon _____ :
and _____ shall be _____ . Thus _____
are the _____ of _____ ."

TRUE OR FALSE: Put either a "T" or "F" in the blanks

_____ 1. Jeremiah very SELDOM alludes to the fact that he was inspired
of God in the messages he gave.
_____ 2. At one time gold was frequently associated with Babylon.
_____ 3. Idolatry is stupidity to the nth degree and then some!
_____ 4. The Babylonian people were totally free of any and all
idolatrous inclinations.
_____ 5. Babylon was successful in resisting defeat by the hands of the
Medo-Persians.

THOUGHT QUESTIONS

1. Why is there great value in repetition and do we find such in
Jeremiah? If so, where and why was it done?

2. Discuss Jeremiah 51:16 in light of Genesis 1.

3. When the Lord speaks, why should this settle the matter and end
all future disputings?

4. Why should national leaders with millions looking to them for a
shield of safety NEVER engage in the kind of actions Belshazzar
and those under him did in Daniel 5?

5. Why was it folly to the nth degree for Babylon to trust in her walls,
gates, mighty warriors etc., when her sins called for justice to be
meted out to her?

CHAPTER TWENTY-SIX

HISTORICAL EPILOGUE OF JEREMIAH
Jeremiah 52

An epilogue is the concluding or completing section of a work. Jeremiah 52 surely fits this definition. This epilogue is historical in that it sets forth many matters of historical interest. It is inspired and may have been penned by the hand of another Spirit-guided scribe other than Jeremiah. Ezra may have penned this chapter subsequent to the Exile. Jeremiah 51:64 seems to indicate the presence of another inspired penman. This chapter does an excellent job of wrapping matters up about which Jeremiah spoke for decade after decade. It would be well for the student to read 2 Kings 24 and 25 as well as 2 Chronicles 36. It also serves as an excellent introduction to Lamentations which shall be covered in a number of appendixes of this volume.

ZEDEKIAH'S REBELLION

Paragraph 1 of Jeremiah 52 reads,

> **Zedekiah was one and twenty years old when he began to reign, and he reigned eleven years in Jerusalem. And his mother's name was Hamutal the daughter of Jeremiah of Libnah. And he did that which was evil in the eyes of the Lord, according to all that Jehoiakim had done. For through the anger of the Lord it came to pass in Jerusalem and Judah, till he had cast them out from his presence, that Zedekiah rebelled against the king of Babylon (52:1-3).**

v. 1. Zedekiah was a son of Josiah by BLOOD line but not by FAITH line. He was the final of the nineteen kings who ruled over Judah subsequent to Solomon. He was twenty-one years old when he ascended David's throne in Jerusalem. He began his reign about 597 B. C. It lasted for eleven years which means he was thirty-two years of age when Jerusalem fell. Hamutal, daughter of Jeremiah of Libnah, was his mother. This Jeremiah is not the prophet by that name. The prophet was from Anathoth; this Jeremiah was from Libnah. Be it further recalled that Jeremiah had been forbidden to marry and have children (Cf. Jeremiah 16:1,2).

v. 2. Like most of his predecessors on Judah's throne since 975 B. C., he pursued evil—not good. The Lord was very much cognizant of the evil he did. He preferred to tread the steps of his older half-brother, Jehoiakim, than the imitation of his eminently just father—Josiah. Zedekiah and Jehoiakim both ruled for a similar period of time—eleven years (2 Kings 23:36).

v. 3. Judah and Jerusalem had sinned so long and so deeply that God's patience would no longer bear with them. They went beyond what the divine panacea would heal. God's anger cast them out of His protective presence, the shield of His security for them. Zedekiah rebelled against Nebuchadnezzar, king of Babylon even though he, earlier, had sworn with an oath that he would maintain loyalty to the Babylonian monarch. A passage in 2 Chronicles 36:13 says of stubborn Zedekiah, "but he stiffened his neck, and hardened his heart from turning unto the Lord God of Israel."

THE LONG SIEGE OF JERUSALEM BY BABYLON

Paragraph 2 of Jeremiah 52 reads,

> **And it came to pass in the ninth year of his reign, in the tenth month, in the tenth day of the month, that Nebuchadrezzar king of Babylon came, he and all his army, against Jerusalem, and pitched against it, and built forts against it round about. So the city was besieged unto the eleventh year of king Zedekiah. And in the fourth month, in the ninth day of the month, the famine was sore in the city, so that there was no bread for the people of the land. Then the city was broken up, and all the**

**men of war fled, and went forth out of the city by night
by the way of the gate between the two walls, which was
by the king's garden; (now the Chaldeans were by the
city round about:) and they went by the way of the plain
(52:4-7).**

vs. 4-6. The tenth month corresponds to our January. Recall that the
Jewish year began in March. So it was in January of Zedekiah's ninth
year as king that Nebuchadrezzar and his army besieged Jerusalem. The
siege lasted till the fourth month of Zedekiah's eleventh year thus making
the siege eighteen months in duration. During this siege, Babylon took
out enough time to send the Egyptians back home in an aborted effort
to aid besieged Jerusalem. Babylon was not about to retreat. Famine
hit hard the besieged Jewish metropolis. Hunger stalked the streets. When
food ran out Jewish resistence to the long siege ceased.

v. 7. Babylon made the successful breach of the walls and gates. The
city fell; military men who had defended the city fled the defeated scene.
They left secretly by night hoping to make good their escape by way
of the Jordan plain to the east. This would be in the direction of Jericho.

ZEDEKIAH QUICKLY APPREHENDED

Paragraph 3 of Jeremiah 52 reads,

**But the army of the Chaldeans pursued after the king,
and overtook Zedekiah in the plains of Jericho; and all
his army was scattered from him. Then they took the
king, and carried him up unto the king of Babylon to
Riblah in the land of Hamath; where he gave judgment
upon him. And the king of Babylon slew the sons of
Zedekiah before his eyes; he slew also all the princes of
Judah in Riblah. Then he put out the eyes of Zedekiah;
and the king of Babylon bound him in chains, and carried
him to Babylon, and put him in prison till the day of
his death (52:8-11).**

vs. 8,9. Zedekiah and his military fleers did not escape the sharp
eyesight of the alert Chaldeans even though the escape was attempted
by night. The Chaldeans pursued the fleeing monarch overtaking him
in the Jericho plains. This was not more than fifteen to twenty miles

449

east of Jerusalem. His army was scattered from him. He was then deported to Riblah in the land of Hamath where the Babylonian king headquartered. There the Chaldean monarch would pass judgment upon rebellious Zedekiah.

vs. 10,11. How extremely severe that judgment was is observed in this duet of verses. The Babylonian king, minus all humane or fatherly feelings at all, slew Zedekiah's sons before his very eyes. Along with them were slain all the princes of Judah. Then Zedekiah's eyes were put out. Perhaps the last thing he observed with his eyesight was the inhumane killing of his very sons and the Judaean rulers who had served under him. The now victorious Babylonians bound the captured and blinded Zedekiah and took him to Babylon. In that era of ancient warfare, a chained king of an enemy nation meant victory for the returning warriors and embarrassing defeat for the bound king. Zedekiah faced life imprisonment upon his arrival in Babylon. He could have avoided ALL this by taking earlier heed to the wise counsel of Jeremiah. Now it was too late to listen to God's prophet and really the best benefactor Zedekiah ever had.

It had been predicted that Zedekiah would go to Babylon, would die there and yet would not see Babylon (Cf. Jeremiah 34:3-5; Ezekiel 12:13). There is nothing but strict harmony in all this. He did go to Babylon; he did die there; he never saw Babylon. The reason is supplied—he was blinded long before he arrived in the Chaldean capital. How harmonious are the Scriptures when all the essential facts are gathered and only legitimate conclusions or logical deductions are drawn therefrom.

THE FALL, DESTRUCTION AND DEVASTATION OF JERUSALEM

Paragraph 4 of Jeremiah 52 reads,

Now in the fifth month, in the tenth day of the month, which was the nineteenth year of Nebuchadrezzar king of Babylon, came Nebuzaradan, captain of the guard, which served the king of Babylon, into Jerusalem, And burned the house of the Lord, and the king's house; and all the houses of Jerusalem, and all the houses of the great men, burned he with fire: And all the army of the

450

Chaldeans, that were with the captain of the guard, brake down all the walls of Jerusalem round about. Then Nebuzaradan the captain of the guard carried away captive certain of the poor of the people, and the residue of the people that remained in the city, and those that fell away, that fell to the king of Babylon, and the rest of the multitude. But Nebuzaradan the captain of the guard left certain of the poor of the land for vinedressers and for husbandmen. Also the pillars of brass that were in the house of the Lord, and the bases, and the brasen sea that was in the house of the Lord, the Chaldeans brake, and carried all the brass of them to Babylon. The caldrons also, and the shovels, and the snuffers, and the bowls, and the spoons, and all the vessels of brass wherewith they ministered, took they away. And the basons, and the firepans, and the bowls, and the caldrons, and the candlesticks, and the spoons, and the cups; that which was of gold in gold, and that which was of silver in silver, took the captain of the guard away. The two pillars, one sea, and twelve brasen bulls that were under the bases, which king Solomon had made in the house of the Lord: the brass of all these vessels was without weight. And concerning the pillars, the height of one pillar was eighteen cubits; and a fillet of twelve cubits did compass it; and the thickness thereof was four fingers: it was hollow. And a chapiter of brass was upon it; and the height of one chapiter was five cubits, with network and pomegranates upon the chapiters round about, all of brass. The second pillar also and the pomegranates were like unto these. And there were ninety and six pomegranates on a side; and all the pomegranates upon the network were an hundred round about (52:12-23).

vs. 12-14. The fifth month would correspond to our August. This account has it the tenth day. The account in 2 Kings 25:8 has it the seventh day. The latter may be when he left the Babylonian headquarters at Riblah and the former may be when he arrived at Jerusalem. The distance is quite great between the two spots but he could cover a lot of ground in three days by horseback or in a chariot. This was the nineteenth year of Nebuchadrezzar's reign. Nebuzaradan served as captain of the Babylonian guard. Upon his arrival in Jerusalem, fiery destruction hits the former city of glory. Up in flames go the temple, the palace of the kings, Jerusalem houses and houses of the great men. In the Babylonian destruction of the city the walls are broken down.

vs. 15,16. Into captivity were taken certain of the poor, the residue of the people yet in the city, those who fell away, those who surrendered to the Babylonian king and the rest of the multitude. However, not all the people were taken. The Babylonian captain left some of the land's poor to dress the vineyards and to cultivate the land. He doubtless took the people with enough artizan ability as to be of help to the victorious Babylonians.

vs. 17-23. In these verses, we have a rather detailed list of the valuable things found in the temple that Babylon seized upon and took to their land. Some of the items were small enough that they could be taken intact and this was done. Other things were too large and these were broken up and taken. Objects made of brass (copper), gold and silver would be helpful to this conquering nation. In taking such as they wanted, they pursued the well-known philosophy that "to the victor belong the spoils." Since these were treasures found in the temple of Judah's God, the Babylonians quite likely felt that their idols had given them the victory over Judah's God. If they thought such, they were in gross ignorance. Judah's God is the VERY ONE who allowed Babylon to be victorious in this conflict—not Belus or any other Babylonian idol.

JUDAH TAKEN INTO CAPTIVITY

Paragraph 5 of Jeremiah 52 reads,

> **And the captain of the guard took Seraiah the chief priest, and Zephaniah the second priest, and the three keepers of the door: He took also out of the city an eunuch, which had the charge of the men of war; and seven men of them that were near the king's person, which were found in the city; and the principal scribe of the host, who mustered the people of the land; and threescore men of the people of the land, that were found in the midst of the city. So Nebuzaradan the captain of the guard took**

them, and brought them to the king of Babylon to Riblah. And the king of Babylon smote them, and put them to death in Riblah in the land of Hamath. Thus Judah was carried away captive out of his own land. This is the people whom Nebuchadrezzar carried away captive: in the seventh year three thousand Jews and three and twenty: In the eighteenth year of Nebuchadrezzar he carried away captive from Jerusalem eight hundred thirty and two persons: In the three and twentieth year of Nebuchadrezzar, Nebuzaradan the captain of the guard carried away captive of the Jews seven hundred forty and five persons: all the persons were four thousand and six hundred (52:24-30).

vs. 24,25. The captain of the guard would be Nebazaradan. We would call him the general of the army or field marshal today. He was Nebuchadnezzar's commander-in-chief. Taken were Seraiah, chief priest and Zephaniah (not the prophet by that name who lived earlier), the second priest. The second priest probably was one deputed to serve in the role of high priest when he was unable to officiate in the temple and at the altar. Keepers of the door were temple assistants and probably chargeable for proper temple decorum. Also taken was an eunuch (one minus manly powers to procreate) who headed the men of war. Seven men were taken who had been near King Zedekiah, probably his confidants, i. e., those who gave him counsel relative to difficult matters of state. The account in 2 Kings 25:19 lists only five such men. Two of them might have been considered as less offensive and were allowed to escape the death penalty. Some think these two may have been Jeremiah and Ebelmelech—both of whom were surely spared. Be it recalled that both Jeremiah and Ebelmelech were counsellors of Zedekiah. There is no contradiction when all facts and possibilities are considered and weighed with logical care. Taken also was the principal scribe of the host who had charge of keeping certain records and sixty men of the city.

vs. 26,27. Those mentioned in previous verses were removed from Jerusalem and taken to where the King has his headquarters—Riblah—north and slightly east of Jerusalem. Here they were slain by orders from Nebuchadnezzar. Judah's captivity is again alluded to at the end of verse 27.

453

vs. 28-30. These were evidently three smaller deportations and not to be confused with the three major ones in 605, 597 and 586 B. C. The total of these minor three was four thousand and six hundred. This surely would not be the total of all deportations for there were some ten thousand taken in 597 B. C. when Ezekiel was included (2 Kings 24:14).

JEHOIACHIN'S CAPTIVITY STATUS IN BABYLON

Paragraph 6, final one of this chapter and of the book itself, of Jeremiah 52 reads,

> **And it came to pass in the seven and thirtieth year of the captivity of Jehoiachin king of Judah, in the twelfth month, in the five and twentieth day of the month, that Evilmerodach king of Babylon in the first year of his reign lifted up the head of Jehoiachin king of Judah, and brought him forth out of prison, And spake kindly unto him, and set his throne above the throne of the kings that were with him in Babylon, And changed his prison garments: and he did continually eat bread before him all the days of his life. And for his diet, there was a continual diet given him of the king of Babylon, every day a portion until the day of his death, all the days of his life (52:31-34).**

v. 31. Jehoiachin (also called Coniah and Jechonias) had reigned only three months and was eighteen years of age when he was taken captive by Babylon (2 Kings 24:8). There were some ten thousand captives taken at this time (2 Kings 24:14). This would have been around 597 B. C. Thirty-seven years later would have made him some fifty-five years of age. The year would have been around 560 B. C. The twelfth month would correspond to our February-March period. Remember that the Jewish year began around mid-March. The Jeremiah account says it was the twenty-fifth day of the month. The account in 2 Kings 25:27 says it was the twenty-seventh day. The order probably was given on the twenty-fifth day and its execution was on the twenty-seventh day. There is NO contradiction or problem here as some have imagined there is. Somehow Evilmerodach and Jekoiachin had formed a friendship.

454

There is an old Hebrew tradition that says Evilmerodach administered affairs of state while his father Nebuchadnezzar was deposed as king by God due to his enormous pride (See Daniel 4). When the deposed monarch was restored he heard of his son's misconduct and imprisoned him. While imprisoned, Evilmerodach and Jehoiachin became fast and firm friends. When Evilmerodach became king upon Nebuchadnezzar's death he did not forget his prison friend, like the butler did Joseph for two years, but lifted up his head. This means a change of fortune for the better. Genesis 40:13 speaks of the lifting up of the head of Pharaoh's butler, i. e., his fortune took a great leap upward. The imagery seems to be of a person who in low straits hangs his head low but when an improved status is granted, he lifts high his relieved head again. Jehoiachin had thus kept his head low for an exceedingly long time—nearly four decades. Evilmerodach releases him from his long stay in a Chaldean prison.

v. 32. Speaking kindly to him means that he dealt favorably with him. Setting his throne above the thrones of other captive kings does not mean that he restored to him the throne of ruling or reigning power again but of privileged position of higher treatment than what was granted his other captive colleagues of former royal powers and privileges.

v. 33. There was an appropriate change of apparel to fit his new improved status. A place at the king's table was his lot the remnant of his days on earth. To eat with another and be in his presence at meal time was a major blessing, a coveted honor especially when dining with the monarch was concerned.

v. 34. A generous provision of food was given him by the king's generosity till the day of his death. This possibly referred to the provisions for his family and friends. No mention is made of their eating with the king. Yet we know from 2 Kings 24:12,15 that his mother, his wives, his servants, his princes and his officers were taken to Babylon with him. Quite likely they were allowed to be with Jehoiachin all these captive years. His restoration to a far improved status would likely have been an improved restoration for them also.

POINTS TO PONDER

(1) It is sad, immeasurably so, when the son of a righteous man fails to walk in the pious pathway trod by the father before him.

(2) Man's inhumanity to man is never more evident than in times of cruel, calloused and cold warfare.

(3) Zedekiah is a prime example of a stubborn man who refused to hear and heed sound and sage counsel from the God of heaven.

(4) Jerusalem and Judah paid a high price indeed for rebelling against God and being defiant toward the prophetic counsel of Jeremiah.

(5) Friendship loyalty was not totally lost among the Chaldeans.

DISCUSSION QUESTIONS

1. Summarize introduction and especially what we mean by an Epilogue.

2. What was significant about a victorious army bringing back home in chains the vanquished king?

3. How thorough was the destruction and spoiling of fallen Jerusalem by the victorious Chaldeans?

4. What is meant by the military expression, "To the victor belong the spoils."

5. Relate the old Hebrew tradition as touching how a Babylonian prince—Evilmerodach—and a Jewish prince—Jehoiachin—formed a fast and firm friendship that lasted when there was a reversal in their respective situations.

MULTIPLE-CHOICE: Underline correct answer

1. (A) Ezra; (B) Zerubbabel; (C) Esther; (D) Haggai—may have written Jeremiah 52 subsequent to the Babylonian Exile.
2. (A) Zedekiah; (B) Coniah; (C) Jehoahaz; (D) Jehoiakim—is the final king of Judah prior to Jerusalem's fall in 586 B. C.
3. The number of kings who ruled Judah subsequent to Solomon was: (A) three; (B) ten; (C) forty-one; (D) nineteen.
4. The Chaldean siege of stubborn, defiant Jerusalem lasted: (A) one month; (B) six months; (C) twelve months; (D) eighteen months.
5. (A) Nebuchadnezzar; (B) Nebuzaradan; (C) Belshazzar; (D) Evilmerodach—dealt very humanely with imprisoned Jehoiachin.

SCRIPTURAL FILL-IN: Only one word is required in each blank

1. "And _____ did that which was _____ in the _____ of the _____ , according to all that _____ had _____ ."

2. "And the _____ of _____ slew the _____ of _____ before his _____ : he _____ also _____ the _____ of _____ in _____ ."

3. "Then he _____ out the _____ of _____ ; and the _____ of _____ bound him in _____ , and _____ him to _____ , and put him in _____ till the _____ of his _____ ."

4. "But _____ the _____ of the _____ left _____ of the _____ of the _____ for _____ and for _____ ."

5. "Thus _____ was _____ away _____ out of _____ own _____ ."

TRUE OR FALSE: Put either a "T" or "F" in the blanks

_____ 1. Egyptian efforts to aid besieged Jerusalem turned out to be a totally embarrassing defeat.

_____ 2. Zedekiah was treated very humanely by the Babylonian king at Riblah.

_____ 3. Zedekiah was executed within a few days after he was brought to Babylon.

_____ 4. Belus and the other Babylonian idols had allowed the Chaldeans to be victorious over Jehovah and Jerusalem.

_____ 5. There is a flat contradiction between Jeremiah 52:25 and 2 Kings 25:19 and there is NO way to harmonize the two numbers of seven and five therein.

THOUGHT QUESTIONS

1. Discuss Zedekiah and Josiah from the common link of a BLOOD line and show how they differed greatly from the FAITH line.

2. How does Jeremiah 52 again exhibit the patent fact that wrath is surely one of the attributes of Jehovah God?

3. How do the masses stiffen their necks and harden their hearts against God and His law today?

4. Harmonize Zedekiah's being brought to Babylon, dying there and yet never seeing the city of Babylon.

5. Contrast the treatment Zedekiah received of his Chaldean captors and that afforded Jehoiachin by Evilmerodach, a later Babylonian ruler.

APPENDIX ONE

LAMENTATIONS INTRODUCED AND OUTLINED

There are two cogent reasons for including this material on Lamentations in this volume under Appendixes. (1) The publisher first requested a commentary on Jeremiah with no mention of Lamentations in said work. I wanted the work on Jeremiah to consist of twenty-six chapters which would make it ideal for six-months or twenty-six weeks of study in Bible Class situations. I outlined the material with that in mind. When I was well along in the writing of this manuscript, the publisher, Benny Whitehead, requested that I include Lamentations in the latter part of this commentary. Not wanting to revise the six-months' concept, which would have necessitated the rewriting of much of this material, I decided to make the material on Lamentations into Appendixes. It is hoped sincerely that classes which use this volume for a six-months' study will also include the necessary addition of weeks to get the study on Lamentations also. Ladies' classes which run from fall through spring will find the twenty-six chapters plus the seven Appendixes just about right for their entire session. There will be six Appendixes on Lamentations and a final Appendix on Lessons Learned from both of these powerful, prophetic products. (2) The book of Lamentations, without doing any damage at all to this literary product, is really an Appendix (addition) to the book of Jeremiah. A number of commentators have so considered it. I am definitely of this number. It is of no lesser value than that to which it is appended for both Jeremiah and Lamentations are the works of an inspired prophet who wrote faithfully the words Jehovah, by the Spirit of Inspiration, put into his mouth (cf. Jeremiah 1:9). It, Lamentations, is somewhat of an inspired P. S. (postscript) to this larger prophetic work. It is an inspired complement to the book of Jeremiah.

THE AUTHORSHIP OF LAMENTATIONS

Students of a more liberalistic bent have decided, quite arbitrarily, that Lamentations could not be the work of Jeremiah. They point out that the position of Lamentations in the Hebrew Bible is not next to Jeremiah as in the Greek Version—the Septuagint—or in our English translations but is found in what they called the Hagiographa (the Holy Writings) and includes such books as Ecclesiastes, Canticles (Song of Solomon), Ruth and Esther. Psalms, Proverbs and Job are also poetical books of the Old Testament and are considered Holy Writings. In the Hebrew Bible, Lamentations is placed between Ruth and Ecclesiastes. However, the Septuagint Version (a Greek translation produced in third century B. C.) placed Lamentations as an appendage to Jeremiah. Our English translations have followed the Septuagint placement and correctly so. Rejectors of Jeremiah's authorship of the Lamentations point to some stylistic differences between certain passages in Lamentations and passages in Jeremiah. Modernistic, liberalistic commentators are notorious for doing this with other acknowledged penmen of Holy Writ. Such commentators seem to think that a literary penman may NEVER change his style or his selection of words yet he may be speaking of a vastly different subject from what he earlier discussed or may be writing from a totally different vantage point. On just such flimsy grounds as the foregoing liberalistic writers have rejected the Mosaic authorship of the Pentateuch, the uniform authorship of Isaiah for all his prophetic product, Daniel's authorship for the twelve chapters of the book that bears his name, Mark's authorship of the final twelve verses of his gospel record, Paul's authorship of the evangelistic epistles of 1 and 2 Timothy and Titus, of his penning Hebrews or of Revelation as being the final work from the prolific pen of the aged apostle John.

The heavy weight of sound, solid Biblical scholarship through the centuries has been in strong favor for Jeremiah's authorship of this book. This was evidently the position of the Septuagint translators who placed it by Jeremiah. Be it recalled that they were only some three centuries removed from the actual writing time of Lamentations. The style is definitely Jeremiah's though in Lamentations he writes as an eye-witness of what has sadly transpired and the book of Jeremiah found him largely the prophetic predictor of coming punishment to Judah and Jerusalem. The vantage point of time difference can easily account for slight stylistic

460

differences the liberalistic writers have claimed to notice. Lamentations breathes the spirit of a man who could be touched deeply with grievous afflictions. The weeping prophet of Anathoth surely fits this very literary disposition. Who else, except Jeremiah, was in position to write such a book as this? An insensitive and uninformed stranger would hardly have been Heaven's choice to pen these funeral dirges, these elegies of stunning sadness, these statements of sin, suffering and solitude.

Without serious quibble or questioning to the contrary, Jeremiah is the earthly, inspired penman. The Holy Spirit is the heavenly author even as he is of all sixty-six books of the Bible—God's Grand Old Volume.

THE WHY OF ITS COMPOSITION

Every Biblical book has either a stated or inferred purpose. Lamentations is no exception to this general rule. Lamentations presents the fulfilled picture of what Jeremiah had predicted throughout his prophetic product, i. e., Jerusalem shall be destroyed by the Chaldean conquerors coming from the north. Lamentations shows that such has now transpired. It exhibits very forcefully that no prediction of Jeremiah relative to Jerusalem's destruction fell to the ground void of minute, precise fulfillment. Jews of the B. C. era, acquainted with both Jeremiah's predictive prophecies in his longer work and of their striking fulfillment in the shorter work, could look down the much longer corridor of time and know for a greater certainty that his predictive prophecies about the Messianic Branch and the new covenant would be fulfilled ultimately with the same amazing accuracy.

Jeremiah's peers thought they could sin and get away with it. They turned up their nose at Heaven's Almighty and dared Him to do something about it. The book of Lamentations shows with force and finality what He did do.

Sin brings sorrow, shame and separation. Every chapter of Lamentations is permeated with sorrow. Every paragraph is punctuated with the shame of sin. Every sentence, with almost no exception, shows that sin separates man from God. Several decades earlier Isaiah, the statesman prophet, had declared that Judah's sins and Jerusalem's transgressions had separated them from the God of holiness and purity (Isaiah 59:1,2).

Lamentations shows just how sensitive one man can be toward the grievous nature of sin and what it does to a nation, to a city and to an individual. An earlier writer by the name of Lowth once wrote relative to Lamentations, "Every letter is written with a tear, every word the sound of a broken heart." This is a poignant portrait of Jeremiah in Lamentations.

THE WHEN OF ITS COMPOSITION

Lamentations was written by an eye-witness, an ear-witness and an inspired witness of Jerusalem's desolations. It seems almost necessary to insist that he wrote it within days or perhaps weeks after the city fell. A number of highly respected and veteran students of this Biblical book think that he wrote it within the month of the city's fall and not later than three months. Soon after the fall and the assassination of the Babylonian-appointed Governor, Gedalaiah, Jeremiah is forced to accompany the Judaean rebels into forbidden Egypt. It seems highly likely that he wrote it prior to their unwise migration into the land of Nile. The time would have been around 586 B. C.

THE LITERARY UNIQUENESS OF LAMENTATIONS

Lamentations is a bit like Psalm 119, the longest chapter in the Bible with its twenty-two divisions and each division that begins with a letter of the Hebrew alphabet. Recall that there are twenty-two letters in the Hebrew alphabet.

Lamentations is composed of five chapters and one hundred fifty-four verses. There are twenty-two verses in chapters one, two, four and five. There are thrice this number in chapter three for a total of sixty-six verses. The verses in chapters one and two are considerably longer than in chapters three through five. Chapters one through four are alphabetical with the verses beginning with a letter of the Hebrew alphabet except in a very few instances where there is a transposition of two letters. In chapter three, each of the three lines forming a stanza begins with the same letter. Chapter five, though it too has twenty-two verses, is not alphabetical as the previous four are. Why this type of literary arrangement? A number of students of Lamentations think it was a literary device to aid the memory.

ONE LINE SUMMARIES OF THE FIVE CHAPTERS

Each of one hundred fifty-four lamentations is a rather complete unit in and of itself. Chapter one treats the sorrowful desolation which has gripped the holy city. Chapter two sets forth the reason for Zion's sufferings—her sins. Chapter three sets forth Jerusalem's basis for hope— the marvelous mercy of Jehovah. Chapter four presents the easily discernible contrast between the past prosperity the famed city once enjoyed and the deeply deplorable condition presently characteristic of it. Chapter five unfolds an humble application for the return of divine favor. Dixon Analytical Bible summarized the book in three words— sin, suffering and sorrow.

LAMENTATIONS OUTLINED

I. Chapter One
  A. The Solitary City in mourning and the why (vs. 1-11).
  B. "Is it nothing to you, all ye that pass by?" (vs. 12-17).
  C. Jehovah's judgment is seen to be just (vs. 18-22).

II. Chapter Two
  A. The prophet's lamentation over Jerusalem's mounting misery (v. 1-19).
  B. The prophet's complaint (vs. 20-22).

III. Chapter Three
  A. Jeremiah's agonizing affliction and genuine grief (vs. 1-21).
  B. Jeremiah's blessed assurance of hope (vs. 22-36).
  C. The prophetic portrayal of Zion's deep afflication (vs. 37-54).
  D. Jeremiah's dependence upon Jehovah (vs. 55-63).
  E. A clear, clarion call for God's justice to be administered (vs. 64-66).

IV. Chapter Four
  A. Zion mourns her severe state (vs. 1-12).
  B. Sins and iniquities confessed (vs. 13-20).
  C. The cup reserved for Edom (vs. 21).
  D. Edom to be punished for her sins (v. 22).

V. Chapter Five
  A. Zion's complaint due to the weighty woes upon her (vs. 1-18).
  B. The eternal Jehovah (vs. 19-22).

463

Conclusion: These five elegies on sin, sorrow and solitude should impress all of us with just how exceedingly sinful sin really is.

POINTS TO PONDER

(1) Theological liberalism cannot keep its unholy and deeply injurious hands off even a tiny Old Testament product like Lamentations.

(2) Theological liberalism is little or no help at all in determining who wrote what books in the Bible.

(3) The Holy Spirit is really the heavenly author of all sixty-six books of the Bible.

(4) The book of Lamentations shows conclusively that defiant man cannot turn up his arrogant nose at God and get away with it.

(5) Lamentations shows that sin is serious, tragic, degrading, demeaning, injurious and ugly.

DISCUSSION QUESTIONS

1. In what sense would Lamentations be something of an inspired postscript to the book of Jeremiah?

2. Give the airtight case that may be assembled for Jeremiah's authorship of Lamentations.

3. What can easily account for the slightly different styles between the book of Jeremiah and the book of Lamentations?

4. Discuss the dual authorship of Lamentations, i. e., the heavenly author and the earthly penman.

5. Discuss in some detail the comprehensive WHY of this book's composition.

MULTIPLE-CHOICE: Underline correct answer

1. The literary link between Lamentations and the book of Jeremiah is: (A) totally non-existent; (B) of very slight kin; (C) that of an Appendix; (D) by common authorship alone.

2. The Greek Version of the Hebrew Old Testament Scriptures is known as the: (A) Hagiographa; (B) Septuagint; (C) Pentateuch; (D) Decalogue.

3. The Septaugint translators evidently agree that the book of Lamentations was written by: (A) Ezra; (B) Jeremiah; (C) a group of redactors; (D) an unknown writer.

4. Sin brings: (A) real meaning for life; (B) the good life in the here and now and heaven in the there and then; (C) real prosperity to its avid promoters and practitioners; (D) sorrow, shame and separation.

5. A literary devise used very effectively in the book of Lamentations is that of: (A) story telling; (B) questions asked with answers demanded; (C) parabolic teaching; (D) alphabetical usage with most of its verses beginning with a letter of the Hebrew alphabet and kept almost always in order.

SCRIPTURAL FILL-IN: Only one word required in each blank

1. Lamentations is as much inspired as Jeremiah wherein we read in Jeremiah 1:9, "_____ , I have _____ my _____ in thy _____ ."

2. "_____ it _____ to _____ , all _____ that _____ by?"

3. We read in Lamentations 3:26, "It is _____ that a _____ should both _____ and quietly _____ for the _____ of the _____ ."

4. We read in Lamentations 3:48, "Mine _____ runneth _____ with _____ of _____ for the _____ of the _____ of my _____ ."

5. Lamentations 5:19 states, "_____ , O _____ , _____ for ever; thy _____ from _____ to _____ ."

TRUE OR FALSE: Put either a "T" or "F" in the blanks

_____ 1. The placement of Lamentations between Ruth and Ecclesiastes in the Hebrew Bible is an airtight case against Jeremiah's authorship of this book.

465

_____ 2. The Pentateuch refers to the opening five books of the Old Testament—Genesis—Deuteronomy.

_____ 3. Jeremiah was an eye-witness to the desolation and misery visited upon Zion by the cruel and calloused Chaldeans.

_____ 4. A lamentation is an elegy or funeral-like dirge.

_____ 5. It is extremely difficult to determine either the stated or implied purpose of any Biblical book.

THOUGHT QUESTIONS

1. In the name of stylistic differences what has religious liberalism done to the authorship of the Pentateuch, Isaiah, Daniel, Mark, the evangelistic epistles, Hebrews and Revelation?

2. Why is it highly unlikely that anyone else but Jeremiah would be commissioned by Heaven to write Lamentations?

3. Why would a total stranger and deeply insensitive person NOT have been an acceptable choice of penning the elegies of Lamentations?

4. Those who saw Jeremiah's book fulfilled in Lamentations could possess a far greater certainty of what coming events in later centuries?

5. How comprehensive are sin, sorrow and shame in the book of Lamentations?

APPENDIX TWO

"IS IT NOTHING TO YOU, ALL YE THAT PASS BY?"
Lamentation 1

This opening chapter establishes the tone and tenor for the remainder of these sorrow-filled elegies or funeral-like dirges. "How" is the opening word of chapter one, chapter two and chapter four. "How" derives from the Hebrew term **Eachah** and is the title Jewish leaders for many centuries have given this book. Permeating this forlorn chapter are Jerusalem's misery, the solemn meditation of her grievous afflictions and yet Jehovah's judgment upon her as being entirely just and deserved.

THE SOLITARY CITY IN MOURNING AND WHY

Paragraph 1 of Lamentations 1 reads,

How doth the city sit solitary, that was full of people! how is she become as a widow! she that was great among the nations, and princess among the provinces, how is she become tributary! She weepeth sore in the night, and her tears are on her cheeks: among all her lovers she hath none to comfort her: all her friends have dealt treacherously with her, they are become her enemies. Judah is gone into captivity because of affliction, and because of great servitude: she dwelleth among the heathen, she findeth no rest: all her persecutors overtook her between the straits. The ways of Zion do mourn, because none come to the solemn feasts: all her gates are desolate: her priests sigh, her virgins are afflicted, and she is in

467

bitterness. Her adversaries are the chief, her enemies prosper; for the Lord hath afflicted her for the multitude of her transgressions: her children are gone into captivity before the enemy. And from the daughter of Zion all her beauty is departed: her princes are become like harts that find no pasture, and they are gone without strength before the pursuer. Jerusalem remembered in the days of her affliction and of her miseries all her pleasant things that she had in the days of old, when her people fell into the hand of the enemy, and none did help her: the adversaries saw her, and did mock at her sabbaths. Jerusalem hath grievously sinned; therefore she is removed: all that honoured her despise her, because they have seen her nakedness: yea, she sigheth, and turneth backward. Her filthiness is in her skirts; she remembereth not her last end; therefore she came down wonderfully: she had no comforter. O Lord, behold, my affliction: for the enemy hath magnified himself. The adversary hath spread out his hand upon all her pleasant things: for she hath seen that the heathen entered into her sanctuary, whom thou didst command that they should not enter into thy congregation. All her people sigh, they seek bread; they have given their pleasant things for meat to relieve the soul: see, O Lord, and consider; for I am become vile (1:1-11).

v. 1. This verse begins with the Hebrew letter—**Aleph.** She now sits in a lonely, solitary and forlorn condition. She who once possessed fulness of population now faces a great void of people. Her grief is like that experienced by a widow who is bereft of him who was her husband, breadwinner, lover, shield and constant companion. Formerly, she was great among the nations but no more! She was once princess among the provinces. Tribute flowed into her rich coffers from conquered neighbors during the golden days of David and Solomon. Now she pays tribute. She who was once a conqueror is now the conquered. She who once was the victor is now the vanquished. She who was once spoiler is now the spoiled.

v. 2. The beginning letter here is **Beth.** Weeping and wailing, anguish and agonizing fill her nights. Streaming tears soil the face that once beamed with brightness. None of her former lovers (political allies) remain as current comforters. Friends to whom she confidently looked for needed aid forsook her. They became her enemies. They chose treachery over truth in their dealings with the once blessed city. Her former friends became hinderers and no longer helpers.

v. 3. This verse begins with **Gimel.** The mourning man from Anathoth laments Judah's exile. Her sins brought on the captivity—a captivity filled with humbling serfdom and continuous affliction. Yet that captivity would cure them permanently of iniquitous idolatry. Never again would they be idolatrous as they formerly had been. The Babylonian Captivity cured them permanently of this besetting sin of such a long standing and deeply embedded nature. She has been removed from the cherished land of her nativity and dwells among the nations minus any rest. She had been taken in the straits or in a narrow place. There may be an allusion here to her fleeing leaders who sought escape but were promptly apprehended by Chaldean soldiers just east of Jerusalem.

v. 4. Daleth is the beginning letter here. The ways (streets) of Zion (Jerusalem) are personified as multiple mourners. Worshippers no longer travel them on their ways to the temple for appointed times and set feasts. Entrances and exits no longer characterize her once busy gates as when vast throngs of people came and went daily. Her priests sigh and sorrow; there is no more need for their sacrificial services as officiants at temple services. Her virgins have seen happiness vanish; now only affliction faces them. In bitterness, Zion sits and recalls happier days of the pleasant and prosperous past.

v. 5. The beginning letter here is **He.** Enemies of Zion now bear rule; they are the victors and God's people are the vanquished. Judah had been captured; she had been embarrassed and humiliated. Enemies enjoy prosperity; Judah knows poverty of flesh and spirit. Her sins have caught up with her; they have found her out (Cf. Numbers 32:23). The God of heaven she defied and forsook has now visited her with deserved, severe punishment. Her transgressions have been many; now her reaped punishment is deep and deserved. Young people of the land have now been taken by the enemy into exile.

v. 6. Vau is the initial letter here. The grieving prophet laments the loss of Jerusalem's once possessed majesty. She who was once beautiful is now ugly. Her leaders are likened to animals who find no pastures; they are robbed of all strength by the relentless pursurers.

v. 7. The opening letter is **Zain.** Jerusalem is in miserable affliction and is portrayed as remembering the past when happiness abounded and prosperity was her daily lot. How frequently do we take things for granted until we are deprived of them. Some verses in Psalm 137 are certainly appropriate here,

> **By the rivers of Babylon, there we sat down, yea, we wept, when we remembered Zion. We hanged our harps upon the willows in the midst thereof. For there they that carried us away captive required of us a song: and they that wasted us required of us mirth, saying, Sing us one of the songs of Zion. How shall we sing the Lord's song in a strange land? If I forget thee, O Jerusalem, let my right hand forget her cunning. If I do not remember thee, let my tongue cleave to the roof of my mouth; if I prefer not Jerusalem above my chief joy (137:1-6).**

But Zion's enemy came and no friend rushed to her rescue. Her enemies viewed her with derision; they mocked her desolate, forlorn state—her pathetic plight indeed! Enemies mocked her sabbaths—the rest of every seventh day and every seventh year. For centuries Judah even mocked these sabbaths in a flagrant failure to keep them. The seventy years of captivity took care of the four hundred ninety years in which there had been no sabbath year rests observed.

v. 8. The first letter here is **Cheth.** The prophetic weeper describes the WHY of it all. Grievous indeed had been Jerusalem's sin. She had majored in transgressions—not in God's truth. God's justice, long delayed but now had come in fulness of force through Babylonian agency, removed her as the unclean thing she had become. Once honored she now is deeply despised. Her nakedness is evident to every beholder and it is utterly revolting. She sighs and is cast downward. Her shameful past has caught up with her.

v. 9. Teth is the first letter here. The verse graphically portrays how her filthiness abounded and affected all her being. It was no longer concealed. She failed to remember just how fatal sin is and how sure payday for transgression always is. In her downward plunge, no helper or aide appeared. She is void of all comfort. Sin makes loners; sooner or later it breeds isolation and contempt from all others. Judah breaks into the lamentation to plead for the Almighty to behold her affliction, to take awareness of the enemy's magnification of himself. In God and God alone could impoverished and enslaved Judah take hope. To look upward is the stricken sinner's only recourse.

v. 10. The small **Jod** is the initial letter here. Revealed here is a sad portrait indeed of the enemy's destruction of the city. Nothing was off limits to the calloused Chaldeans. Nothing was deemed as being sacred. The hands of the enemies were upon all the pleasant things of Jerusalem. Possibly there is a reference to her sacred things. These conquering pagans paid no attention to Mosaic restrictions about invading the sacred worship area in the temple. No Jew, unless of Levitical and priestly links, was allowed in the sacred sanctuary. The invaders went in nevertheless. It mattered not a particle to them that they violated, and violated most seriously, a law of the Most High in entering such hallowed chambers. These heathen soldiers impiously tramped into places where no unauthorized Jew dared go at all. An earlier king of Judah, Uzziah, found out quickly how lethal such location could be to an unauthorized Jew (Cf. 2 Chronicles 26:16-21).

v. 11. Caph is the first letter here. Described here is the people's pathetic plight as a result of the eighteen months' siege. Unmitigated hunger plagued the besieged city as supplies ran low and out. Their most precious jewels, goods and other property were gladly and gratefully relinquished for just enough food to keep life and limb together and even this was a losing proposition. The plea is made for God to be a witness to the sad conditions prevailing.

"IS IT NOTHING TO YOU, ALL YE THAT PASS BY?"

Paragraph 2 of Lamentations 1 reads,

> **Is it nothing to you, all ye that pass by? behold, and see if there be any sorrow like unto my sorrow, which is done unto me, wherewith the Lord hath afflicted me in the day of his fierce anger. From above hath he sent fire into my bones, and it prevaileth against them: he hath spread a net for my feet, he hath turned me back: he hath made me desolate and faint all the day. The yoke of my transgressions is bound by his hand: they are wreathed, and come up upon my neck: he hath made my strength to fall, the Lord hath delivered me into their hands, from**

whom I am not able to rise up. The Lord hath trodden under foot all my mighty men in the midst of me: he hath called an assembly against me to crush my young men: the Lord hath trodden the virgin, the daughter of Judah, as in a winepress. For these things I weep; mine eye, mine eye runneth down with water, because the comforter that should relieve my soul is far from me: my children are desolate, because the enemy prevailed. Zion spreadeth forth her hands, and there is none to comfort her: the Lord hath commanded concerning Jacob, that his adversaries should be round about him: Jerusalem is as a menstruous woman among them (1:12-17).

v. 12. The opening letter of this verse is **Lamed.** In deep despair, the bitter cry goes forth as to whether the passers-by feel any sympathy at all for Jerusalem's misery. Can you behold such and treat it with lightness? The challenge is presented to see if a parallel to Jerusalem's desolations can be found anywhere. The destroyed city has become the afflicted victim of God's fierce anger, His deep wrath. Those who think there is no wrath to God's character have never read carefully Lamentations or have read it to almost no profit at all!

v. 13. Mem is the first letter here. Jeremiah is the spokesman for the desolate city. The shafts of God's anger were not directed at Jeremiah directly or personally though he did face the consequences that came to the city. Destruction from the Lord is set forth in three figures. (1) There is the fiery destruction that has descended. It sank or pentrated into the very bones; it prevailed or was victorious in its punishing purposes. (2) A net is spread much like a hunter for the game he plans to entrap. Jerusalem did not escape the trap at all. (3) Desolation and sickness are next presented as a unit. Being faint all the day refers to a loss of bodily vigor and physical stamina.

v. 14. The opening letter here is **Nun.** The mass of Jerusalem's sin has become a mighty yoke placed upon the neck of the vanquished nation. The imagery is of a husbandmen who had his work animal under a heavy yoke with the rope, wreathed or knitted together and which is held firmly by his authoritative hand. God caused Jerusalem to be weak when the enemy came, God was the one who caused Jerusalem to fall. Had the Lord been on Zion's side there would not have been enough power in all of Babylon to take her. The defeat to the Chaldean was so complete that the besieged city had been totally unable to rise up. She was a city put down and put down completely.

v. 15. Samech is our initial letter here. Jerusalem's warriors had not fallen out on a battlefield in Judah's countryside but in the very midst of Jerusalem. This was a sure sign of the divine wrath at work against her. The called assembly by Jehovah was not a throng of Israelite worshippers as formerly had gathered in the once highly favored, flourishing city. This assembly was composed of the Chaldeans. They were there to crush Jerusalem's young men. Virgin or daughter stands for the people. The conquering Chaldeans had trodden Jerusalem's people as though they were a winepress; blood, like wine, burst forth at every pore. The intense imagery was graphic for Palestine had been a land of grape vineyards and many were the presses that could be found therein.

v. 16. The first letter here is **Ain.** Jerusalem is personified as speaker here. The destroyed city weeps; tears flow down her cheeks. The comforter was far removed and not nearby at all. Jerusalem's children or population are filled with desolation. The enemy, Chaldea, has prevailed or been totally victorious.

v. 17. Our opening letter here is **Pe.** Zion spreads forth hands of desperation seeking help, enlisting aide, entreating sympathy. None is forthcoming. Her idols are impotent to the nth degree and then some; so are all her former allies such as the Egyptians. Jehovah has cut off all such by giving charge to the adversaries that Jacob was to be surrounded and that no sympathy was to be extended at all. Jerusalem is likened to a menstruous woman who is ceremonially counted as unclean. Jerusalem is looked upon as an abomination, as a city totally abandoned and without friend or helper.

JEHOVAH'S JUDGMENT SEEN TO BE JUST

Paragraph 3 of Lamentations 1 reads,

> **The Lord is righteous; for I have rebelled against his commandment: hear, I pray you, all people, and behold my sorrow: my virgins and my young men are gone into captivity. I called for my lovers, but they deceived me: my priests and mine elders gave up the ghost in the city, while they sought their meat to relieve their souls. Behold,**

O Lord; for I am in distress: my bowels are troubled; mine heart is turned within me; for I have grievously rebelled: abroad the sword bereaveth, at home there is as death. They have heard that I sigh: there is none to comfort me: all mine enemies have heard of my trouble; they are glad that thou hast done it: thou wilt bring the day that thou hast called, and they shall be like unto me. Let all their wickedness come before thee; and do unto them, as thou hast done unto me for all my transgressions: for my sighs are many, and my heart is faint (1:18-22).

v. 18. Tzaddi is the first letter of this verse. Recognition of Jehovah's righteousness and our own sinfulness is one of the first imperative parts of true repentance. Jeremiah speaks for the nation. The nation now recognizes that Jehovah has been right in the punishment He has brought upon the land by His avengers—the Chaldeans. Jerusalem has now paid the high cost for her rebellion, her wayward ways. The prayerful petition goes forth to be heard. Her sorrows are to be noted. Among the deepest, most grievous sorrows was the taking of her virgins and young men into captivity. Youth are the hope of any city or nation. When they are gone procreation powers for continuation are eliminated totally. This serves as an ancient picture in a modern setting. The writer of these notes speaks in a dozen or more gospel meetings and twenty or more lectureships each year. Annually, I see congregations in fifteen or more states composed almost entirely of older members with few younger couples and almost no children at all in many places. Unless youth are soon brought in and solidified for the future of such churches, congregational extinction is written on the walls of their very meetinghouses. Such is sad; it is immeasurably sad. It grieved destroyed Jerusalem that her youth were no more in her streets.

v. 19. Our initial letter here is **Koph.** Jerusalem's former lovers are summoned to help in the hour of grievous sorrow. These would have been her allies such as Egyptians to the southwest. They met the call with deception. They have washed their hands, as we would express it currently, of Jerusalem and Judah. Food was so scarce and at such a premium that priests and elders died of starvation. Giving up the ghost is a Biblical depiction of demise. Meat (food) was sought desperately to sustain life and could not be found anywhere. The condition of solitary Jerusalem (v. 1) almost defies apt description.

v. 20. Resh is our first letter here. Jeremiah is still the voice depicting Jerusalem's deepest of afflictions. The fallen city cries out with a confession of being in deep distress. Bowels here is rendered heart in the ASV. The seat of affections is the thrust of the heartrending remark. Jerusalem was sufferng from heart ailments. Her transgressions have come home to trouble her with grievous wages paid. We would say, "the chickens have come home to roost." A second description is given of her heart malady. Her heart is turned within her. This depicts deeply the gravity of her grief—grief that refused to go away. Again the city confesses rebellion and this time adds that they "have grievously rebelled." Their sins had not been shallow by any means. They had been wilful, deliberate, presumptuous and yet their greatest king, David, had written more than four centuries earlier, "Keep back thy servant also from presumptuous sins; let them not have dominion over me: then shall I be upright, and I shall be innocent from the great transgression" (Psalm 19:13). Their grievous dangers were not just confined to the desolate city. Outside Jerusalem people died by the sword, a lethal weapon; inside the city people perished by the masses as a result of the famine, i. e., by starvation. Unrelieved sorrow fills each one of these elegies or funeral-like dirges.

v. 21. The first letter of this verse is **Schin.** The sighing becomes even more grievous because no comforter arises. Enemies were minus all care and concern. They heard what God had done to the apostate capital of His people and it gladdened their hearts. Yet the day would come when these jubilant nations would reap their own punishment. Jehovah has never tolerated jubilation from a beholding nation when He punishes an apostate nation. Soon these celebrating rebels would be like Jerusalem—brought to the depths of despair themselves.

v. 22. Tau is our opening letter here. This is a recognition of the just judgment that the gloating beholders deserved and a clear, clarion charge that it come. Judah had to pay for his transgressions; neighboring nations must do the same. The chapter closes with the recital of Jerusalem's many sighs and a heart that is faint (very weak).

POINTS TO PONDER

(1) Lamentations 1 shows very graphically the high cost of defying God and rebelling against His law.

(2) The sure fruit of sin is always captivity of one kind or another.

(3) Other sure fruits of sin are isolation, solitude and lingering loneliness.

(4) Sinners have no other way to look than toward God and His plan of merciful pardon.

(5) Sooner or later the "chickens always come home to roost" for those who have sowed their wild oats.

DISCUSSION QUESTIONS

1. Summarize introduction.

2. Of what persistent and long practice did the Exile permanently cure the Jews?

3. Discuss in detail how this chapter depicts the deep depths to which Zion has fallen.

4. How is destruction from the Lord set forth in three graphic figures?

5. Discuss the heart trouble that afflicted Jerusalem.

MULTIPLE-CHOICE: Underline correct answer

1. The Hebrew word **Eechah** is translated in this book as: (A) "How;" (B) "elegy:" (C) "dirge;" (D) "sin."
2. The book of Lamentations deals with: (A) temple worship; (B) Levitical sacrifices; (C) sin, sorrow, solitude and shame; (D) happiness and prosperity.
3. In the book of Lamentations, Jerusalem is pictured as: (A) powerful; (B) prosperous; (C) peaceful; (D) desolate.
4. The opening letter of the Hebrew alphabet is (A) Alpha; (B) Omega; (C) Aleph; (D) Jod.
5. Jewish adversaries saw her and mocked her: (A) temple; (B) annual feasts; (C) ten commandments; (D) sabbaths.

SCRIPTURAL FILL-IN: Only one word in each blank

1. "_____ doth the _____ sit _____ , that was _____ of _____ !"

2. "_____ hath _____ sinned; _____ she is _____ :. . ."

3. "_____ it _____ to _____ , all ye that _____ by?"

4. "_____ spreadeth _____ her _____ , and there _____ none to _____ her; . . ."

5. "Let _____ their _____ come _____ thee; and _____ unto them, as thou hast _____ unto me for _____ my _____ : for my _____ are _____ , and my _____ is _____ ."

TRUE OR FALSE: Put either a "T" or "F" in the blanks

_____ 1. At her fall Jerusalem had an abundance of friends desirous of aiding her.

_____ 2. Psalm 137:1-6 is an excellent commentary on much of Lamentations 1.

_____ 3. Lamentations is one book of the Bible in which there is not so much as a particle of God's wrath exhibited.

_____ 4. Chaldea had been very humane in her capture of Zion.

_____ 5. Giving up the ghost is a Biblical description of physical demise.

THOUGHT QUESTIONS

1. Contrast PAST Jerusalem with PRESENT Jerusalem during the time this book was penned.

2. In times of deep crises, why do so many past helpers become present hinderers?

3. Discuss some of the sure ways in which sin always finds us out (Numbers 32:23).

4. What is so very destructive and pathetic about widespread fatalties to youth?

5. What is sure to be the bleak future of current congregations who are totally minus any young couples and young children? What can and should be done to alleviate this critical, crucial situation?

APPENDIX THREE

JEREMIAH'S LAMENT OVER
JERUSALEM'S MISERY
Lamentations 2

Zion is suffering because Zion has sinned and sinned grievously. The sensitive Seer knows why great suffering has descended the city on four hills but he still mourns the solitary site and grieves over the desolate metropolis. His heart is at the breaking point. This chapter is pungently punctuated with graphic and vivid lamentations that almost defy parallels.

PROPHETIC LAMENTATION OVER
JERUSALEM'S MOUNTING MISERY

Paragraph 1 of Lamentations 2 is lengthy covering almost the whole chapter. It reads,

> **How hath the Lord covered the daughter of Zion with a cloud in his anger, and cast down from heaven unto the earth the beauty of Israel, and remembered not his footstool in the day of his anger! The Lord hath swallowed up all the habitations of Jacob, and hath not pitied: he hath thrown down in his wrath the strong holds of the daughter of Judah; he hath brought them down to the ground: he hath polluted the kingdom and the princes thereof. He hath cut off in his fierce anger all the horn of Israel: he hath drawn back his right hand from before the enemy, and he burned against Jacob like a flaming fire, which devoureth round about. He hath bent his bow like an enemy: he stood with his right hand as an adversary, and slew all that were pleasant to the eye in**

the tabernacle of the daughter of Zion: he poured out his fury like fire. The Lord was as an enemy: he hath swallowed up Israel, he hath swallowed up all her palaces: he hath destroyed his strong holds, and hath increased in the daughter of Judah mourning and lamentation. And he hath violently taken away his tabernacle, as if it were of a garden: he hath destroyed his places of the assembly: the Lord hath caused the solemn feasts and sabbaths to be forgotten in Zion, and hath despised in the indignation of his anger the king and the priest. The Lord hath cast off his altar, he hath abhorred his sanctuary, he hath given up into the hand of the enemy the walls of her palaces; they have made a noise in the house of the Lord, as in the day of a solemn feast. The Lord hath proposed to destroy the wall of the daughter of Zion: he hath stretched out a line, he hath not withdrawn his hand from destroying: therefore he made the rampart and the wall to lament; they languished together. Her gates are sunk into the ground; he hath destroyed and broken her bars: her king and her princes are among the Gentiles: the law is no more; her prophets also find no vision from the Lord. The elders of the daughter of Zion sit upon the ground, and keep silence: they have cast up dust upon their heads; they have girded themselves with sackcloth: the virgins of Jerusalem hang down their heads to the ground. Mine eyes do fail with tears, my bowels are troubled, my liver is poured upon the earth, for the destruction of the daughter of my people; because the children and the sucklings swoon in the streets of the city. They say to their mothers, Where is corn and wine? when they swooned as the wounded in the streets of the city, when their soul was poured out into their mothers' bosom. What thing shall I take to witness for thee? what thing shall I liken to thee, O daughter of Jerusalem? what shall I equal to thee, that I may comfort thee, O virgin daughter of Zion? for thy breach is great like the sea: who can heal thee? Thy prophets have seen vain and foolish things for thee: and they have not discovered thine

iniquity, to turn away thy captivity; but have seen for thee false burdens and causes of banishment. All that pass by clap their hands at thee; they hiss and wag their head at the daughter of Jerusalem, saying, Is this the city that men call The perfection of beauty, The joy of the whole earth? All thine enemies have opened their mouth against thee: they hiss and gnash the teeth: they say, We have swallowed her up: certainly this is the day that we looked for; we have found, we have seen it. The Lord hath done that which he had devised; he hath fulfilled his word that he had commanded in the days of old: he hath thrown down, and hath not pitied: and he hath caused thine enemy to rejoice over thee, he hath set up the horn of thine adversaries. Their heart cried unto the Lord, O wall of the daughter of Zion, let tears run down like a river day and night: give thyself no rest; let not the apple of thine eye cease. Arise, cry out in the night: in the beginning of the watches pour out thine heart like water before the face of the Lord: lift up thy hands toward him for the life of thy young children, that faint for hunger in the top of every street (2:1-19).

v. 1. The first letter of this verse is **Aleph.** "How" begins this chapter as well as chapters one and four. It is a powerful term with which to begin the elegies or funeral dirges of chapter two. The daughter of Zion is simply a reference to God's people. Verse 1 uses "daughter of Zion;" verse 2 uses "daughter of Judah." They refer to the same people. Jehovah is portrayed as one who in His wrath has covered Zion with a cloud—a dark cloud, a thick cloud. Jerusalem has been made obscure. The once great city has been cast down from heaven (an exalted state) to earth (a lowly, humiliated, miserable state). We are reminded of our Lord's denunciation of Capernaum which had been exalted to heaven and was to be brought down to Hades (Matthew 11:23—ASV). The beauty of Israel may well refer to her once magnificent and majestic temple— now in the debris of destruction. The footstool may refer to the most glorious piece of furniture in the temple—the ark of the covenant that was housed in the Most Holy Place and that only the high priest could approach, as representative of the people, one day a year—the day of atonement which was the seventh month and tenth day (Cf. Leviticus 16). This verse closes with a reference to God's anger. Those who deny Jehovah's wrath apparently are strangers to such passages as Lamentations 2:1.

v. 2. Our opening letter here is **Beth.** The swallowing up of Jacob's habitations is a graphic description of the widespread destruction and thorough overwhelming Jehovah permitted Chaldea to make of the apostate city. For century after century, God took pity on His people but not this time. His pity was turned away this time. The bastions of her strongholds no longer enjoyed His bequeathed blessing. In His aroused wrath, He threw them down; He brought them even with the ground. The description is graphic; it is very vivid. They first polluted His kingdom by their gross idolatry, their ever-increasing immorality and their flagrant failure to honor Him and respect His statutes. Now He has polluted them with their leaders.

v. 3. Gimel is our initial letter here. His wrath is again in the forefront here in the lively language of "fierce anger"—an anger that refused to subside until just retribution came their way. "The horn of Israel" had been cut off. The imagery is drawn from the horns of animals—sources of power and means of self-defense. Jehovah had cut off Israel's power, her means of national defense. For centuries, His right hand (symbol of power) had been extended to help them; now it had been withdrawn. Chaldea did not have to fight God in this battle; He helped them—not apostate Judah. God's fierce anger became a flaming fire devouring on all fronts.

v. 4. The first letter here is **Daleth.** Archery was an ancient way of waging warfare. Jehovah is pictured as an archer with bow bent and with the arrows of His destruction aimed at defiant Jerusalem. With the power of His right hand He became as Jerusalem's adversary—no longer her deliverer. Slain in the fall of the city had been those pleasant to the eye—her youth, her talented, her people of rank, power and prestige. This was done in their very capital. "Daughter of Zion" refers to Jerusalem's teeming population. His fury (more of His aroused wrath) was poured out like fire. Through all this God had employed an agent—Chaldea.

v. 5. He is our first letter here. Jehovah, long Judah's deliverer and Jerusalem's shield, has now become the adversary, the enemy. Israel, His covenant people and called by that noble name once given to Jacob and then to his descendants, has been swallowed up, thoroughly destroyed. Note the sad specifics. (1) Her palaces have been destroyed. (2) Her strongholds (means of national defense) are no more. (3) There has been a great increase of her mourning and lamentation. Her sorrows and sighings mount higher and higher.

v. 6. Vau is the first letter here. The stately temple, once the place where His name was registered and He met with His people, has not been spared. With His presence removed, the temple was nothing but a hollow framework, an empty edifice, a building now void of meaning. The temple experienced a violent destruction. Nothing could Chaldea do that would show her total subjection of Judah more than the total destruction of the towering temple—the very symbol of Judah and Jerusalem. God allowed the removal of the temple much like a man removes a garden. The temple is no longer a place of religious assembly. Solemn feasts such as Passover, the feasts of weeks (Pentecost in the New Testament) and the feast of tabernacles are no more. The weekly sabbaths (Saturday or seventh day) are no longer remembered in Zion. Deposed are both king (royalty) and priest (religious leadership).

v. 7. The first letter here is **Zain.** Temple demolition is still the thrust here. The altar is cut off and this is where Israel, represented by the priesthood, drew nigh to God and He to them. God abhored His sanctuary—the holy and most holy places. The temple precincts were given to the enemy—the Chaldeans. Noise permeates the house of the Lord but it is not the joyful refrain of worshippers, as in the former feasts of solemnity, but of foreign invaders who triumphed their tones of total victory over Judah's and Jerusalem's most sacred spot—the glorious temple on Mount Moriah.

v. 8. Cheth is our first letter here. Jehovah's purposing to destroy Zion's wall simply means He forsook the city as Heavenly Shield and Divine Protector allowing Chaldean warriors success in their besieging Jerusalem. Ancients stretched lines both in building and in destroying. This meant the city was destroyed thoroughly, by design, systematically and methodically. The destroying hand was not withdrawn until the collapse of the city occurred. The rampart (lower part of wall) and the remainder of the wall are spoken of as lamenting, as languishing together, as being mutual twins of sorrow. In their personification, they pour out their common sighing with and to each other.

v. 9. Teth is the opening Hebrew letter. The sinking of Zion's walls into the ground means they no longer stood as a defense against the besieging Chaldeans. The breaking and destroying of her bars is a further portrait of the utterly defenseless nature of the once well-fortified metropolis. Zion is now minus political leadership since her king (Zedekiah) and his princes are among the Gentiles, i. e., the Chaldeans. The law is no more due to there being no entrenched power to execute such. Prophets are minus any revelations from Jehovah and thus have no messages for the people.

v. 10. Jod, smallest letter of Hebrew alphabet, opens this verse. Israelite elders who once flourished as counsellors and confidants of a mighty city are now pictured as ground occupiers. Silence grips their once busy tongues. To show their deep sorrow, they have cast dust upon their heads and chosen as sorrowful apparel sackcloth. Proverbially, through the Bible, this was symbolic of the deepest of sorrows. Virgins, known for their happy and cheerful outlook on life, now hang their saddened heads to the ground. There is nothing to cheer their sorrow-filled countenances.

v. 11. Caph is the initial letter here. The prophet had wept so much that his reservoir of tears was totally diminished. His bowels (heart— ASV) was overwhelmed with trouble. Jeremiah could well have related to the very familiar expression that closes Job 3, ". . .yet trouble came" (v. 26). Allusion to his liver being poured upon the earth possibly refers to the bitter anguish that permeated his whole personality. The liver produces bile and this reflects something very bitter. Anguish punctuated Jeremiah's whole frame due to the heavy destruction visited upon his people—people who had sinned grievously and yet people he loved devoutly. Children and sucklings (those still of nursing age) swoon or perish in the streets of the doomed city.

v. 12. Lamed is the first Hebrew letter here. In desperation these starving children cry out to their mothers for corn and wine (for the food they needed so desperately). They were dying before the riveted eye of the prophet upon their anguish. They died while seeking nourishment from the breasts of their exhausted mothers—nourishment not forthcoming. Their dying breath was at their mother's empty bosoms!

v. 13. Mem is our first Hebrew letter in this verse. Jeremiah wished to comfort his distraught contemporaries but found no way so to do. No other calamity came to his troubled mind with which a comparison could be made. Sometimes we can assuage sorrow with assurance that others are suffering similarly or even more deeply. Peter does this in 1 Peter 5:9 and Paul does so in Hebrews 12:1ff. About the only thing that came to the agitated prophet's mind was the measureless sea with which to compare their immeasurable agonies. Zion's breach is great like the sea. Clarke has this interesting and well-worded observation on this verse, "Thou hast a flood of afflictions, a sea of troubles, an ocean of miseries." None could heal. What an immeasurably sad analysis of the once glorious city.

v. 14. Nun opens the verse as first Hebrew letter. Note that Jeremiah refers to these prophets as "thy prophets" and not as Jehovah's prophets. Jeremiah here inveighs against these pseudo prophets as he did throughout his long prophetic product (the book of Jeremiah). They were not seers of truth but seers of vain (empty) and foolish (minus any and all wisdom) things in efforts to please their auditors with smooth sayings and pleasing platitudes. These false teachers never exposed Judah's sins and Jerusalem's iniquities. Had they joined Jeremiah as seers of truth and opponents to any and all errors Judah might have repented. Then the captivity could have been averted and this widespread destruction to the city would never have materialized. Instead the burden of their false messages was to offer peace when there was no peace, hope when all was hopeless, cheer when all was cheerless. Now it was too late. The river of no return had been reached; the exile could not be avoided.

v. 15. The first letter of this verse is **Samech.** This verse graphically details the heightened joy Zion's enemies experienced when they witnessed the Jewish capital amidst the debris of total destruction. They clapped their hands with glee; they hissed the city or expressed great contempt for it. They wagged their heads with a sense of satisfaction. They interrogated in great jest and ridicule, "Is this the city that men call The perfection of beauty, The joy of the whole earth?" Solomon's temple had graced the city with unparalleled beauty for more than four eventful centuries. It was perhaps the most beautiful city in all the world of that era. The perfection was no more; the joy had departed the demolished metropolis. What a spectacle of sadness it must have presented to every Jewish beholder in general and to Jeremiah in particular.

v. 16. **Pe** is our initial Hebrew letter here. This verse links with the previous one in depicting how the enemies reacted to Zion's fall, to Jerusalem's destruction. They opened their mouth but not to express sympathetic sorrow. There was no empathy on their part toward Jerusalem's pathetic population. Hisses leave their lips. They gnash or grind their teeth in the fiendish delight of a competitor now humiliated, now destroyed. They gladly took credit for her swallowing or total destruction. They had longed for the day when detested Zion would fall in humiliation and embarrassment. That day was now and they saw it with a great gleam of satisfaction. This is neighborly indifference gone to seed and then some!

v. 17. Ain is the initial Hebrew letter here. Jehovah had now done what he long had threatened to do—destroy Jerusalem. Babylon was simply his chosen agent. Had God fought for Jerusalem the Chaldeans would have never been successful in conquering Jerusalem. Fulfillment of what He had promised of old possibly refers to the punishments Moses set forth as warnings when the people of the future would abandon God (Deuteronomy 28). They apostatized and God caused their collapse. No pity was shown them in the Chaldean capture of the once impregnable city (as long as God was shield and protector). By enabling the Chaldean nation to be victorious, he had made it possible for Babylon to exult in her destructive work. The setting up of the horn of her adversaries simply means that God invested Babylon with power and reduced Zion to NO power at all. Jerusalem fell much like ripened grain before a modern combine.

v. 18. Tzaddi is the first letter here. In their distress, the vanquished turned to the Lord. They should have done this earlier and this widespread destruction could have been averted. Zion's wall is here addressed and charged to weep profusely with regretful tears flowing like a river day and night. More than one commentator has objected to the wall as being addressed. Some even have chosen to rewrite the text to remove an objection they have concocted. The text needs to be left alone and accepted as the prophet wrote it nearly twenty-six centuries ago. It is figurative language with a part (the wall) put for the whole of the entire city and all its population. It is precisely what we have in Isaiah 14:31 where Isaiah, the great statesman prophet, wrote, "Howl, O gates; cry, O city; . . ." If gates may howl and a city may cry, then may walls shed tears in the vividness of figurative language. It is a powerful figure of speech charging that there be no abatement in the tears of sorrow shed over desolate Zion. There is to be neither rest nor respite from such tearful expressions of grief. The apple of the eye is to continue its profuse production of tears. The weeping prophet had known such all his prophetic life—weeping over Judah and Jerusalem and the punishment he saw coming over forty years of preaching to the adamant rebels.

v. 19. Koph is the opening letter there. The charge to weep continues here in this verse. Tearful petitions are to be sent to the throne of God in the night and its watches. In the Old Testament there were three—sunset till ten, ten till two and two till sunrise. In the New Testament, and due to Roman influence, the watches became four—three hours each. The charge is to preface each of the three watches with a prayer lifted to Jehovah. Prayers are to be prayed in fervency for young children who were starving throughout the city now deprived of food. The plight is great indeed.

THE PROPHET'S LAMENTATION IN PRAYER

Paragraph two, the final and very short, of Lamentations 2 reads,

> **Behold, O Lord, and consider to whom thou hast done this. Shall the women eat their fruit, and children of a span long? shall the priest and the prophet be slain in the sanctuary of the Lord? The young and the old lie on the ground in the streets: my virgins and my young men are fallen by the sword; thou hast slain them in the day of thine anger; thou hast killed, and not pitied. Thou hast called as in a solemn day my terrors round about, so that in the day of the Lord's anger none escaped nor remained: those that I have swaddled and brought up hath mine enemy consumed (2:20-22).**

v. 20. Resh is the initial letter here. From the depths of his moved heart the prophet addresses God with the magnitude of their miseries. He requested the Lord to consider how bad conditions were. Starvation was such a threat that mothers might even consume the very fruit of their bodies—their own children, children a span long—babies who were still very small. Moses predicted such (Deuteronomy 28:53ff). Such had occurred during a great famine in the Northern Kingdom (2 Kings 6:28,29). Would there have to be a repeat of this? Next he inquired if priest and prophet were to be slain in the Lord's very sanctuary.

487

v. 21. Shin is our opening letter here. Death en masse had come to both young and old. Their corpses lined the streets suggestive of even no burials. The lethal sword has cut down both virgins and young men. These were the hope of the nation's future. The prophet refers to the slaying of such as God's anger and as being minus pity. It is always hard for man to understand the wrath of God. But the slayings could have been averted if these people had repented. Sin brought on death in mass form and pity was no longer retained by God toward his rebellious nation.

v. 22. Tau opens this verse. The imagery seems to be as if the Lord had called all them into the one location—Jerusalem—for a solemn day so that none might escape. The prophet speaks for the people. Babies they had swaddled and then brought up were consumed by conquering Chaldeans.

The elegies or funeral dirges of this chapter are punctuated with how desperate the plight of a God-forsaken people can be.

POINTS TO PONDER

(1) Jerusalem's once radiant beauty had been spoiled by the repulsive ugliness of sin.

(2) When Jehovah vacated the temple, that magnificent building was an empty edifice robbed of its real redeeming value.

(3) There is a river of no return for sinners today when they lose all interest in Deity and Deity's law.

(4) Sin has a sure way of destroying everything that possesses beauty in the human personality.

(5)Like abandoned Judah, the masses frequently wait too late to turn to Jehovah.

DISCUSSION QUESTIONS

1. Summarize introduction.

2. In what grievous ways did Jerusalem pollute the Lord's kingdom and what was the recompense with which He repaid them?

3. Show how extremely difficult it was for the distraught prophet to comfort his people.

4. What well-worded observation is made by the learned Clarke?

5. Discuss in some detail the weeping as done by the wall of Jerusalem.

MULTIPLE-CHOICE: Underline correct answer

1. Jerusalem was built on: (A) a flat plain; (B) seven hills; (C) four hills; (D) one large mountain.
2. (A) "How;" (B) "When;" (C) "Why;" (D)"Where"—begins Lamentations 1,2 and 4.
3. Jesus spoke of: (A) Nazareth; (B) Jerusalem; (C) Chorazin; (D) Capernaum—in His day as being exalted to heaven but would be brought down to Hades.
4. The one piece of furniture placed in the Most Holy Place of the tabernacle and later the temple was the: (A) table of showbread; (B) altar of incense; (C) candlestick; (D) ark of the covenant.
5. (A) Chaldea; (B) Egypt; (C) Assyria; (D) Syria—was Jehovah's chosen agent in destroying Jerusalem in 586 B. C.

SCRIPTURAL FILL-IN: Only one word required in each blank

1. God "poured _____ his _____ like _____ ."

2. Jeremiah wrote that "the _____ is no _____ ; her _____ also _____ no _____ from the _____ ."

3. "O _____ daughter of _____ ? for thy _____ is _____ like the _____ : who _____ heal thee?"

4. "Is this the _____ that men _____ The _____ of _____ , The _____ of the _____ earth?"

5. "O _____ of the _____ of _____ , let _____ run _____ like a _____ day and _____ : give _____ no _____ ; let not the _____ of thine _____ cease."

TRUE OR FALSE: Put either a "T" or "F" in the blanks

_____ 1. The High Priest could approach the ark of the covenant any day of the year and with Jehovah's full approval.

_____ 2. Chaldea had to fight both Jehovah and Jerusalem in the besieging and capture of the metropolis.

_____ 3. Jehovah became Jerusalem's adversary—not deliverer—when Chaldea attacker her.

_____ 4. Jod, tenth letter of the Hebrew alphabet, was the smallest letter of their alphabet.

_____ 5. "Yet trouble came" applied both to Job and Jeremiah though circumstances greatly differed between the pious pair of Old Testament worthies.

THOUGHT QUESTIONS

1. Discuss the sad specifics of Jerusalem being swallowed up and what lessons we can derive from the same.

2. What did the total demolition of the temple really signify in Chaldea's triumph over Zion?

3. What exhibits the deeply sensitive nature of Jeremiah's weeping and how should sins (ours and others) cause weeping on our part?

4. What are some things false teachers will never do in the teaching they present their auditors?

5. Give a summation of Lamentations 2:20-22.

APPENDIX FOUR

ONLY IN JEHOVAH IS THERE HOPE AND ASSURANCE
Lamentations 3

This chapter has thrice as many verses as do chapters one, two, four and five. Yet it is not that much longer of actual material than chapters one and two because the verses are much shorter. In this chapter, we have the prophetic bewailing of the calamities, the acknowledgment of Jehovah's justice and the prophet's fervent prayer.

JEREMIAH'S AGONIZING AFFLICTION AND GENUINE GRIEF

Paragraph 1 of Lamentations 3 reads,

I am the man that hath seen affliction by the rod of his wrath. He hath led me, and brought me into darkness, but not into light. Surely against me is he turned; he turneth his hand against me all the day. My flesh and my skin hath he made old; he hath broken my bones. He hath builded against me, and compassed me with gall and travail. He hath set me in dark places, as they that be dead of old. He hath hedged me about, that I cannot get out: he hath made my chain heavy. Also when I cry and shout, he shutteth out my prayer. He hath inclosed my ways with hewn stone, he hath made my paths crooked. He was unto me as a bear lying in wait, and as a lion in secret places. He hath turned aside my ways, and pulled me in pieces: he hath made me desolate. He

hath bent his bow, and set me as a mark for the arrow. He hath caused the arrows of his quiver to enter into my reins. I was a derision to all my people; and their song all the day. He hath filled me with bitterness, he hath made me drunken with wormwood. He hath also broken my teeth with gravel stones, he hath covered me with ashes. And thou hast removed my soul far off from peace: I forgat prosperity. And I said, My strength and my hope is perished from the Lord: Remembering mine affliction and my misery, the wormwood and the gall. My soul hath them still in remembrance, and is humbled in me. This I recall to my mind, therefore have I hope (3:1-21).

vs. 1-3. Each of these three introductory verses begins with the first Hebrew letter—**Aleph.** Though Jeremiah was a good, godly and great man personally, yet he had seen (experienced) affliction by the wrath of God's rod. He knew the affliction of rejection, loneliness, being misunderstood, imprisonment and seeing beloved Zion fall to the Chaldeans. His example in handling afflictions should have been emulated by all his fellow Jews but alas, it was not that way. The darkness into which he had been led here is not a symbol of sin, as frequently it is in Holy Writ, but into gloom and calamity. The light into which He had not been led symbolizes prosperity. Representing the entire nation Jeremiah recognized that the powerful Jehovah who was once with them had turned from them. No longer was He their deliverer; now He had delivered them into the hands of their captors. The heavenly hand that once shielded them now stood as their adamant adversary. Repeated afflictions are herein portrayed.

vs. 4-6. Each of this trio begins with the second letter of the Hebrew alphabet—**Beth.** So deep were the afflictions that weighed constantly upon the persecuted prophet that he felt his flesh and skin (his body) had become old before its time. The breaking of his bones refers to the depth of pain he bore. Mounds and ramparts had been built by the determined Chaldeans in their successful besieging of walled and well-fortified Zion. These compassed Zion with gall (bitterness) and travail (great, persistent weariness). Chaldea wore Zion down and then out. The dark places would be the graves or sepulchres where dead bodies are interred. The dead of old are those long consigned to oblivion. The dead are soon forgotten and quick will come the time when all who did know them will not even be here to do any remembering. They, too, have a destiny with oblivion.

vs. 7-9. Each of these three verses begins with the third Hebrew letter—**Gimel.** Jeremiah portrays himself as being enclosed in such fashion that escape is out of the question. He is fettered with an unbreakable chain. Prayerful petitions sent to the heavenly throne of grace are short-circuited before arriving at their destined destination. Perhaps he alludes to the prohibitions that he not pray for apostate Judah for Jehovah said He would not hear (Cf. Jeremiah 7:16; 11:14). The enclosing of his ways with hewn stone and the making of his paths crooked suggest that obstacles were before him and his ways were uncertain.

vs. 10-12. Each of these three verses begins with the fourth Hebrew letter—**Daleth.** Minus Heaven's help, which had now vacated them, Jeremiah and Judah were as weak and helpless as one facing a bear lying in wait or the lion of prey lurking in secret places. Jeremiah had been turned aside from his ways; he had been pulled into pieces much like the prey is of wild animals. Desolation is now his persistent lot. It would not go away. Bow and arrow formed a prominent part of enemy warfare and many are the allusions to archery within Holy Writ. We have one here in verse 12. It was natural imagery growing out of the previous allusions to being prey to bears and lions. Clarke has this interesting comment on this verse, "This was the state of poor Jerusalem. It seemed as a butt for all God's arrows; and each arrow of calamity entered into the soul, for God was the unerring marksman." Verse 12 is reminiscent of Job 7:20 wherein the persecuted and perplexed patriarch of Uz uttered, ". . .why hast thou set me as a mark against thee, so that I am a burden to myself?"

vs. 13-15. These three verses all begin with the fifth letter of the Hebrew alphabet—**He.** Arrows, not singular but a plurality, are suggestive of afflictions and persecutions that were his. Entering into reins would indicate the depth of the sorrow and affliction. Jeremiah had become a derision to all his people. Jeremiah 20:7 is an excellent commentary upon verse 14. It reads, "O Lord, thou hast deceived me, and I was deceived: thou art stronger than I, and hast prevailed: I am in derision daily, every one mocketh me." Jeremiah knew rejection from his people much like a greater than Jeremiah—Jesus Christ—would know it six centuries later (John 1:11). They treated him sneeringly and shabbily. Their songs contained lyrics about Jeremiah but not to his praise. Even their lyrics exhibited their cruel, calloused and cold contempt for him. He did not experience a **smattering** of bitterness (sorrow, trouble, distress, affliction) but an **overwhelming** of it. He was an inebriated man though not on alcohol. Wormwood symbolized something very bitter much like quinine does to a modern mind. So engulfed was he in his bitterness that he spoke graphically of being intoxicated on such! It is a portrayed picture of poignant plight.

vs. 16-18. Each of this trio of verses begins with the sixth letter of the Hebrew alphabet—**Vau.** His intake of food had been mixed so much with gravel stones or grit that his teeth were broken. The picture of teeth grinding on gravel till they were all broken up is graphic indeed. Covered with ashes is likewise vivid. Eyes are blinded by such; ears are stopped by such. The mouth is filled with such. Nostrils gasp in vain for fresh air in such a setting. It is a suffocating portrait indeed painted by the agonizing man from Anathoth. Peace is far removed from him. Prosperity is so far in the past that it seems as though he had never been its fortunate possessor. It was with difficulty that he could ever remember the blessed state of happiness. There has to be a heaven in the rightness of things for people like Jeremiah who knew a lifetime of sorrow and sighing. The bottom brink of deep despair is reached when he referred to the very perishing of strength and hope. And yet in the next trio of verses resilient hope will again be kindled in the despairing disciple of Deity. The rainbow of hope frequently does not appear until one is at the end of trouble's tunnel.

vs. 19-21. Each of this trio of verses begins with the seventh letter of the Hebrew alphabet—**Zain.** The depths of despair felt so pentratingly by Jeremiah are graphically portrayed by four words in verse 19—affliction, misery, wormwood and gall. Retaining such in remembrance was an humbling experience to Jeremiah. He had complained bitterly; now he returns to the plateau of hope once again with rousing resiliency.

JEREMIAH'S BLESSED ASSURANCE OF HOPE

Paragraph 2 of Lamentations 3 reads,

> **It is of the Lord's mercies that we are not consumed, because his compassions fail not. They are new every**

morning: great is thy faithfulness. The Lord is my portion, saith my soul; therefore will I hope in him. The Lord is good, unto them that wait for him, to the soul that seeketh him. It is good that a man should both hope and quietly wait for the salvation of the Lord. It is good for a man that he bear the yoke in his youth. He sitteth alone and keepeth silence, because he hath borne it upon him. He putteth his mouth in the dust; if so be there may be hope. He giveth his cheek to him that smiteth him: he is filled full with reproach. For the Lord will not cast off for ever: But though he cause grief, yet will he have commission according to the multitude of his mercies. For he doth not afflict willingly nor grieve the children of men. To crush under his feet all the prisoners of the earth, To turn aside the right of a man before the face of the most High, To subvert a man in his cause, the Lord approveth not (3:22-36).**

vs. 22-24. These verses begin with the eighth letter of the Hebrew alphabet—**Cheth.** Jeremiah begins to see a brighter and better side. Jehovah's mercy comes before the battered prophet. Had Jehovah not extended mercy, Judah would have been consumed or exterminated in totality. Faith is again on the throne of Jeremiah's heart and he sees Jehovah's compassions as failure-proof. Evidence of His new mercies and compassions appears daily. Jeremiah now looks away from his persecutions to his God on holy high as his portion. In Him alone could the encompassed prophet find hope. From the valley of deep depths, he is climbing the mountain of hope again.

vs. 25-27. This trio of verses is begun with the ninth letter of the Hebrew alphabet—**Teth.** More than one commentator has pointed out the interesting observation how that GOOD inheres these three verses. In our English translation, good is the fourth word in verse 25 and the third in verses 26,27. Jehovah's goodness (with God goodness is always absolute and perfect) is exhibited to those who wait for Him and seek Him with their souls. Here are the valiant virtues of patience and zeal. Israel's sweet Psalmist says, "Wait on the Lord: be of good courage, and he shall strengthen thine heart: wait, I say, on the Lord" (Psalm 27:14). Relative to seeking Isaiah has this interesting statement, "Seek ye the Lord while he may be found, call ye upon him while he is near" (Isaiah 55:6). In verse 26 we have linked the lovely language of good, hope, a quiet wait and salvation. Hope is anticipation, expectation, desire. It is a weak and failing hope if it is agitated or troubled; it is a resilient, victorious and strong hope when it rests in the beautiful bosom of a quiet and sustained wait for Jehovah's salvation. Note where Jeremiah places salvation—in the state or sphere of the Lord. Good is pronounced upon a man who learns well to bear the yoke in youth. Discipline taught and accepted in youth paves the way for its proper reception and application in advanced age. Hardships and afflictions faced and accepted in youth help to make such much more bearable in later life. None of these experienced in youth makes the facing of such more difficult in later life. Two verses from the Bible's longest chapter, Psalm 119, serve as excellent and inspired commentaries on Lamentations 3:27. They read. "Before I was afflicted I went astray: but now have I kept thy word. . .It is good for me that I have been afflicted; that I might learn thy statutes" (vs. 67,71). Disciplined youth is very rare today. Such surely paves the sure way for a mass of undisciplined senior citizens in a few short years.

vs. 28-30. These three verses begin with the tenth letter of the Hebrew alphabet—**Jod**—the smallest of the Hebrew letters (Cf. Matthew 5:18—called jot but still the same Hebrew letter). The docile suppliant for Jehovah's salvation is independent in that he seeks his quest alone and in silent submission. He resigns himself to whatever his lot may be. Like Paul in Philippians 4:11,12, he has learned contentment either with much or with little. Putting the mouth to dust was an Oriental way of quiet and humble submission. The mouths would have to be dumb if embedded in dust. This he does in the attainment of hope. The doubt is not whether there is hope in God but whether he is doing God's will that will allow such hope to develop in his searching, seeking soul. Some people know well how to take chastisement from God but lose any and all patience if the afflictions come from man. The wise admonition here is for the seeker of salvation, the person of patience, the recipient of hope, to give his cheek to the smiter. Jesus taught such in Matthew 5:39. Predictive prophecy said He would give His back to the smiters, His cheeks to them that plucked off the beard and would not hide His face from shame and spitting (Isaiah 50:6). All this was fulfilled in His passion (the trials and crucifixion). Facing fulness of reproach does not detour him in his quest for salvation.

vs. 31-33. This section is begun with the eleventh letter of the Hebrew alphabet—**Caph.** Three grounds of assurance are set forth by the prophetic penman in these verses. (1) The afflictions are temporary—not permanent. He will not cast off forever. When His people repent and turn to Him again, He will graciously pardon and tenderly accept them again. (2) Any grief or affliction will be mixed with compassion that flows freely from the multitude of His mercies. His mercy is not sparce; it is abundant and unfailing. (3) Whatever affliction or chastisement God brings upon His people or allows to be brought upon them is not done gladly or with a joyful heart. He receives NO pleasure in such but knows that such is for the ultimate good of His people. Like the loving, caring and knowing parent that He is, He knows that discipline is a must and that suffering can be the very fire that burns away the worthless dross in our lives and leaves us with the pure gold of His approval. Judah would later sense that current exile in Babylon would be for their long-term good in weaning them away permanently from their besetting sin of idolatry and all the trimmings of transgression it triggered.

vs. 34-36. This triplet of verses is the **Lamed** section—the twelfth letter of the Hebrew alphabet. Be it observed that this trio of verses does not consist of three sentences but of one extended sentence. There are three well-known evils none of which receive approbation of righteous Jehovah. (1) The crushing under feet of prisoners He approveth not (see verse 36). (2) A refusal to give a man his rightful due in a court of law where the Almighty is considered as being a present yet unseen witness does not receive his approval (see verse 36). (3) To wrong a man generally is something of which He does not approve at all. The Lord will do right and never engage in that which is wrong (Cf. Genesis 18:25).

PROPHETIC PORTRAYAL OF ZION'S DEEP AFFLICTIONS

Paragraph 3 of Lamentations 3 reads,

> **Who is he that saith, and it cometh to pass, when the Lord commandeth it not? Out of the mouth of the most High proceedeth not evil and good? Wherefore doth a living man complain, a man for the punishment of his sins? Let us search and try our ways, and turn again to**

the Lord. Let us lift up our heart with our hands unto God in the heavens. We have transgressed and have rebelled: thou hast not pardoned. Thou has covered with anger, and persecuted us: thou hast slain, thou hast not pitied. Thou hast covered thyself with a cloud, that our prayer should not pass through. Thou hast made us as the off-scouring and refuse in the midst of the people. All our enemies have opened their mouths against us. Fear and a snare is come upon us, desolation and destruction. Mine eye runneth down with rivers of water for the destruction of the daughter of my people. Mine eye trickleth down, and ceaseth not, without any intermission. Till the Lord look down, and behold from heaven. Mine eye affecteth mine heart because of all the daughters of my city. Mine enemies chased me sore, like a bird, without cause. They have cut off my life in the dungeon, and cast a stone upon me. Waters flowed over mine head; then I said, I am cut off (3:37-54).

vs. 37-39. This triplet of verses is the **Mem,** the thirteenth letter of the Hebrew alphabet, section of Lamentations 3. No man can predict something that will occur if it be not the Lord's will that it one day materialize. Jeremiah had known many false prophets of his era that attempted such but all became flagrant failures as touching the fulfillment category. Evil in verse 38 very likely means calamity and good symbolizes prosperity. Both proceed from the Lord as His wisdom may dictate. A man who still possesses life should prize it highly and not descend to the low base of complaining, whining, repining. Instead of repining due to his sorrows and sufferings, he should be concerned with his sins. All sorrow and suffering, directly or indirectly, result from sin. Man knew neither sorrow nor suffering until he sinned in Edenic excellency. Since then he has known sorrow and suffering on a daily scale.

vs. 40-42. This trio of verses is the **Nun,** fourteenth letter of the Hebrew alphabet, section of this lengthy chapter. Instead of repining over sorrow and suffering, it is a hundred times better that man rivet his attention on repentance. The prophetic penman urges all his fellow Jews to search and try their ways. Let us determine just what our sins and transgressions to God are. Then the next imperative step is turning to God. In sincerity of soul, not in hypocrisy or pretence, let us lift heart (center of affections) with hands (instruments of action) to the God of the high and holy heavens. Verse 42 is a recognition of where their real problem lay—in their transgression of rebellion. Transgression is a going beyond; rebellion is a refusal to be guided and governed by God's law. One astute commentator on this verse said that when one CALLS sin transgression and rebellion, he has not MISCALLED it. Jehovah had not pardoned; the exile was still in its early stages; it would not be concluded for another half century.

vs. 43-45. This triplet of verses is begun by **Samech,** fifteenth letter of the Hebrew alphabet. The long practiced transgression and flagrant rebellion of verse 42 must be punished. These three verses detail that more-than-deserved punishment. (1) Jehovah covered with anger; this is an expression of His righteous indignation. (2) He persecuted His people, i. e., allowed Babylon to capture them and captivate them for seventy years. (3) He had slain or allowed the cruel, calloused Chaldeans to kill en masse multitudes of them. (4) He had not pitied, i. e., allowed them to escape the long exile. (5) Their sins had become a cloud that hid God's face from them. Isaish 59:1,2 is an excellent commentary on verse 44. Sin separates from God and hides His face from His people. (6) Sin became such a barrier between apostate Judah and faithful Jehovah that their very prayers were short-circuited, as we might express it in modern parlance, from the prayer-hearing God on holy high. (7) God had made them the offscouring and refuse in the midst of neighboring beholders. All spectators held them in derision; they treated fallen Judah with utter contempt. PROUD Judah has now become PROSTRATE Judah—a people humiliated and embarrassed.

vs. 46-48. Here there is a break in the alphabetical usage with **Pe,** seventeenth letter of the Hebrew alphabet, coming before **Ain,** sixteenth letter. Verses 46,47 continue with the detailed punishment already begun in verses 43-45. The enemies were not MUTE beholders of Judah's calamities. They OPENED their mouths to express their contempt, derision and disdain. It was not the case of a portion or a few so engaged but all of Judah's enemies were so engaged. The imagery of verse 47 is of fleeing, fearful animals who fall into the snare or trap of destruction. Such had come with fulness of force upon fleeing, fearful Judah—the Chaldean snare or trap of capture and captivity. Verse 48 is one of the reasons why Jeremiah has frequently been styled the weeping prophet and with good reason. From his sensitive, sympathetic, caring and concerned eye there ran down rivers of water (multiple tears) for the destruction of the daughter (the nation) of his people. He wept unashamedly except for the shame of sin that triggered it all. Did ever another Hebrew prophet feel the depths of sorrow and sighing for God's people as did Jeremiah? Not likely. Little wonder then that some saw in the Sympathetic Saviour a striking similarity to Jeremiah (Matthew 16:13,14).

vs. 49-51. This triplet of verses is the **Ain,** sixteenth letter of Hebrew alphabet, section of this extended chapter. Profuse tears of great grief had been mentioned in verse 48. Their continuation is the thrust of verse 49. The waters (tears) continued to trickle down his weary face with no abatement; there was no intermission of their continuous flow. There would be no appreciable relief till the Lord's look of mercy and compassion came from heaven. Jeremiah possessed hope that this would not be long in delay but soon would materialize. Eye and heart were linked in the grieving prophet. Clarke well says, "What I SEE I feel. I SEE nothing but MISERY; and I FEEL, in consequence, nothing but PAIN" (All emphases—his). Allusion to the daughters of his city has been variously understood. Some see the reference as being the neighboring cities in and around Jerusalem. This is not likely the real meaning. Much more probable is that the allusion is to the maidens or young women in Jerusalem. Note that he uses "my city" and this whole book has Jerusalem's desolation as its literary thrust.

vs. 52-54. This section, in each of its verses, is begun with the eighteenth letter of the Hebrew alphabet—**Tzaddi.** Though some think Jeremiah personifies himself in this triplet of verses as representative of the people, yet it seems more likely he is depicting his own sufferings and persecutions. Innocency is set forth in verse 52. This fits Jeremiah before his enemies but NOT Judah before her enemy—Chaldea. Enemies chasing him sorely and minus justifying causes would fit the whole of Jeremiah's treatment by calloused, cold and cruel Jerusalem and Judah. What Chaldea did to Judah and Jerusalem was not without cause. Judah and Jerusalem deserved what came by God's appointed agent of destruction—Babylon. Jeremiah had spent time in a dungeon (Jeremiah 38:6ff) and the intent of the enemies was to cut off his life though he was spared by God's providence. Placement of the stone above it simply meant his enemies meant to make it escape-proof. The flowing of waters over his head referred to all the mental anguish that was his in such lethal surroundings with death always near at hand due to the painful and unwholesome surroundings.

JEREMIAH'S DEPENDENCE UPON JEHOVAH

Paragraph 4 of Lamentations 3 reads,

> **I called upon thy name, O Lord, out of the low dungeon. Thou hast heard my voice: hide not thine ear at my breathing, at my cry. Thou drewest near in the day that I called upon thee: thou saidst, Fear not. O Lord, thou hast pleaded the causes of my soul; thou hast redeemed my life. O Lord, thou hast seen my wrong: judge thou my cause. Thou hast seen all their vengeance and all their imaginations against me. Thou hast heard their reproach, O Lord, and all their imaginations against me; The lips of those that rose up against me, and their device against me all the day. Behold their sitting down, and their rising up; I am their musick (3:55-63).**

vs. 55-57. This triplet of verses is begun in each verse with the nineteenth letter of the Hebrew alphabet—**Koph.** From the LOW dungeon Jeremiah lifted his prayer to the hearing Jehovah in the HIGH heavens above. It was not a prayer prayed in vain for God heard his desperate entreaty as He does all prayers of His faithful children IF prayed in harmony with His holy will. Jeremiah pleads for God to hear whether the prayer be a whisper or a loud cry. Jeremiah was drawing near God in prayer; God drew near him in a prompt, precious response. Jehovah tenderly, lovingly charged him to ''Fear not''—a delightful duet of words often given by Deity to humanity. The inspired James wrote, "Draw nigh to God, and he will draw nigh to you" (James 4:8).

vs. 58-60. This triplet of verses, each one, is begun with the twentieth letter of the Hebrew alphabet—**Resh.** Genuine gratitude wells up within the prophet's heart because God had pleaded in his behalf and redeemed his life. The imagery of the allusion to the pleading seems to be a poor man in court against a wealthy man with no advocate to advance his cause. The Lord came to plead Jeremiah's cause. Verse 59 seems to portray Jeremiah as representing Judah. God had been merciful to him personally. He would also be mindful of and helpful toward His people. God knew only too well their wrongs. In equity, He would judge their cause. After a period in exile, He would redeem them. Judah had wronged God and also His great prophet. Jehovah in His omniscience knew of all Jewish vengeance and imaginations of iniquity against the faithful prophet. A better day loomed for Judah when they repented and turned back to the Gracious God they had snubbed so long.

vs. 61-63. This is the **Schin** section. This is the twenty-first letter of the Hebrew alphabet. Verse 61 is largely a repeat of verse 60. No reproachful language or imagination of evil had been devised against obedient and reverent Jeremiah but what the Lord was fully cognizant of the same. In both language and devices they opposed Jeremiah. It was an all day or continuous harangue against him. Their sitting down and rising up simply referred to all their actions. Jeremiah entreated that the Lord behold all such from his enemies. He had become the taunting object of their music or their songs.

A CLEAR, CLARION CALL FOR JEHOVAH'S JUSTICE TO BE ADMINISTERED

Paragraph 5, the final and shortest one in Lamentations 3, reads,

Render unto them a recompence, O Lord, according to the work of their hands. Give them sorrow of heart, thy curse unto them. Persecute and destroy them in anger from under the heavens of the Lord (3:64-66).

This is the **Tau,** twenty-second letter of the Hebrew alphabet, section of Lamentations 3. Sin truly has a payday. As men and/or nations sow, they shall also surely reap. Here is an entreaty for the Lord to render unto them a recompense; it is to be according to the work of their hands. Judgment is always proportionate to the sins men commit. Sorrow of heart is a blindness or hardness which their sins have called down upon them as they rushed toward destruction. Jehovah's curse or punishment had to come in the name of retributive justice. No longer could there be the delay that His mercy and patience had granted for so long. Judah and Jerusalem had long despised that mercy, that patience, that delayed justice. Jeremiah knew that in His righteous indignation the holy wrath of an aroused, offended Jehovah must persecute, must destroy. This greatly deserved wrath on their part would be observed by all who live "under the heavens of the Lord." It would serve to emphasize to all that there is the Great Judge of the Universe who rules and reigns from above the heavens—the heaven above us where birds soar and clouds collect and the heaven above it where sun, moon and stars have their appointed orbits of heavenly functions.

Relative to the triplet acrostic characteristic of this chapter, Adam Clarke observed as he brought his comments on this chapter to a crisp close,

> **It has already been noticed in the INTRODUCTION, that this chapter contains a TRIPLE ACROSTIC, THREE, lines always beginning with the same letter; so that the Hebrew alphabet is thrice repeated in this chapter TWENTY-TWO multiplied by THREE being equal to SIXTY-SIX (All emphases—his).**

POINTS TO PONDER

(1) A people must be far, Far, FAR gone into apostasy when Jehovah gives the prohibition to cease any and all praying for them.

(2) For the patient and pious there will always be a rainbow of hope though it may be long in being detected.

(3) Jeremiah was an amazing man in being able to bounce back in resiliency when cast so low by powerful, persistent persecutions.

(4) Blessed assurance is one of the greatest gifts tendered us by our Gracious God on holy high.

(5) If we expect God to draw near to us, then we MUST draw nigh to Him.

DISCUSSION QUESTIONS

1. Summarize introduction.

2. What interesting observation does Clarke make relative to Lamentations 3:12?

3. How is Jeremiah 20:7 an excellent commentary on Lamentations 3:13-15?

4. List and discuss the seven points relative to their more-than-deserved punishment.

5. Judgment is always proportionate to what?

MULTIPLE-CHOICE: Underline correct answer

1. In Lamentations 3 a: (A) duet; (B) trio; (C) quartet; (D) full paragraph—of verses is begun with the same letter of the Hebrew alphabet.
2. The darkness into which Jeremiah had been led was: (A) the night as opposed to daylight hours; (B) ignorance; (C) sin; (D) gloom and calamity.
3. John 1:11 is spoken of: (A) the apostles; (B) Jesus Christ; (C) John the Baptist; (D) Jeremiah.
4. Bible hope is: (A) minus any evidence to undergird it; (B) an ever evasive thing; (C) anticipation, expectation, desire; (D) millennial in content and scope.
5. (A) Aleph; (B) Jod; (C) Caph; (D) Vau—is the smallest letter of the Hebrew alphabet and the very letter to which Jesus referred in Matthew 5:18.

SCRIPTURAL FILL-IN: Only one word in each blank

1. "I _____ a _____ to _____ my _____ ; and their _____ all the _____ ."
2. "It is _____ that a _____ should both _____ and quietly _____ for the _____ of the _____ ."
3. "_____ us _____ and _____ our _____ , and _____ again to the _____ ."
4. "Mine _____ runneth _____ with _____ of _____ for the _____ of the _____ of my _____ ."
5. "Thou _____ near in the _____ that I _____ upon thee; thou _____ , Fear _____ ."

504

TRUE OR FALSE: Put either a "T" or "F" in the blanks

_____ 1. Things can happen on earth which will short-circuit our prayers to heaven.
_____ 2. God's goodness is just as relative and imperfect as man's.
_____ 3. Man is NEVER required to do any seeking of the Lord.
_____ 4. There is never any good which can come out of affliction.
_____ 5. The Judge of the earth will always do right and of that we can be fully assured.

THOUGHT QUESTIONS

1. Why does there have to be a heaven to right all the wrongs done to good, great and godly men like Jeremiah who were maligned and mistreated all their lives?

2. Why should we never cease climbing the majestic mountain of faith, hope and love?

3. What blessings accrue to those who quietly and patiently wait on the Lord according to Psalm 27:14 and Lamentations 3:25,26?

4. Where was salvation placed by Jeremiah and where is it placed by apostolic authority in New Testament Scripture?

5. Why is undisciplined youth one of the real tragedies of modern times?

APPENDIX FIVE

SORROWS AND SUFFERINGS OF THE CHALDEAN SIEGE
Lamentations 4

In this chapter, we go back to the twenty-two verses which had characterized chapters one and two, but from which a triple departure, sixty-six verses, had been made in chapter three. Chapter four has four paragraphs. Dixon Analytical Bible gives this summary heading of these four divisions, (1) "Zion bewaileth her pitiful estate;" (2) "She confesseth her sins;" (3) "Edom is threatened;" and (4) "Zion is comforted."

Brother Wayne Jackson, able preacher and writer par excellent, had a very fine article on Lamentations in the GOSPEL ADVOCATE, October 21, 1976. Here is his accurate analysis of chapter 4,

> **The Suffering of the Seige (sic)—as mentioned earlier during the eighteen month seige (sic) of Jerusalem, conditions became intolerable. Famine was acute. "The tongue of the suckling child cleaveth to the roof of his mouth for thirst: The young children ask bread, and no man breaketh it unto them." Conditions were so horrible that "the hands of pitiful women have broiled their own children," so that "they that are slain with the sword are better than they are slain with hunger." But Judah was only reaping what she had sown. Her iniquities were many; the prophets and priests had been corrupt and the people rejoiced therein" (Jeremiah 5:30) (p. 683).**

ZION MOURNS HER SEVERE STATE

Paragraph 1 of Lamentations 4 reads,

How is the gold become dim! how is the most fine gold changed! the stones of the sanctuary are poured out in the top of every street. The precious sons of Zion, comparable to fine gold, how are they esteemed as earthen pitchers, the work of the hands of the potter! Even the sea monsters draw out the breast, they give suck to their young ones: the daughter of my people is become cruel, like the ostriches in the wilderness. The tongue of the suckling child cleaveth to the roof of his mouth for thirst: the young children ask bread, and no man breaketh it unto them. They that did feed delicately are desolate in the streets: they that were brought up in scarlet embrace dunghills. For the punishment of the iniquity of the daughter of my people is greater than the punishment of the sin of Sodom, that was overthrown as in a moment, and no hands stayed on her. Her Nazarites were purer than snow, they were whiter than milk, they were more ruddy in body than rubies, their polishing was of sapphire: Their visage is blacker than a coal; they are not known in the streets: their skin cleaveth to their bones; it is withered, it is become like a stick. They that be slain with the sword are better than they that be slain with hunger: for these pine away, stricken through for want of the fruits of the field. The hands of the pitiful women have sodden their own children: they were their meat in the destruction of the daughter of my people. The Lord hath accomplished his fury; he hath poured out his fierce anger, and hath kindled a fire in Zion, and it hath devoured the foundations thereof. The kings of the earth, and all the inhabitants of the world, would not have believed that the adversary and the enemy should have entered into gates of Jerusalem (4:1-12).

v. 1. This verse begins with **Aleph**—first letter of the Hebrew alphabet. Highly figurative language appears in this opening verse. Gold was the most precious element known to the ancient Jew. It symbolized Jerusalem in former ages of prosperity. The dimming of the gold is the abject loss of that once prestigious prosperity. Now the city lies in the throes of destruction and devastation. Most fine gold represents the peak of her prosperity; the changing represents her current status—a besieged city that has fallen in humiliating defeat. Stones of the sanctuary represent the priests and Levites who formerly officiated and served in the temple. These are deposed—they "are poured out in the top of every street"—a very graphic description of their fall from priestly and Levitical duties in the holy areas of the once glorious temple.

v. 2. This verse begins with **Beth**—second Hebrew letter. Zion's precious sons, once comparable to find gold, are now likened to earthen vessels, work of but a potter's hands. The contrast is strong and startling—fine gold and piece of clay! This graphically portrayed the tragic fall and loss Jerusalem had sustained.

v. 3. This verse is begun with **Gimel**—third letter of the Hebrew alphabet. There is a textual problem here as to whether sea monsters (KJV) or jackals (ASV) is the true rendering. Regardless of which is the correct rendering, the idea is the same. He speaks of animals who give suck to their offspring. They do not withhold the breast of milk from their young. Cruel, cold and calloused Judah was unlike these suckling mothers among the animal world. They had become like the ostriches, proverbially known for the oblivious neglect they give their eggs. During the desperate siege, calloused Jewish mothers neglected the very children they had brought into the world. It is not a pretty picture the pained prophet paints with his pen of potency.

v. 4. Daleth, fourth Hebrew letter, begins this verse. Extreme cruelty to children continues from verse 3 on into this verse. The famine has removed milk from the mother's breast. A dry breast offered no milk to the starving child. There was no moisture for his dry mouth; there was no food for his shriveled stomach. In the child's dry mouth his tortured tongue cleaves (is glued) to the roof of his mouth. The thirst was great and grievous. Young children old enough to request bread begged for such but none was forthcoming. Their plight is beyond our power to grasp it living as we do in a land of affluence and abundance.

v. 5. He, fifth Hebrew letter, begins this verse. Here the picture changes from children to adults but not from worse to better by any means. They who once fed and feasted on dainties and delicacies now perish with hunger on the desolate streets of fallen Zion. They who were brought up amidst scarlet (represenative of riches and prosperity) now embrace dunghills. We would style such in modern parlance as garbage dumps. Many people have gone from rags to riches. With these people there was a reversal—from riches to rags!

v. 6. Vau, sixth Hebrew letter, begins this verse. No verse in all this book, and there is a total of one hundred fifty-four verses, depicts more strongly Zion's severity of sufferings than does this one. The prophet styles it as by-passing even the severity that descended upon sinful, sensual Sodom around thirteen centuries earlier. Sodom was destroyed around 1898 B. C. Jeremiah writes this around 586 B. C. Sodom's destruction came in a moment or day and was over though its accountable citizens have suffered in the sorrows of Sheol or the horrors of Hades since. Zion's siege lasted for eighteen months. Sodom knew no siege, no sorrow, no thirst, no hunger. Zion knew all these. Zion had been destroyed by slow degrees. Zion had far more light and opportunity to repent than did Sodom in the patriarchal morning of time. Therefore, her punishment was proportionately greater. No hands stayed on Sodom with a protracted siege as had been the case of the Chaldeans against Jerusalem.

v. 7. Zain, seventh Hebrew letter, begins this verse. Nazarites were separated ones according to certain regulations as outlined in Numbers 6. The ASV here has nobles. Eminent men were at times so designated. Whether men under the vow or men of great eminence the contrast is the same. Their once possessed glory is described in verse 7. Their departed glory and the calamity that overtook them form the thrust of verse 8. A quartet of descriptions is given of their former glory and eminence. (1) They were purer than snow (eminence of piety). (2) They were whiter than milk (eminence of wholesomeness). (3) They were more ruddy in body than rubies (eminence of great health). (4) Their polishing was of sapphire (eminence of their brilliance).

v. 8. Cheth, eighth letter of Hebrew alphabet, begins this verse. Set against the fourfold picture of former glory and prestige in verse 7 is a fivefold depiction of the demeaned and degraded state they now experienced. (1) Their visage is blacker than a coal (a strong, descriptive contrast with the pure-as-snow delineation in verse 7). (2) They are not known in the streets (oblivion is now their lot). (3) Their skin cleaveth to their bones (a marked contrast to the health and vigor formerly theirs).

(4) They are in a withering condition (near starvation). (5) They have become like a stick (a dry stick minus all sap or moisture).

v. 9. Teth, ninth letter of Hebrew alphabet, begins this verse. Graphically portrayed here is the contrast between a quick death by the lethal sword and one by starvation which takes many days. The former is better than the latter. There is much more suffering connected with the slow death by starvation. Those dying by sword do not linger; their blood flows out with rapidity and death soon occurs. Due to their being stricken through, they no longer have any need of food from the fruits of the field.

v. 10. Jod, tenth letter of the Hebrew alphabet and the smallest of any of the twenty-two letters (cf. Matthew 5:18), begins this verse. Pitiful women refer to women ordinarily compassionate but who, in the straits of the siege, would sod (boil or cook) their own children and use such for food. Moses predicted such a horrible thing in Deuteronomy 28:56,57. It was fulfilled in the Chaldean siege as well as the Roman siege under Titus six centuries later or in A. D. 70. This became their meat (food) in the siege. Adam Clarke crisply comments, "From these horrible scenes, it is well to pass with as hasty a step as possible." Indeed it is too sad a scene to linger long thereabout.

v. 11. Caph, eleventh letter of the Hebrew alphabet, is the beginning letter of this verse. This verse is potently punctuated with a fourfold affirmation of Jehovah's aroused wrath. (1) Jehovah has accomplished what He set out to do in the fulness of His fury. (2) His fierce (very deep) anger had been poured out. This is reminiscent of Romans 1:18 which states, "For the wrath of God is revealed from heaven against all ungodliness and unrighteousness of men, who hold the truth in unrighteousness; . . ." (3) Jehovah has kindled a fire in Zion. This destructive fire had been ignited by the wrath of God against the apostate city. (4) The fire just alluded to had been thorough in its devastation. It had devoured the very foundations. The collapse of the city could not be depicted any more strongly or sadly than in this expressive statement.

v. 12. Lamed, twelfth letter of the Hebrew alphabet, begins this verse. Jerusalem was a city built on hills; it was a walled city; it was a well-fortified city; it was considered to be an impregnable citadel. It had this well-earned reputation among surrounding kings and neighboring nations who viewed the city as being secure against capture. If asked, they in unison would have said, "No opposing city or country will enter Zion's gates." But Chaldea did enter her gates; the city fell; it now lay in ruins as Jeremiah penned these sorrow-filled elegies, these funeral-like dirges, these lamentations of weight and woe.

GRIEVOUS SINS AND INIQUITIES CONFESSED

Paragraph 2 of Lamentations 4 reads,

For the sins of her prophets, and the iniquities of her priests, that have shed the blood of the just in the midst of her. They have wandered as blind men in the streets, they have polluted themselves with blood, so that men could not touch their garments. They cried unto them, Depart ye; it is unclean; depart, depart, touch not: when they fled away and wandered, they said among the heathen, They shall no more sojourn there. The anger of the Lord hath divided them; he will not more regard them: they respected not the persons of the priests, they favoured not the elders. As for us, our eyes as yet failed for our vain help: in our watching we have watched for a nation that could not save us. They hunt our steps, that we cannot go in our streets: our end is near, our days are fulfilled; for our end is come. Our persecutors are swifter than the eagles of the heaven: they pursued us upon the mountains, they laid wait for us in the wilderness. The breath of our nostrils, the anointed of the Lord, was taken in their pits, of whom we said, Under his shadow we shall live among the heathen (4:13-20).

v. 13. Mem, thirteenth letter of Hebrew alphabet, begins this verse. True prophets and holy priests are not portrayed in this verse. Conversely, we have depicted here murderous prophets and iniquitous priests. These latter groups were always baneful elements in Israelite society. They shed blood; they shed innocent blood; they shed innocent blood in the very midst of Jerusalem—the city of the Great King—a place where limb and life should have enjoyed the supremacy of safety and the sureness of security.

v. 14. Nun, fourteenth letter of Hebrew alphabet, begins this verse. In panic, confusion and bewilderment they wandered Zion's streets as though they were blind men. Not only were they aimless leaders but also were polluted leaders. So polluted were they with blood that men were prohibited from so much as touching their garments. A Mosaic mandate almost a thousand years earlier had stated, "And whosoever toucheth one that is slain with a sword in the open fields, or a dead body, or a bone of a man, or a grave, shall be unclean seven days" (Numbers 19:16).

v. 15. Samech, fifteenth letter of Hebrew alphabet, begins this verse. Such blood guiltiness did not go unnoticed. Quite to the contrary, these blood-polluted leaders found no welcome wherever they went. They were viewed as unclean much like lepers who had to call out to near passers-by, "Unclean, unclean." These men of blood were told in no uncertain terms to depart, depart, depart. This thrice-mentioned depart is full of emphasis. Those polluted were not to be touched at all. When they left Jewish habitats they found no word of welcome and no summons to sojourn among heathen or pagan neighbors. They were not even deemed worthy of pagan reception, heathen recognition, non-Israelite fellowship. Their ostracism was total. They were men without a country.

v. 16. Ain and **Pe** are transposed here even as they were in the two previous chapters (2:16,17; 3:46-51). **Pe,** seventeenth letter of Hebrew alphabet, begins this verse. Pagan Gentiles are the spokesmen here and give their observed analysis of what had happened. In the dispersion of the Jews, their observant pagans recognized the stirred-up wrath of Jehovah at work. These dispersed Jews no longer have the Lord's regard at work for them though He had not cast them off permanently. These dispersed Jews had reached such a low depth that they did not even respect the persons of righteous priests. They felt no responsibility toward the elders of their land. This verse is disrespect personified as touching these irreverent, rebellious and adamant apostates.

v. 17. Ain, sixteenth letter of Hebrew alphabet, begins this verse. Judah is setting forth the address here. In vain their eyes looked for approaching help from allies and especially from Egypt but none was forthcoming—not a particle of help! Egypt was nothing but a broken reed as far as being an ally to Judah was concerned. Jehovah willed the captivity for His apostate people and neither Egypt nor any other ally would thwart His purpose.

v. 18. Tzaddi, eighteenth letter of the Hebrew alphabet, begins this letter. Judah here is portrayed in her complaints. She has become the prey of her enemy—the Chaldeans. They had become the hunted. No safety lies in the streets. The Chaldeans were able to pick off one by one any careless Jews who ventured upon Zion's streets. Their polity as a nation was numbered with the end in sight. The captivity began around 606 B. C. when Jehoiakim was king. It would last till near 536 B. C. or a full seventy years. Apostate Judah is now paying dearly for her sins.

v. 19. Koph, nineteenth letter of Hebrew alphabet, begins this verse. Judah is still the speaker here. The Chaldean invaders are described. Warriors from the Babylonian army are swifter in their military pursuits than soaring eagles from heaven who have spotted their prey and zoomed down upon the same. No safety was afforded in mountainous retreats for there the enemies successfully pursued fleeing Jews. In the wilderness, the enemies lurked awaiting any fleeing Jew.

v. 20. Resh, twentieth letter of Hebrew alphabet, begins this verse. "Breath of our nostrils" refers to the final breath of life as a nation. The anointed of the Lord would have been their final king—Zedekiah. Yet he could not even extend their life as a nation for he was apprehended in his planned exit from besieged Jerusalem in the plains of Jericho just a few miles east of Jerusalem. Any hopes that had lodged in him were now dashed to the ground. He could have no semblance of a government over them among the pagans. He became a blind captor himself soon after their apprehension of him in the Jericho plains.

EDOM'S CUP OF PUNISHMENT: SURE AND SEVERE

Paragraphs 3 and 4 of Lamentations consist of one verse each and touch one basic theme—Edom's coming punishment of her sins and transgressions. They read,

> **Rejoice and be glad, O daughter of Edom, that dwellest in the land of Uz; the cup also shall pass through unto thee: thou shalt be drunken, and shalt make thyself naked. The punishment of thine iniquity is accomplished, O daughter of Zion; he will no more carry thee away into captivity: he will visit thine iniquity, O daughter of Edom; he will discover thy sins (4:21,22).**

v. 21. Schin, twenty-first letter of Hebrew alphabet, begins this verse. The Edomites were descendants of Esau. They lived south of the Dead

Sea and south of Canaan. Hatred and hostility early erupted between the two founders of these people—Jacob and Esau—and their descendants continued the hatred and hostility with little or no abatement at ANY period of the two nations. Edom rejoiced when Zion fell to Chaldea. In deep irony they are told to rejoice and feel their gladness for it was to be short-lived. The Edomites who dwelt in Uz had their day of punishment coming. The cup (symbol of Jehovah's wrath) would soon come their way. They would be drunken or intoxicated men, i. e., confused, stumbling around and unsure of themselves much like people in a drunken stupor. Nakedness is often associated with drunkenness as here, in Noah's case in Genesis 9, in Habakkuk 2:15, etc. Drunkenness and the licentiousness of nakedness have a natural affinity for each other. They always HAVE, still DO and always WILL!

v. 22. Tau, twenty-second and final letter of Hebrew alphabet, begins this verse. The day would come when Zion's punishment would reach its conclusion. They were not to be permanent captives in a strange land. Restoration would surely come their way. It did under Zerubbabel, Ezra and Nehemiah. Edom would NOT be so fortunate though. Her day to receive God's visitation of wrath is soon to come. She has sown iniquity and must reap its sure harvest. When God covers sins He pardons or remits them; when He discovers sins He reveals such and brings proper punishment upon such adamant sinners. Spiritual aspects of the Abrahamic promises would come through restored Judah—not a restored Edom.

POINTS TO PONDER

(1) It is especially poignant when children have to suffer hunger, pain, mistreatment and neglect.

(2) It is folly to the nth degree to reject God as helper throughout life and to depend upon puny, weak, fickle and vacillating man as aide.

(3) Sinners have to pay a dear price for the allegiance and service they give Satan.

(4) Jehovah never intended for Judah to remain in permanent captivity to the Chaldeans.

(5) The restoration promises were fulfilled in the eras of Zerubbabel, Ezra and Nehemiah; they have NO reference to a premillennial framework of modern times.

DISCUSSION QUESTIONS

1. Summarize in some detail the Introduction.

2. What contrast is made in Jeremiah's usage of gold and earthern vessels?

3. In what ways did Zion's punishment far exceed that visited upon sensual Sodom?

4. In Lamentations 4:7,8 give the marked contrasts between their former glory and their current calamity.

5. Discuss the Edomites as touching origin, where they lived, what their disposition was and why mention is made of them here.

MULTIPLE-CHOICE: Underline correct word

1. Zion's punishment was greater than that of the ancient city of: (A) Nineveh; (B) Damascus; (C) Jericho; (D) Sodom.
2. Zion's citizens in Lamentations 4 had gone from: (A) impiety to piety; (B) rags to riches; (C) riches to rags; (D) captors to victors.
3. The sorrows of Sheol or the horrors of Hades refer to: (A) punishment for sin in this life; (B) punishment for sin between death and judgment; (C) punishment for sin in Eternal Gehenna; (D) a very brief period of mental anguish for personally committed sins.
4. Zion was besieged by Babylon for: (A) three years; (B) thirteen years; (C) one month; (D) eighteen months.
5. The years of 586 B. C. and A. D. 70, refer to: (A) a golden period of glory to the Jews; (B) the destruction of Jerusalem by Chaldeans and Romans respectively; (C) the most important dates in all the Bible; (D) the dedication of the two temples on Moriah.

SCRIPTURAL FILL-IN: Only one word required in each blank

1. "_____ that did _____ delicately are _____ in the _____ : they that were _____

515

up in _____ embrace _____ ."

2. "The _____ hath _____ his _____ ; he hath _____ out his _____ anger, and hath _____ a _____ in _____ , and it hath _____ the _____ thereof."

3. "They _____ our _____ , that we _____ go in our _____ : our _____ is _____ , our _____ are _____ ; for our _____ is _____ ."

4. "Our _____ are _____ than the _____ of the _____ : they _____ us upon the _____ , they laid _____ for _____ in the _____ ."

5. "The _____ of thine _____ is _____ , O _____ of _____ ; he will no more _____ the _____ into _____ ; he will _____ thine _____ , O _____ of _____ ; he will _____ thy _____ ."

TRUE OR FALSE: Put either a "T" or "F" in the blanks

_____ 1. The ostrich is especially concerned and watchful over the eggs she has laid.

_____ 2. Sin always causes glory to fade and calamity to descend.

_____ 3. **Jod** is the largest letter of the Hebrew alphabet.

_____ 4. Jerusalem was known as the city of the Great King.

_____ 5. Egypt, as far as helping Judah was concerned, was nothing but a broken reed.

THOUGHT QUESTIONS

1. Discuss various ways that some modern mothers now mistreat and abuse their children. Do the same with some modern fathers.

2. How does this chapter prove conclusively that God will punish sin with great enormity and severity?

3. How do Lamentations 4:11 and Romans 1:18 relate to each other?

4. Discuss why no individual, city, state or nation is impregnable when sin dominates.

5. Show how sin ultimately isolates the man who majors therein.

APPENDIX SIX

ZION'S CALAMITIES SUMMARIZED
Lamentations 5

Though this chapter has the same number of verses as do chapters 1, 2 and 4, yet in actual material, it is by far the shortest chapter of the book. Each of the verses is shorter than the majority of the verses composing chapters 1, 2 and 4. The alphabetical arrangement found uniquely in the first four chapters is lacking here. My Bible entitles this chapter as "A Complaint of Zion In Prayer to God." It is a short summary of the sorrows and calamities that had descended the once glorious city but now the devastated capital of Canaan, the collapsed center of Jewish dreams, aspirations, etc. Some of the ancients called this chapter "The Prayer of Jeremiah."

The KJV does not divide this chapter by paragraphs. There are two paragraphs of it in the ASV. I shall employ the two paragraph sections used by the ASV though the quoted verses will be from the revered KJV, the best beloved and most widely read of all English translations to date.

ZION'S COMPLAINTS DUE TO THE
WEIGHTY WOES UPON HER

Paragraph 1 of Lamentations 5 reads,

Remember, O Lord, what is come upon us: consider, and behold our reproach. Our inheritance is turned to strangers, our houses to aliens. We are orphans and fatherless, our mothers are as widows. We have drunken our water for money; our wood is sold unto us. Our necks are under persecution: we labour, and have no rest. We

518

have given the hand to the Egyptians, and to the Assyrians, to be satisfied with bread. Our fathers have sinned, and are not; and we have borne their iniquities. Servants have ruled over us: there is none that doth deliver us out of their hand. We gat our bread with the peril of our lives because of the sword of the wilderness. Our skin was black like an oven because of the terrible famine. They ravished the women in Zion, and the maids in the cities of Judah. Princes are hanged up by their hand: the faces of elders were not honoured. They took the young men to grind, and the children fell under the wood. The elders have ceased from the gate, the young men from their musick. The joy of our heart is ceased; our dance is turned into mourning. The crown is fallen from our head; woe unto us, that we have sinned! For this our heart is faint; for these things our eyes are dim. Because of the mountain of Zion, which is desolate, the foxes walk upon it (5:1-18).

v. 1. God Almighty is addressed in prayer and called upon to remember His people as touching the desperate distress that had descended upon them. They besought the Lord to consider their plight. They plead with Him to behold their reproach or their disgrace. Sin had brought about their reproach. Their greatest ancestor of wisdom, Solomon, had taught that righteousness exalts nations but sin is reproachful to any people (Proverbs 14:34). Their disgrace in all forms is traceable to their transgressions and iniquities.

v. 2. Their inheritance had been taken over by strangers (the Chaldeans). Canaan had been promised to Abraham, Isaac and Jacob (Acts 7:2-5; Genesis 12:1-3; 26:3-5; 28:13-15). They received it as a precious promise fulfilled under General Joshua (Joshua 21:43-45). Moses made clear it was a conditional gift. They forfeited it by their adamant rebellions against the Giver of Canaan—Jehovah Himself. No longer were even their houses in their possession but were in the hands of the alien invaders. Many of their houses were not even standing; they had been destroyed in the Chaldean capture of Judah and Jerusalem.

v. 3. Orphans, fatherless and widows set forth the depths of their plight. Orphans or the fatherless are deprived of parental care, protection and guidance. They were in a most calamitous condition. Widows were deprived of husbands who loved, cared and provided for them. Nothing would be more descriptive of their bereft condition than the usage of this trio of terms.

v. 4. Water used to be free for the fetching of it but not now. We have to purchase this absolute necessity with hard-to-come-by money. Wood is no longer free for the taking. Now this essential is ours only if we shell out the money for its acquisition.

v. 5. Necks under persecution refer to the galling yoke now theirs because independence is lost and slavery to a pagan power is our unenvied lot. Life is filled with labor and no rest is provided. There was no rest at night when it is normally expected. Not even the sabbath day of rest is ours. Chaldean control of them made no provisions for a seventh day of rest weekly.

v. 6. For years they had courted aid from the Egyptians to the southwest (called a broken reed in Isaiah 36:6 by an Egyptian enemy) and the Assyrians to the northeast who had always been minus of any real dependability. In the hour of crucial, critical need, Egypt gave Jerusalem no real hand of help and from Assyria no bread (food) was forthcoming. Egypt and Assyria were both broken reeds as far as desperate Judah was concerned.

v. 7. For generation after generation their ancestors had sinned. Their forefathers were dead before these Chaldean calamities were visited on them. They were suffering the consequences of these ancestral sins but not the guilt. Sons do not suffer the guilt of sins committed by their fathers or fathers the guilt of sins committed by their sons.

Ezekiel, in this same framework of time, taught that,

> **The soul that sinneth, it shall die. The son shall not bear the iniquity of the father, neither shall the father bear the iniquity of the son: the righteousness of the righteous shall be upon him, and the wickedness of the wicked shall be upon him (18:20).**

By no stretch of the imagination was Jeremiah's generation innocent. They were now suffering the guilt of their own sins plus the consequences of both their sins and those of their flagrant forefathers.

v. 8. The Chaldeans were now their masters. Proud Jews deemed these pagans as servants and yet they were now the masters, the rulers. No power was present to deliver captive Jews out of their hands.

v. 9. To obtain food meant leaving the city and yet risking dangers to limb and life by the calloused citizens of the wilderness. The sword of the wilderness was the lethal weapon employed by these cruel people.

v. 10. This verse describes the condition of their skin as the long siege of starvation took its heavy toll upon their once fair and flourishing complexion. Jamieson, Fausett and Brown have this comment on this verse, "Hunger dries up the pores so that the skin becomes like as if it were scorched by the sun." In a closely akin statement Job says, "My skin is black upon me, and my bones are burned with heat" (Job 30:30). Severe hunger does terrible things to a body that once bloomed in health and flourished in prosperity. Starvation works shambles to bodies once known for their beauty or their handsome qualities.

v. 11. Zion's women and Judah's maidens had to pay an additional penalty in the Chaldean conquest—sexual assaults in mass form. Virile Chaldean soldiers, long gone from home and sexual companionship from their wives, took out their pent-up passions on Jewish women. This has frequently been one of the cold and calloused cruelties of warfare—victorious soldiers taking captive women for their sporting pleasures. The women either gave them what they wanted or they took it by force, i. e., rape. Moses predicted such in Deuteronomy 28:30ff and so did Jeremiah early in his prophetic book (6;12).

v. 12. The Chaldeans exhibited their severe, insensitive cruelty by hanging Jewish rulers by their hands till the torture and sheer exhaustion finally brought on their demise. Aged men were shown no honor but treated with extreme cruelty as well. "Man's inhumanity to man makes countless millions mourn" receives an apt illustration in this verse.

v. 13. Grinding at the millstone was usually the work of the lowest female slaves. Young Jewish males were assigned that thankless task. Children were given the assigned task of bearing loads of wood—the loads were so heavy that they sank under their weight. It is a graphic picture as to how low their fortunes had sunk.

v. 14. Elders or older men no longer assembled at the gate for judicial matters pertaining to the city or for social concourse. The elders were either now in captivity or there was no city business for them to discuss or conduct. Young men were no longer found at such sites with their musical instruments. The young men were now in exile. Any still left had nothing over which to make joyful music.

v. 15. Joy that formerly permeated our heart has now gone. Only sadness and sorrow remain. Dancing, associated with happiness, had been replaced by something much more appropriate the lot of desolate Zion—mourning.

v. 16. The crown of a once happy, prosperous, flourishing and independent people no longer adorns our head; it has toppled. "We have sinned" is the bottom line of all that had come upon them. On this verse, brother DeHoff wisely comments, "It is good when men stop confessing the sins of others and confess their own sins!"

v. 17. Zion was weak and exhausted. They had wept so much that their eyes were now dim. The picture drawn is a very vivid one indeed!

v. 18. Flourishing Zion of the prosperous past is no more. She is now desolate. Foxes or jackals walk in her midst. They would not be there unless the city was minus people. They now roamed where great throngs of people once walked in pride and prosperity.

THE ETERNAL JEHOVAH

The second and final paragraph (as divided in the ASV) of Lamentations 5 reads,

> **Thou, O Lord, remainest for ever; thy throne from generation to generation. Wherefore dost thou forget us for ever, and forsake us so long time? Turn thou us unto thee, O Lord, and we shall be turned; renew our days as of old. But thou hast utterly rejected us; thou art very wroth against us (5:19-22).**

v. 19. The eternality of Jehovah is herein recognized and praised eloquently and excellently. He is without beginning; He is without end. From generation to generation, His throne continues in its sovereign sway over all His creation. An excellent commentary on this verse reads,

> **Lord, thou hast been our dwelling place in all generations. Before the mountains were brought forth, or ever thou hadst formed the earth and the world, even from everlasting to everlasting, thou art God (Psalm 90:1,2).**

v. 20. It seemed to desolate Zion that the time was very long in which Jehovah left them to suffer for their grievous sins. But it was not to be a permanent abandonment of them.

522

v. 21. Here the plea is presented for a return of Jehovah's favor to Zion and for Zion to be a converted or truly turned people. To return to the coveted position of olden times is desired.

v. 22. For seventy long years, God did reject them and let them pay dearly for their sins. His wrath was heavy and severe in that period but a return of His favor would ultimately be theirs.

POINTS TO PONDER

(1) A sure fruit of transgression and iniquity is the disgrace that comes to every adamant sinner.

(2) Sin brings the most galling slavery of all.

(3) We are only guilty of the sins we personally commit—not of Adamic sin or ancestral transgressions; sin is NOT inherited either remotely or immediately.

(4) Isolation and desolation sooner or later follows sinful indulgences.

(5) Lamentations, significantly, ends upon the note of wrath—the very attribute of God denied by the spineless masses of religionists today.

DISCUSSION QUESTIONS

1. Summarize introduction.

2. How does the mention of widows and the fatherless show the bereft condition of devastated Zion?

3. What informative statement is offered on Lamentations 5:10 by Jamieson, Fausett and Brown?

4. What extreme cruelties do women often have to pay in cold, cruel, calloused warfare?

5. What wise observation is made by brother DeHoff on Lamentations 5:16?

MULTIPLE-CHOICE: Underline correct answer

1. Devastated Judah now calls upon: (A) Jehovah; (B) Baal; (C) Moloch; (D) Chemosh—for aid.

2. (A) Solomon; (B) David; (C) Josiah; (D) Hezekiah—taught in Proverbs 14:34 that righteousness exalts a nation but sin is a reproach to any people.
3. (A) Egypt; (B) Chaldea; (C) Phoenicia; (D) Syria—was a broken reed on which Judah foolishly leaned.
4. In Lamentations 5, Zion is: (A) prosperous; (B) independent; (C) weak and exhausted; (D) victorious over Chaldea.
5. Jehovah kept Judah in Babylonian Captivity for: (A) two years; (B) twenty years; (C) four hundred thirty years; (D) seventy years.

SCRIPTURAL FILL-IN: Only one word required in each blank

1. "_____ , O _____ , what is _____ upon _____ : consider, and _____ our _____ ."

2. "Our _____ have _____ , and are _____ ; and we have _____ their _____ ."

3. "The _____ is _____ from our _____ : woe unto _____ , that _____ have _____ ."

4. "Thou, O _____ , remainest for ever; thy _____ from _____ to _____ ."

5. "_____ thou _____ unto _____ , O _____ , and _____ shall be _____ ; _____ our _____ as of _____ ."

TRUE OR FALSE: Put either a "T" or "F" in the blanks

_____ 1. Canaan was an unconditional gift to Israel, i. e., they were required to do nothing in its reception.

_____ 2. The Chaldeans were happy to provide rest at night and on the sabbath for the captured Jews.

_____ 3. Jeremiah's generation was guilty of enormous sins and as a result were being properly punished.

_____ 4. The conquering Chaldeans were quite humane in their treatment of captured Zion.

_____ 5. "Man's inhumanity to man makes millions mourn" is a very true observation.

THOUGHT QUESTIONS

1. How does Lamentations 5:2 refute the premillennial plank that Israel NEVER received the land promise of Canaan in the Old Testament?

2. Discuss the difference in the guilt of sin and suffering the consequences of others' sins.

3. Contrast the eternal, powerful and living Jehovah with temporary, impotent and lifeless idols.

4. Show the beautiful harmony between Lamentations 5:19 and Psalm 90:1,2.

5. Why must we become a truly turned or conscientiously converted people to receive Jehovah's multiple mercies?

APPENDIX SEVEN

TWENTY-FIVE LESSONS LEARNED FROM JEREMIAH AND LAMENTATIONS

Throughout this commentary on Jeremiah and Lamentations, I have closed each chapter and appendix with some five points to ponder. These were lessons that could and should be learned. It is appropriate that the conclusion of this lengthy volume should likewise close on this same note of nobility—lessons learned. Twenty-five lessons will be numbered and noted.

(1) GOD'S WORD IS PLENARILY AND VERBALLY INSPIRED

Plenary inspiration is complete, entire and total inspiration; verbal inspiration is word inspiration. Such great passages as 2 Timothy 3:16,17 and 1 Corinthians 2:13 affirm both for the whole of God's word. A man that has not been prejudiced by modernistic tenets cannot help but see plenary inspiration and verbal inspiration upon every page, in every line, in each word and in each syllable of Jeremiah and Lamentations. At the very beginning of Jeremiah, Jehovah said to the youthful appointee to the prophetic post, "Behold, I have put my words in thy mouth" (Jeremiah 1:9). He did and that is where they stayed till the final syllable of Lamentations stood in literary completion and perfection.

(2) JEREMIAH SERVED GOD FOR A LIFETIME

He is an eloquent exhibition of one who remembered God in youth, in his mature years and in his sunset years. He did in early youth what the Wisest of the Ages, Solomon, counseled—remember God in youth (Ecclesiastes 12:1). In his mature and sunset years, he did not cast off the God he had served and worshipped in youth. Like Paul would do six hundred years plus in the future, Jeremiah began well, continued well and concluded well. Jeremiah becomes a stern rebuke to everyone who accepts God in youth and casts Him off later in life. Jeremiah was not fickle; he was not seasonal in his religion. It was his spiritual bread and butter over an entire lifetime.

(3) JEREMIAH WAS UNBENDING, UNYIELDING AND UNCOMPROMISING IN HIS PROPHETIC ROLE

It is said of the three Hebrew children in the book of Daniel—Hananiah, Mishael and Azariah—that they would not BREAK; they would not BOW; they would not BURN (Daniel 3). Jeremiah, an older contemporary of these three valiant youths, was of the same holy order. He bent in only one direction—the heavenly one. Toward all other directions, he was the unbending one. He yielded to only one person—God. Toward all others he was the adamant one who refused to yield. Compromise was a total stranger to his whole framework. The masses could not bend him away from God; the peer pressure from powerful princes could not move him from the realm of righteousness. Four vacillating kings, Jehoahaz, Jehoiakim, Jehoaichin and Zedekiah, were totally inept in separating from truth the unmovable man from Anathoth.

(4) ABANDONING JEHOVAH ALWAYS LEADS TOWARD TURNING TO THAT LESS THAN GOD

It did so for apostate Israel nearly all the two and one-half centuries they existed as a separate polity and under nineteen ungodly monarchs. Idolatry was their constantly besetting sin between 975 B. C. and 722 B. C. It did the same for apostate Judah. Jeremiah 2:13 is one of the saddest statements ever made relative to Judah. It reads with sadness permeating every sorrow-filled syllable, "For my people have committed two evils; they have forsaken me the fountain of living waters, and hewed them out cisterns, broken cisterns, that can hold no water." The broken cisterns were the idols they accepted in lieu of Jehovah—"the fountain of living waters." Who would want to forsake crystal clear, living waters for insipid, lifeless, brackish water? Men who turn from God always, without exception, turn to that less than God.

(5) REAL MEN ARE SCARCE IN EVERY AGE

Jehovah mourned their scarcity in Jeremiah 5:1 by charging the faithful seer, "Run ye to and fro through the streets of Jerusalem, and see now, and know, and seek in the broad places thereof, if ye can find a man, if there be any that executeth judgment, that seeketh the truth; and I will pardon it." Ezekiel, a younger contemporary of Jeremiah, found equal difficulty in finding a true man, a real man, a courageous man, a competent man to stand in the gap (Ezekiel 22:30). The cynical Diogenes of ancient Athens once walked the city streets of that Grecian metropolis with lighted lantern in broad open daylight. Inquired of by interested observers as touching the why of such, he responded that he was looking for a man, a real man, a honest man in Athens. One wonders if the philosopher's quest ever materialized in his era. Real men are equally scarce in our day also. Very few measure up to the nobility of real men who are willing to stand in the gap.

(6) THERE IS AN INTENSELY IMPERATIVE NEED TO RETURN TO THE OLD PATHS

This was Jeremiah's clarion cry and poignant plea to his own apostate-bent generation. His plain, pointed and powerful words read,

Thus saith the Lord, Stand ye in the ways, and see, and ask for the old paths, where is the good way, and walk therein, and ye shall find rest for your souls. But they said, We will not walk therein. Also I set watchmen over you saying, Hearken to the sound of the trumpet. But they said, We will not hearken (6:16,17).

Jeremiah knew this was the great need of that era. But his calloused contemporaries were not buying his weighty, wonderful words of sage counsel. Likewise, it is the crying need of our evil era, our wicked world. Our plea for the old paths is a plea for the Bible, for its Godhead, for the church, for the gospel and for the unity of the Spirit in the bond of peace.

(7) THE FOLLY OF SUBSTITUTING TRUST IN A PHYSICAL EDIFICE FOR A LIFE OF FAITH, TRUST AND OBEDIENCE

Yet this is what materialistic Judah did in Jeremiah's age. Jeremiah wrote, "Trust ye not in lying words, saying, The temple of the Lord,

The temple of the Lord, The temple of the Lord, are these" (7:4). Both before this verse and after it the Lord stressed the type of life they should be living. They thought a visit to the temple would sugarcoat all the glaring sins of which they were guilty.

Church going on Sunday will not take care of six days of ungodly living the remainder of the subsequent week. Worship is imperative but it must be linked loyally with dedicated deportment as a disciple of Deity.

(8) APOSTASY IS POSSIBLE AND IS ALWAYS AN EVER PRESENT DANGER FOR GOD'S PEOPLE

Calvinism would have a difficult time in dealing with Jeremiah for apostasy runs the full gamut of the book. Jeremiah fought apostasy among his peers in Judah and Jerusalem all his prophetic life. There would have been no cause for the Exile if apostasy had been impossible for God's sons and daughters under the Mosaic Age. Jeremiah's Jewish peers were filled with idolatry, adultery, impiety, pride, dishonesty, rebellion and greed. Can God's children practice such hideous actions and still be approved in His sight? All of Jeremiah and Lamentations respond with a quick negative.

(9) JEREMIAH'S DENIAL OF MARRIAGE AND A FAMILY: A SUPREME SACRIFICE

Celibacy among Hebrew prophets of the Old Testament was a clear exception to the rule. Many of God's great prophets of the Old Testament were married men and had families. Moses was married and had children; Samuel was married and had children; Isaiah was married and had children; Ezekiel was a married man; Hosea was married and had a number of children; those who belonged to the schools of the prophets under Samuel, Elijah and Elisha could be married as we learn in 2 Kings 4:1ff. Jeremiah was prohibited from taking a wife and having children in apostate Judah (16:1ff). Jeremiah puts up no question and offers no quibble to the contrary. God had spoken and Jeremiah accepted with promptness the no-marriage and no-family prohibition. Had he married and begat children, their sufferings would likewise have been as deep and painful as that which came to the persecuted prophet all his prophetic life.

(10) THE DEPTHS OF A DECEITFUL AND DESPERATELY WICKED HEART

There is really no way we can plumb the devilish depths of a heart that is deceitful above all things and desperately wicked. This is the very graphic manner and vivid language employed by Jeremiah in depicting such. Our world is filled with that which is very deceitful because we have a world full of deceitful hearts. Our world is overwhelmed with desperate wickedness because we have a world of hearts that are desperately wicked. Solomon the Sage counsels us, "Keep thy heart with all diligence; for out of it are the issues of life" (Proverbs 4:23). A far greater than Solomon expressed it this way,

> **O generation of vipers, how can ye, being evil, speak good things? for out of the abundance of the heart the mouth speaketh. A good man out of the good treasure of the heart bringeth forth good things: and an evil man out of the evil treasure bringeth forth evil things (Matthew 12:34,35).**

Wicked words and devilish deeds all spring from hearts that are unholy and impious. Someone has well written,

> **There is no peace in the world because there is no order in the nation.**
> **There is no order in the nation because there is no harmony in the home.**
> **There is no harmony in the home because there is no beauty in the character.**
> **There is no beauty in the character because there is no righteousness in the heart.**

Impious hearts make for a wicked world in both language and deeds departments.

(11) IDOLATRY IS PERHAPS THE GREATEST INSULT MAN CAN HURL AT HIS MAKER—GOD

Commandments one and two of the Decalogue in Exodus 20 and Deuteronomy 5 prohibit any others gods or the making of any graven images (Exodus 20:1-6; Deuteronomy 5:7-10). Idolatry was the besetting sin of the pagan, heathen nations in Old Testament times. It became the ever present and always occurring transgression of God's people in Old Testament times. Injunction after injunction in the New Testament give stringent warning to God's saints to keep themselves ever aloof from damnable idolatry. Idolatry is so silly and void of all rationality. Dagon, Philistine god in the time of the Judges, could not even protect himself against an embarrassing fall on his face (to all his devotees) and mutilation of his head and hands when beside Jehovah's ark of the covenant to say nothing of shielding an entire nation of superstitious worshippers (1 Samuel 5:1ff). All the idols in aggregate among the Amorites, Canaanites, Hivites, Hittites, Jebusites and Perizzites could protect neither the land nor their superstitious manufacturers when Jehovah was ready for Israel to conquer Canaan. Baal could not protect himself from an aroused Gideon in Judges 6 or a fierce, fearless champion like Elijah in 1 Kings 18.

The idols have to be made. Hands and feet are supplied them by their makers but those hands can neither bless nor curse; those feet neither can move nor trample upon an enemy in times of warfare. Ears can be put into the idol but they will never hear any entreaties from the maker of the same. Eyes can be put therein but they cannot see. A mouth can be fashioned into the object but it will never speak a message of either weal or woe.

Modern idolatry, anyone or anything accepted in place of Deity, is no better—not a whit! It cannot solve sin for us for it is sinful to the nth degree itself. It cannot answer prayers; it cannot offer true comfort; it cannot mend broken hearts; it cannot solidify marriage and the home, it cannot mold better children; it cannot atone for sins; it cannot take us home to heaven at last. One thing it can do for us is to take us straight to hell at last!

Idolatry is senseless and silly. It is an officious affront and inexcusable insult to the true and living Jehovah—Maker and Preserver of all. Idolatry is stupidity personified and then some!!

(12) GOD'S WORD: A BURNING FIRE IN ONE'S WHOLE BEING THAT CANNOT BE CONTAINED

Jeremiah found this to be the case. He wrote, "Then I said, I will not make mention of him, nor speak any more in his name. But his word was in mine heart as a burning fire shut up in my bones, and I was weary with forebearing, and I could not stay" (20:9). A sincere soul saturated with the word of God and on fire for His cause on earth will feel as did the pent-up prophet here. The word cannot be contained inwardly; it will have to have a way to become outward in proclamation and practice.

(13) THE WAY OF LIFE AND THE WAY OF DEATH: MAN'S EVER PRESENT ALTERNATIVES

Jeremiah 21:8 reads tersely and truthfully, "Thus saith the Lord; Behold, I set before you the way of life, and the way of death." Like two threads these opposite alternatives run from Genesis through Revelation. Every generation from Adam and Eve to the current one has had life and death alternatives—life if we hear and heed Jehovah, death if we hear and heed Satanic counsel and devilish devices. Sadly and yet surely, the masses of every generation have usually chosen death over life. It is no different for our generation.

(14) PREMILLENNIALISM IS SOUNDLY REFUTED IN JEREMIAH 22:30

Of fickle, wicked and rebellious Coniah, Jehovah prompted Jeremiah to pen, "Write ye this man childless, a man that shall not prosper in his days: for no man of his seed shall prosper, sitting upon the throne of David, and ruling any more in Judah" (22:30). This Coniah is the same as Jechonias in Matthew 1:12 who begat Salathiel and Salathiel begat Zorobabel. Coniah is in the regal seed line from which came the Christ according to Matthew's genealogy. Salathiel and Zorobabel are in the seed line according to Luke's genealogy in Luke 3:27. Jeremiah said none of Coniah's seed would ever prosper again on David's throne and ruling in Judah. But Judah is the very geographical location that poisonous, pernicious premillennialism has the Christ scheduled to reign or rule for a thousand literal years. Were such to occur, which it will not, his whole reign would be minus any prosperity to Himself and to any of His subjects. Premillennialism is soundly refuted right here in the tremendous book of Jeremiah.

(15) THE TRAGIC END OF HANANIAH SHOULD BE A SOBERING WARNING TO EVERY FALSE TEACHER

In Jeremiah 28 Hananiah spued out his venom against God and against God's faithful seer—Jeremiah. With reckless abandonment, he assured the people that Babylon's yoke would be broken in two years and that all captives now in Babylon will be back in Judah again. Very graphically he even took the yoke of wood from Jeremiah and broke it saying that in similar fashion God would break Nebuchadnezzar's yoke in two years. Jeremiah answered him forthrightly but God later gave the death message to be delivered personally to the pseudo prophet who was pompously puffed up with his own inflated sense of personal pride. Jeremiah 28:15-17 must have hit Hananiah like a bolt of lightning when Jeremiah said to him,

> **The Lord hath not sent thee; but thou makest this people to trust in a lie. Therefore thus saith the Lord; Behold, I will cast thee from off the face of the earth: this year thou shalt die, because thou hast taught rebellion against the Lord. So Hananiah the prophet died the same year in the seventh month.**

It is a very serious indictment against any man when he causes the people "to trust in a lie" (28:15). Preachers, priests and rabbis en masse do that very thing.

(16) JEREMIAH KNEW THE LAW OF MOSES WAS TEMPORARY AND WOULD BE SUPERCEDED BY A BETTER LAW

Jeremiah 31:31-34 is one of the clearest prophecies in the Old Testament relative to the certain-to-come abrogation of the Mosaic Dispensation and the sure-to-transpire new covenant that would one day grace Jehovah's green footstool. It would be a new covenant—not an annex to the Israelite covenant that began at Sinai. Some of its basic and beautiful benefits are delineated here quite dynamically. There would be distinctive differences between the covenant in effect when Jeremiah lived and that later to come under Christ beginning in Acts 2 upon that memorable Pentecost. Those who contend that the law of Moses is still in effect, do not believe what Jeremiah wrote here and what Hebrews 8 affirms as fulfilled. Churches of Christ are frequently maligned by saying that we do not believe the Old Testament. We are about the only religious people who DO believe it. We believe what it says about itself, i. e., it would be repealed, annulled and abrogated in order that a better covenant in EVERY way might take its place.

(17) THOSE AMAZING RECHABITES PRESENT A BEAUTIFUL PORTRAIT OF LONGEVITY IN FILIAL OBEDIENCE

Jeremiah 35 depicts their precious portrait. For more than three centuries, they had adhered faithfully to the counsel and commands of their famed, esteemed ancestor—Jonadab, the son of Rechab. They were total abstainers from any wine products. For a surety there were no drinkers, drunks or alcoholics among them!! They were tent dwellers; they were sojourners in the land. Generation after generation they had adhered to Jonadab's words of weight and wisdom. God commended their obedience and chided His own people who had failed to give Him the filial obedience this people gave their ancient ancestor. God rewarded them in abundant fashion for this show of submission, this longevity of loyalty.

(18) JEHOIAKIM: AN ANCIENT DESTROYER OF GOD'S WORD WHO HAS MANY MODERN COUNTERPARTS

Jehoiakim is one of the most wicked men in all of Holy Writ. Yet he had one of the best fathers who ever lived—the just Josiah. Jehoiakim was as bad as Josiah was good. Jeremiah 36 depicts Jehoiakim as hater and destroyer of God's word. When Jeremiah's inspired role of Sacred Scripture was read before the mad, malicious monarch, the disturbed king took his lethal penknife and cut God's word to pieces. To exhibit even further contempt for Deity's word, he burned what he had cut to pieces.

All Jehoiakims did not die in 597 B. C. when this wicked man expired in infamy. We have an army of them today and they have a ready arsenal of penknives which they use freely to destroy God's word. Many of the modern day translators are taking knives and scissors and cutting out of the Bible what they disbelieve and/or dislike. READER'S DIGEST BIBLE, correctly named for it is NOT JEHOVAH'S BIBLE AT ALL,

534

cut out some 300,000 words before they wore out an entire case of Jehoiakim penknives. Such is a literary crime that defies apt description, accurate appraisal. The hottest chambers of Eternal Gehenna surely are reserved for people who hate and despise God's precious words to these extents.

(19) THERE IS WORD FROM JEHOVAH BUT THE MASSES DISLIKE IT AND DISOBEY IT WHEN THEY LEARN WHAT IT IS

In one of his most desperate moments weak and vaccilating, Zedekiah asked of informed Jeremiah, "Is there any word from the Lord?" (Jeremiah 37:17). In essence Jeremiah said, "There is but you are not going to like it when I tell you what it is." And sure enough, he did not like it when informed of its contents! Jehovah has filled a whole book, the Holy Bible, with words of weight and wisdom from Him and addressed to feeble and frail man. Yet the masses are totally disinterested in any and every word that derives from Deity. Even among the few who do inquire as touching whether there is word from the Lord or not, they dislike it as soon as it is submitted for their attention. This is sad; it is immeasurably sad. Yet it is realistically true of adamant humanity. We should learn a permanent lesson from Zedekiah and pursue the converse of what he did, viz., honor and obey God's will as we study, learn and believe it.

(20) EBEDMELECH'S CHARACTER AND FRIENDSHIP LOYALTY ARE BRIGHT SPOTS IN THE WHOLE BOOK OF JEREMIAH

In fact they are two of the VERY BRIGHTEST spots in the whole of Jeremiah. This saintly servant is only mentioned in two Biblical chapters—Jeremiah 38 and 39. He was an Ethiopian eunuch whose name meant "servant of the king." He courageously befriended Jeremiah by delivering him from prison in Jeremiah 38. Jehovah rewarded him in Jeremiah 39 and paid striking tribute to him, "because thou hast put thy trust in me, saith the Lord" (39:18). Other than his faithful secretary, Baruch, Jeremiah never had a more loyal, sacrificing friend than this man from Ethiopia. We recall another eunuch from Ethiopia who demands our ardent appreciation and earnest esteem—the Queen's

Treasurer in Acts 8 who became a convert under Philip's powerful preaching.

(21) THE AMENABILITY OF ALL NATIONS TO GOD RECEIVES AN INTENSE IMPETUS IN JEREMIAH'S PROPHETIC BOOK

This is seen in his being a prophet "unto the nations" (1:5). It is seen throughout the book and especially in the latter chapters where prophecies after prophecies are given the nations of that day. Punishments are portrayed again and again because they had sinned against Jehovah. They could not have sinned against Him unless they had been under law to Him. Where there is no law there is no transgression (Romans 4:15; 5:13). They had transgressed. Therefore, they must have been under law to God. Patriarchal law continued for all non-Israelites (who were NOT under Sinaitic statues from Moses till Calvary) until they became amenable to Christ and Christianity. No people from Adam to the present have been minus law to God. From Christianity onward all have been amenable to the gospel as God's law for ALL humanity—NOT some evasive so-called law of the heart or some great moral law of the heart separate and apart from the gospel.

(22) JERUSALEM IN LAMENTATIONS SHOWS WHAT SIN CAN DO TO A ONCE PROSPEROUS, POWERFUL METROPOLIS

The city now sits in a solitary stance (1:1). Sin is to blame. The city is now a grieving widow (1:1). Sin is to blame. The city is no longer a recipient of tribute; now she is a giver of it (1:1). Sin is to blame. The city is bereft of her former friends and past allies (1:2). Sin is to blame. The city has seen its citizens go into captivity (1:3,5). Sin is to blame. The city is void of the worshipful throngs who once populated her streets during festival periods (1:4). Sin is to blame. The city has lost the beauty that once adorned it (1:6). Sin is to blame. The city is left only with memories; now she knows affliction, misery and distress (1:7). Sin is to blame. The city has witnessed the enemy mock her sabbaths and defile her sanctuary (1:7,10). Sin is to blame. The city has been left destitute (1:11). Sin is to blame. The city has drunk deeply of sorrow's cup (1:12). Sin is to blame. The city now knows weakness, frailty and failure (1:14). Sin is to blame. The city is void of comfort and comforters (1:17). Sin is to blame. The city is inundated with transgression and rebellion (1:18,20). Sin is to blame. Enemies of the city rejoice in its downfall and gloat over its humiliating capture (1:21). Sin is to blame. The succeeding four chapters repeat much of the same. What an exceedingly high price sin extracts from its willing, eager patrons.

(23) JERUSALEM IN LAMENTATIONS IS GETTING THE KICKBACK OF HER SINS

A young man once found great delight in fulfilling the lusts of the flesh, the eyes and life's pride or vainglory (1 John 2:15-17). He frequently boasted of all the KICKS he was getting out of his licentious lifestyle. Years later a friend met him and inquired if he were still getting a kick out of his sins. His reply in essence, was, "A kick indeed! I am now getting the kickbacks from my sins!" The kicks of sin are very temporary. Soon they turn to permanent kickbacks. The reversal of these roles cannot be extended very long.

Jerusalem found that to be the case. It had long been a city given to idolatry, greed, immorality, violence, selfishness, pride, etc. Now their sins had caught up with them. Like Israel, neighbor to the north, they had sown to the wind and now were reaping the whirlwind (Hosea 8:7). They had thought they could mock God (turn up their spiteful noses at Him in utter contempt and disdain) and get away with it. They had sown to the flesh; now they were reaping the grievous consequences (Galatians 6:7,8). Lamentations says in big, bold words that sins pays a wage; transgression today will have its kickbacks on some sure tomorrow.

(24) SIN SHOULD PROVOKE GRIEF—NOT LAUGHTER

A plain and pointed proverb from Solomon's pen states that "Fools make a mock at sin: . . ." (Proverbs 14:9). Much of so-called comedy today makes sin a laughingstock, the butt of endless jokes designed to evoke laughter. The eighteen months in which Zion was besieged by determined Chaldeans were not laughable to hard-pressed Judah. No laughter appeared on their tormented lips as they faced sword, famine and pestilence. Subsequent to the fall of Zion, there was no laughter on the lips of Jeremiah as he penned the sad elegies of Jerusalem's utter desolation. A physical death in sins, Hadean suffering and eternal Gehenna are not laughing matters to any serious person. We should grieve over our own sins and the sins of others as well. That grief should then take the course of pardon's pathway as we walk the way of obedience to God's prescribed conditions. We should do all we can to influence others to follow in similar submission.

(25) JEHOVAH IS STILL ON HIS THRONE

This is the tremendous thrust of Lamentations 5:19. Jehovah is eternal; His throne of sovereignty continues from generation to generation. DEATH will not remove Him from its august occupancy for He is deathless. DEFAULT will not remove Him for He is ever faithful. Dereliction will not remove Him for neglect has NEVER been one of His attributes. DISLODGMENT due to pressure from an aggressive usurper will never materialize for He is all-powerful and neither Satan nor man will ever be in position to make the Eternal One abdicate the Eternal throne. Even God the Son during the Christian religion is at the RIGHT HAND of God the Father who ever occupies that august throne preeminently His.

CLOSING PRAYER

Our Holy Father in Heaven. Hallowed be thy name in all the earth. May thy will be done completely, joyfully and promptly on earth even as it is in heaven on high.

We thank thee for thy word in general and the two books of Jeremiah and Lamentations in particular. We thank thee for Jeremiah, a good and faithful servant of thine in an ancient age. We thank thee for the example of patience and piety he left us upon the sands of time. We thank thee for his faith, hope and charity. We thank thee for the profound, powerful and profitable lessons he taught us. We thank thee for every person who has studied this volume, either in a class setting or individually, about him and his writings. May we catch a generous glimpse from him of what it means to be faithful to thee regardless of sacrificial costs and what it means to be a servant of others as preeminently he was. May we follow him as he followed Thee. In the name of Jesus Christ our Lord we pray. Amen.

POINTS TO PONDER

(1) The masses today are no more interested in the old paths than was Jeremiah's obstinate generation.

(2) There are few Jeremiahs today who view God's word as a fire shut up in the bones and who just have to proclaim it fervently and faithfully.

(3) Modern Jehoiakims in the role of modern day Bible translators are still destroyers of God's word.

(4) Zedekiah was like some people in inquiring if there is word from the Lord and dislike and detest it when learning what it is.

(5) The account of Ebedmelech is one of the brightest spots in the whole book of Jeremiah and shows what a foreigner did in spiritual development under tremendously difficult pressure.

DISCUSSION QUESTIONS

1. Discuss Jeremiah as a LIFETIME servant of God.

2. What two grave evils characterized Judah as per Jeremiah 2:13?

3. Discuss Jeremiah's charge to remain unmarried in contrast with many other Hebrew prophets of the Old Testament.

4. What is the greatest insult man can hurl at his Heavenly Maker and why?

5. Show conclusively how Jeremiah 22:30 is a rousing refutation of premillennialism.

MULTIPLE-CHOICE: Underline correct answer

1. It has been said of: (A) Korah, Abiram and Dathan; (B) Ahab, Ahaz and Manasseh; (C) Herod the Great, Judas Iscariot and Diotrephes; (D) Hananiah, Mishael and Azariah—that they would not break, bow or burn.

2. Jehoahaz, Jehoiakim, Jehoiachin and Zedekiah were: (A) vacillating kings; (B) strongly supportive of Jeremiah; (C) kings of righteousness; (D) field generals of Babylon's army.

3. Jeremiah's peers placed their trust in: (A) God; (B) truth; (C) the temple; (D) righteous lives.
4. (A) Dagon; (B) Molech; (C) Belus; (D) Chemosh—was totally impotent when in the powerful presence of the mighty ark of Jehovah God.
5. Hananiah of Jeremiah 28 was: (A) supportive of Jeremiah; (B) a false prophet; (C) promised many more years of life; (D) a faithful prophet of Jehovah.

SCRIPTURAL FILL-IN: Only one word required in each blank

1. "_____ , I have _____ my _____ in thy _____ ."
2. "_____ ye in the _____ , and _____ , and _____ for the _____ paths, where is the _____ way, and _____ therein, and ye shall find _____ for your _____ ."
3. "_____ , I _____ before you the _____ of _____ , and the _____ of _____ ."
4. "_____ make a _____ at _____ : . . ."
5. We read in Lamentations 1:12, "_____ it _____ to _____ , all _____ that _____ by?"

TRUE OR FALSE: Put either a "T" or "F" in the blanks

_____ 1. Plenary, verbal inspiration receives NO particle of help from the fifty-seven chapters of Jeremiah and Lamentations.
_____ 2. Men who turn from God invariably turn to that less than God.
_____ 3. One of the cardinal teachings of Calvinism has been the ever present possibility of apostasy for God's people.
_____ 4. Jeremiah predicted that the law of Moses would last forever.
_____ 5. The kicks of sin today are sure to become the kickbacks on some certain tomorrow.

THOUGHT QUESTIONS

1. Why have real men always been scarce among humanity's teeming masses?

2. Why is the root of our problems traceable to deceitful and desperately wicked hearts?

3. Just how silly and absurd was ancient idolatry? Is modern idolatry any more rational? Why or why not?

4. How do people misrepresent us when they say churches of Christ do not believe the Old Testament?

5. What lesson should drinking and drunk America derive from the Rechabites of Jeremiah's era?

Space for Personal Notes

Commentaries From Quality Publications